Greek and Roman Antiquity in First World War Poetry

OXFORD CLASSICAL RECEPTION COMMENTARIES

The Oxford Classical Reception Commentaries Series provides texts of and commentaries on selected authors writing in English who make extensive use of classical material. The commentaries analyse intertextualities with and between the ancient texts. They also go beyond these to map and discuss many types of classical connections, recognising the role of intervening texts that mediate between ancient and modern, malleability, and the varied perspectives and starting points of new writers, readers and scholars. Digital versions of the Series volumes provide on-line links to other relevant classical and modern texts, archival resources and paramaterial.

Greek and Roman Antiquity in First World War Poetry

Making Connections

LORNA HARDWICK, STEPHEN HARRISON,
AND ELIZABETH VANDIVER

OXFORD
UNIVERSITY PRESS

OXFORD
UNIVERSITY PRESS

Great Clarendon Street, Oxford, OX2 6DP,
United Kingdom

Oxford University Press is a department of the University of Oxford.
It furthers the University's objective of excellence in research, scholarship,
and education by publishing worldwide. Oxford is a registered trade mark of
Oxford University Press in the UK and in certain other countries

Published in the United States of America by Oxford University Press
198 Madison Avenue, New York, NY 10016, United States of America

British Library Cataloguing in Publication Data
Data available

Library of Congress Control Number: 2023945592

ISBN 978–0–19–890787–9 (hbk.)
ISBN 978–0–19–890788–6 (pbk.)

DOI: 10.1093/oso/9780198907879.001.0001

Contents

Oxford Classical Reception Commentaries and Their Aims   vii
Acknowledgements   ix
List of Abbreviations   xi
Archival Sources   xiii

Introduction   1
Lorna Hardwick

Rupert Brooke (1887–1915)   23
Stephen Harrison

Charles Sorley (1895–1915)   41
Stephen Harrison

Isaac Rosenberg (1890–1918)   57
Lorna Hardwick

Wilfred Owen (1893–1918)   113
Elizabeth Vandiver

Works Cited   213
Index of Classical Writers   223
Index of Biblical Passages   225
Index of Poems   226
General Index   228

Oxford Classical Reception Commentaries and Their Aims

Series page: https://global.oup.com/academic/content/series/o/oxford-classical-reception-commentaries-ocrc

This book is part of a substantial project to create and publish digitally and in print new kinds of commentary on key works in English literature that draw on and rework Greek and Roman material. The project marks a further development in the commitment of Oxford University Press to publication in the field of classical reception, the multifaceted afterlife and re-imagining of the classical texts and artefacts of Greece and Rome, both in antiquity and in later cultures. Other examples from OUP include the five-volume reference work *The Oxford History of Classical Reception in English Literature* (*OHCREL*), the series *Classical Presences* (approaching one hundred volumes published since 2005), and the new series *Postclassical Interventions*, which showcases radical new ideas and approaches.[1]

There is a close relationship between the structures and underlying principles of the digital form of *OCRC* and the printed volumes. Digital technology enhances possibilities for the close reading of literature and exploration of the abundance of meaning embedded in and generated by the text under consideration and its relationship to other works. Literary relationships and resonances may be actualized by readers in different ways and at different times, as when a reader knows both (or several) of the source works and reads each in the light of the other(s). Such readers might be scholars or writers, or both, and might triangulate meanings that do not depend on direct dialogue between the source writers involved (who might not even be aware of one another's work). Enabling words, texts, and 'the company they keep' to be tracked and annotated gives maximum flexibility to commentary users to read texts forwards, backwards, and sideways and to reflect on their own experiences of reading over time and across contexts.

---

[1] https://global.oup.com/academic/content/series/p/postclassical-interventions-pci

The *OCRC* commentator is *both* a reader of Greek and Roman texts and their receptions *and* a reader of texts written in English and their antecedents and therefore has to be able to envisage either or both of these as starting points for analysis. The printed versions of *OCRC* will reflect that interplay. They are self-contained and also introduce and complement the digital site, where readers can use links to pursue their own interests, and to read further texts and more detailed theoretical critique. The authors of the *OCRC* commentaries start from the assumption that they are not the sole (let alone the dominant) reader. Nor do they direct their analysis to an 'assumed' or 'ideal' reader. The point of *OCRC* is to recognize the importance of multiple readerships and the range of starting points and perspectives thus generated. Neither the *OCRC* project as a whole nor individual commentary authors adopt a closed approach that privileges particular theoretical frames. The aim is rather to be exploratory and critical. This requires transparency about why certain questions are being asked, and about the strengths and weakness of the extant evidence and the conceptual tools for their enquiry. Most of all, the commentaries, printed and digital, aspire to foster the excitement of encountering new texts, revisiting familiar ones and exploring routes that connect or distance them (an odyssey in itself).[2]

---

[2] See Heslin 2016 and (with special reference to mediation and digital media) Michelakis 2020.

Acknowledgements

We are grateful for the support and insights of the International Advisory Board for *OCRC*.

We thank our colleagues in the *Classics and Poetry Now* research network and all the participants in the seminar series organized jointly by *CAPN* and the *Archive of Performances of Greek and Roman Drama* at the Classics Centre in Oxford in autumn 2019 for their constructive comments on earlier versions of this material.

We thank Charlotte Loveridge at OUP for her support of this project over a long period, and our project editor Cathryn Steele, our copy-editor Tim Beck, and our typesetter Dolarine David at Straive for their efforts and contributions. We are also particularly grateful for the insights offered by the anonymous external reader, and to Amanda Saladine of the Open University Archives for her assistance. For their assistance with the chapter on Wilfred Owen we thank Meg Crane, Stuart Lee, David Lupher, Thomas J. P. Muldoon, Paul Norgate, Jane Potter, Vivien Whelpton, and Oliver House and Sarah Wheale of the Weston Library, as well as Chris Stray for his timely advice.

The text of the poems of Rupert Brooke in this volume is taken from Brooke 1918, that of the poems of Charles Sorley from Wilson 1985a; we are most grateful to Jean Moorcroft Wilson for her kind permission to use her edition of Sorley. Texts of Isaac Rosenberg's poems are taken (with thanks to OUP) from Noakes 2008; we are most grateful to the Wilfred Owen Estate for permission to quote copyrighted material from *Wilfred Owen: The Complete Poems and Fragments* (Chatto & Windus, 2013) edited by Jon Stallworthy. Finally, we are grateful to Michael Longley for kind permission to quote from his work.

List of Abbreviations

AV	The Authorised Version of the Bible, including the Old Testament and the New Testament, translated into English, 1611 [= King James Bible].
CPF	J. Stallworthy, ed., 1983, rev. edn. 2013, *Wilfred Owen: The Complete Poems and Fragments* [2 vols.] (London: Chatto and Windus).
CRJ	*Classical Receptions Journal.* Print and online at https://academic.oup.com.
FWWPDA	First World War Poetry Digital Archive. Until June 2024, at https://oxford.omeka.net. From July 2024, at https://war.web.ox.ac.uk.
IJCT	*International Journal of the Classical Tradition.* Hybrid journal. Online at https://springer.com/journal/12138.
IWM	Imperial War Museum. https://www.iwm.org.uk/
OCD	*Oxford Classical Dictionary*, 4th edn., 2012. General Editor S. Hornblower. Volume editors A. Spawforth and E. Eidinow. Online at https://oxfordreference.com.
OCRC	*Oxford Classical Reception Commentaries.*
ODNB	*Oxford Dictionary of National Biography*, 2004–. General Editor D. Cannadine. Online at https://oxforddnb.com.
OED	*Oxford English Dictionary.* 1st edn. 1884–1928; 2nd edn. 1989; 3rd edn. in preparation. Online at https://www.oed.com.

Archival Sources

The Papers of Rupert Chawner Brooke, Archive Centre, King's College, Cambridge, https://archivesearch.lib.cam.ac.uk/repositories/7/resources/1261.

George Henry Bonner Papers, Magdalen College Archives, Oxford, https://archive-cat.magd.ox.ac.uk/records/P429.

Gurney = [Ivor] Gurney Archive, Gloucester Public Records Office.

The Hydra Magazine. Transcripts, Napier University, https://www.napier.ac.uk/about-us/our-location/our-campuses/special-collections/war-poets-collection/the-hydra.

Owen Archive = Archive of Wilfred Owen and Family Members. *c.*1820–2003. Oxford, Bodleian Libraries. MSS. 12282/1–59; MSS. 12282 photogr. 1–10; JL 977–984.

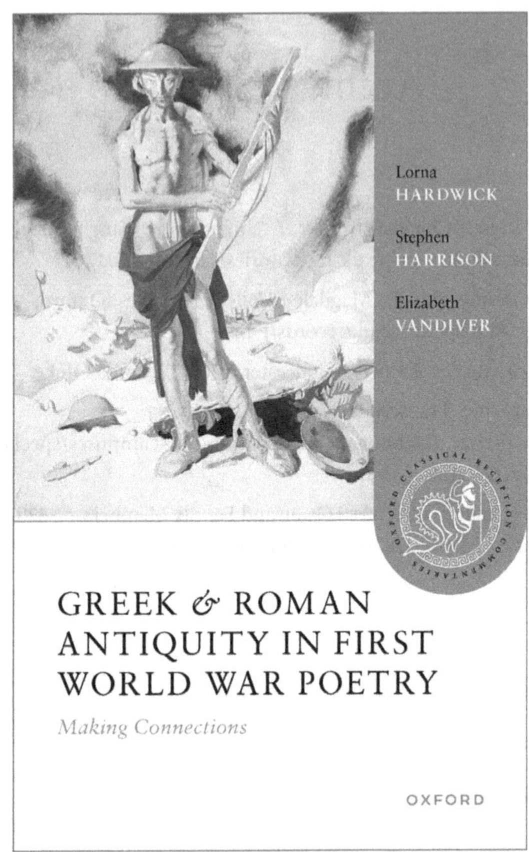

Cover image: *Blown Up*, William Orpen, 1917, Imperial War Museum Art 2376, reproduced by permission. The water colour and pencil image depicts a soldier, wearing only his helmet and boots and carrying a rifle. Most of his clothing has been blown away and his facial expression suggests he is shell-shocked. He stands in front of a dug-out with the remains of a village visible in the background. Orpen's work resonates with Donatello's bronze David (c.1435–40, Florence: Museum Nazionale), which itself was a reception of the free-standing male nude of antiquity. The Old Testament text 1 Samuel 17 references the story of the shepherd boy David who volunteered to fight the Philistine giant Goliath when Israel was threatened. Orpen reworked the pose in the context of the Trenches, signalling the classical connection in the treatment of the anatomy of the abdomen, the pose of the hip and legs, and the draping of the cloth round the groin, but gave the image an elegiac rather than a heroic tone. The Series logo is a modern designer's representation of the figure of Proteus, a deity associated with the seas and able to change shape in response to different environments and journeys.

Introduction

Lorna Hardwick

This book examines how, in what circumstances, and with what effects four First World War poets engaged with Greek and Roman material. It is the inaugural printed volume in the *Oxford Classical Reception Commentaries* series and is designed to be a manageable size that can also be published in paperback. This book will be complemented by a larger printed volume, a complete scholarly edition in which all the classically connected poems by the selected authors will be included and discussed.[1] Both printed volumes herald the digital version but are also designed to be self-standing resources. It is anticipated that further printed commentaries in the *OCRC* series will be published. We have chosen to start with World War I poets for several reasons. These writers have contributed well-known poems that are extensively read by students of poetry in English at schools, colleges, and universities in the UK. The 'war poets' are frequently regarded as a loosely constructed group, constituting a genre of poetry and anthologized as such (as exemplified in Kendall 2013 and Silkin 1979/1981), thus reaching out to students and interested readers in the English-speaking world and beyond.[2] The commentaries in this volume originate from our sense of the value of enabling readers to make a deeper investigation into how these poets encountered, interpreted, and responded to classical material. By extension, the commentaries will help readers of all kinds to become critically aware of how the poems have shaped perceptions not only of WWI (the Great War) but of antiquity in general and *its* wars. The selection of poems included in this printed volume is confined to those written during or

---

[1] Hardwick, Harrison, and Vandiver 2024, *Rupert Brooke, Wilfred Owen, Isaac Rosenberg and Charles Sorley: Classical Connections*, which also includes discussion of the place of *OCRC* in the developing history of classical reception scholarship. The content of the digital version will be the same as that in this full scholarly edition with the addition of a range of informative hyperlinks (https://global.oup.com/academic/content/series/o/oxford-classical-reception-commentaries-ocrc/.

[2] The Introduction to Das 2013 includes valuable discussion and bibliography about how the experiences of the war and the poetry that was written about it go 'beyond Englishness'.

Greek and Roman Antiquity In First World War Poetry: Making Connections. Lorna Hardwick, Stephen Harrison, and Elizabeth Vandiver, Oxford University Press. © Lorna Hardwick, Stephen Harrison, and Elizabeth Vandiver 2024. DOI: 10.1093/oso/9780198907879.003.0001

about the First World War, with the exception of a small number which directly help to inform and explain the war poems. For instance, Rupert Brooke's 'The Old Vicarage, Grantchester' provides insights into the war poems, both because of its treatment of the experiences of German culture available to those who could travel in the pre-war years and also because of its treatment of the English landscape, a dominant theme in Georgian poetry and one which was critically challenged and stylistically modified in war poetry.[3]

The four poets selected for this volume became some of the best known of those who died in the war. They came from diverse social, literary, and cultural backgrounds and provide an interesting range of educational experience, especially in relation to Greek and Roman texts and ideas (for further discussion, see Vandiver 2010: ch. 2). Rupert Brooke and Charles Sorley benefited from privileged backgrounds and received teaching in the classical languages at English public schools (i.e. elite fee-paying schools). Wilfred Owen had a modest technical-school education but also an interest in Latin poetry and productive associations with fellow war poets Siegfried Sassoon and Robert Graves. Isaac Rosenberg came from an artisan Jewish background.[4] As a boy he had only basic formal education but as a young man he went on to hone his artistic and literary talents and developed links with Modernism. The poets' experiences of types and situations of military training and combat also varied. More detail on all these aspects is given in the commentaries on each poet.

The choice of these particular war poets, with their different routes to and modes of use of classical literature, requires a rich taxonomy that reflects the diverse ways in which poets engaged directly or indirectly with the literature of Greece and Rome. We hope this 'stretched' taxonomy (summarized on pp. 8–13) will encourage readers to think about a wide range of possibilities of literary interaction with Greek and Roman material, to appreciate how those interactions were focused in a time of war, and to pursue comparisons with other poets. In the context of World War I poetry comparisons might include Richard Aldington, Robert Graves, Julian Grenfell, Ivor Gurney, Thomas Hardy, A. E. Housman, David Jones, Rudyard

---

[3] Brooke in particular had links with the Georgian poets who were prominent in the years preceding the war. In this volume, commentaries on individual poems indicate how the experience of war led to poetic challenges to simplistic or nostalgic attitudes to place, landscape, flora, and fauna.

[4] Various forms of anti-Semitism and the stereotypical discrimination experienced by Rosenberg are discussed below, pp. 69–71. For an overview of the history and features of anti-Semitism, see Beller 2007.

Kipling, Siegfried Sassoon, Patrick Shaw-Stewart, Edward Thomas, and W. B. Yeats.

There are also informative intersections with poetry written by women, although the relative lack of access to classical learning that was available to women in the culture and education of the period meant that their inter-textual use of Greek and Roman material was less intense than is found in (for example) Brooke and Sorley. However, poetry by women is a significant source for analysis of the impact of physical experience of war, as well as giving a voice to women's experiences in combat zones and as mothers, sisters, wives, and companions of serving soldiers. Catherine Reilly has challenged simplistic generalizations that WWI poetry by women was 'ignorant and idealistic' about the war and points out how women 'were writing protest poetry before Wilfred Owen and Siegfried Sassoon' (Reilly 1997: viii). She notes that it was actually easier for women to publicly take a critical stance towards the war as they were not eligible for active service, and therefore did not run the risk of being accused of cowardice, or worse. Female poets who served in France or in Britain with VADs (Voluntary Aid Detachments) or other nursing organizations included Vera Brittain (1896–1970), Mary Borden (1886–1968, awarded the Croix de Guerre and Legion d' Honneur), May Wedderburn Cannan (1893–1973), Winnifred M. Letts (1882–1971), May Sinclair (1863–1946), Millicent Sutherland (1867–1955, French Red Cross, awarded the Croix de Guerre), and Katherine Tynan (1861–1931).[5] Sylvia Townsend Warner (1893–1978) worked in a munitions factory.[6]

Post-war writing profoundly influenced by the classical engagements, subject matter, and aesthetics of the poetry of the war includes work by H.D. (Hilda Doolittle), T. S. Eliot, Ezra Pound, and Louis MacNeice. More recently the nexus between classical material, conflict, and trauma in many parts of the world has generated poetry by Josephine Balmer, Eavan Boland,

---

[5] Mary Borden, an American, wrote most of her WWI poetry while under bombardment in France. Her prose account, *The Forbidden Zone*, was denied publication in 1917 because of the concerns of the censors that it revealed the full horrors of the war (Kendall 2013: 75). Her work and that of other female poets is discussed in the section on Isaac Rosenberg, *Contemporaries*, pp. 106–9 below. Sinclair provides an interesting example of a woman who relished the prospect of excitement and danger. She wrote of her resentment at not being asked to return to France after her initial service of three weeks in a Field Ambulance unit in 1914 ('I do not call you comrades . . . you have taken my dream'; text in Kendall 2013: 19).

[6] An extensive range of poetry by women written in and about the First and Second World Wars can be consulted in Reilly ed. 1997.

Keith Douglas, Tony Harrison, Ted Hughes, Michael Longley, Alice Oswald, and Derek Walcott.[7]

The poets included or referenced in this volume were not static in their aesthetic explorations of form and language, or in the reading and reflection which underpinned this. The subject matter and diction of the poems analysed here were forged by these developments, as well as by the poets' experience of war. All, in different ways, engaged with a 'classical tradition' of epic war poetry and its associations with empire and heroic masculinity that was by no means confined to the classical education offered in the elite public schools. It was also prevalent in many aspects of bourgeois and popular culture.[8] One important criticism that has been made about any tendency by writers or critics to situate poetic treatments of war in a historical sequence starting with Homer and the Trojan War and continuing through medieval and chivalric battles is that the use of Greek and Roman precedents, motifs, and analogies could be perceived as legitimizing and sanitizing the human, social, political, and environmental devastation of twentieth-century wars.[9] The commentaries in this volume look in detail at the poets' selectivity in respect of the classical material and at the extent to which they revised or adapted norms of continuity and tradition. The commentaries also address the significance, modes, and stages of the poets' reception of Greek and Roman material where this is important for assessment of their work as a whole and for its effect on how readers might perceive the war.

A further contribution of the *OCRC* series to critical discussion is to identify and critique some of the stereotypes that have persisted in both popular and scholarly approaches to the war and to the poetry. Each poet's overlapping social and literary affiliations and senses of identity, how these affected their approach to their war experiences, and how they wrote about them are pervasive themes in the commentaries. Studies of upper-class education in

---

[7] Eliot and Pound wrote in the context of the years after the war, seizing on the combat experience of the war poets as giving authority and authenticity to post-war reflections on cultural and political change (discussed in Howarth 2013: 59). For poets writing in WWII and subsequently, the impact of WWI on attitudes to WWII is also a factor, as is the lasting shadow cast by WWI on even later conflicts (see further Brearton 2013).

[8] See, for example, the discussion of burlesque in Hall and Macintosh 2005; the revisionist chapter Hardwick 2015; and the detailed documentation and analysis in Hall and Stead 2020.

[9] The general comment in Fussell 1975: 144–5 on these implications is discussed in Poole 2013: 150 with special reference to David Jones but the general point holds good for approaching the modes of classical selection and reception in any of the war poets (see also Vandiver 2010). Winter 2013 includes discussion of lexical aspects, such as the reduced occurrence in poetry in English during WWI of words like 'glory', in contrast to French usage.

the late nineteenth and early twentieth centuries have shown (unsurprisingly) that teaching quality varied as did the aptitude and diligence of pupils. Detailed knowledge of Greek and Latin might be more honoured in the breach than the observance and easy allusion to Latin tags might not necessarily indicate sensitivity to the multiple resonances of the languages (Stray 1998). Moreover, allusion to heroic figures such as Achilles might indicate commonality of spheres of reference across classes in society, rather than being an indication of privileged access to knowledge. Nor are such allusions necessarily idealistic: for example, Margaret Adelaide Wilson's poem 'Gervais (*Killed at the Dardanelles*)' centres on the somewhat unwillingly endured classical education of a young man who preferred cricket but 'read of Patroclus' doom / And flower of youth a-dying by far-off windy Troy'. He was killed at Gallipoli. Wilson questions whether 'old tales' that are 'half remembered' have come back to haunt the soldier when he joins 'England's bitter Iliad' and 'frowns with dying wonder up to Hissarlik's sky!' (text in Reilly ed. 1997: 129).[10] The poem provides an interesting example of a combination of cultural and educational context with the poetry of unease.

Another area which *OCRC* series will problematize is the blanket use of class terminology by critics. Terms like 'officer class' have sometimes been used inaccurately or in ways that suggest simplistic divisions into 'officer class' and 'working class', with nothing in between, while some critics have used anachronistic terms like 'underclass'. It is simply not true to say that virtually all the war poets were 'officer class', or to imply that they perceived themselves as such. For example, David Jones, who like Rosenberg and Gurney served as a private soldier, wrote not only from the experiences of what he called 'the essential foot-mob, [...] who endure all things' (*In Parenthesis* 126) but also addressed differences in heritage and social experience with acuity.[11] The term 'officer class' is itself a form of shorthand that covers a range of situations and contested social attitudes, past and present.[12]

---

[10] The poem was included in the anthology edited by Clarke 1919: 391. The author may be the Margaret Adelaide Wilson (later Arnold, 1879–1969) from Portland, Oregon, who matriculated at Bryn Mawr in 1897, in the Greek and German group. Wilson was also the author of the well-known poem 'The Road to Babylon'.

[11] Discussed by Poole 2013: 145.

[12] There is a rare error in the otherwise excellent study by Hall and Stead 2020, which claims (497) that Rosenberg was from the 'officer class'. Moreover, it is clear from works such as Siegfried Sassoon's *Memoirs of a Fox-Hunting Man* that there were considerable gradations in the social standing attached to regular and war-time commissions and to the social background of those holding them (Sassoon, 1975 [1928]: 263–70 and 273–4, including the reference to

The *OCRC* series necessarily explore those issues in relation to individual poets. In addition, the individual commentaries also highlight and excavate multiple issues surrounding chronologies and imaginative temporalities. There are specific chronological questions concerning individual poets, often hinging on the dates when the poems were written and where and when they were published. This in turn influences reader response. That aspect opens out to consideration of the relationship between the poems and attitudes to the war at the time, in the immediate post-war years, and subsequently. The influence of poems on how the war came to be perceived and judged also raise questions about the extent to which evidence from poetry has been privileged or marginalized by subsequent historians and (sometimes contrastingly) in the public imagination.[13]

The commentaries in this book discuss temporalities through a number of lenses. The first is through analysis of internal aspects of the poems such as formal structure, allusion, register and diction. Poetic techniques fold together antiquity and modernity through layering, association, affinity and simile, persuading readers to hold pasts, presents, and futures together in their imaginations. These formal, lexical, and syntactical features are also important for reading how the poets communicate senses of 'place'. For example, the natural world in the war zone may be both materially 'present' and imaginatively a means of transporting the poet and the reader to the places, environment, and natural features that have been left behind at home, and which are now disrupted by the absence of those who are away fighting. Examples of this poetic sense of belatedness include Edward Thomas' poem 'As the Team's Head Brass' (1916). Rosenberg and Sassoon

'temporary gentlemen', who were criticized by the adjutant for their 'manners and accent', 264). Hall and Stead 2020 discuss this in ch. 24 but are too ready to elide working class with non-elite but middle-class officers (496). Such differentiations between different echelons in lower middle-, middle-, upper middle-, and upper-class society continued during the twentieth century (see further Stewart 2016: 73, which focuses on the comparative status of elite regiments, territorial regiments, and negative attitudes to those with military and administrative service in lower-status parts of the British Empire). Such attitudes were not confined to British society. In the context of Irish resistance to British occupation, W. B. Yeats' poem 'Easter 1916' is an apology to those whom he had scorned in the years before the Rising when he encountered them 'Coming with vivid faces / From counter or desk ... And thought before I had done / Of a mocking tale or a gibe / To please a companion / Around the fire at the Club' (see also Foster 2014). Further examples are cited in Hardwick, Harrison, and Vandiver 2024. Up to the battle of the Somme in 1916, major newspapers such the *Daily Telegraph* and the *Morning Post* printed the names of all casualties. After the Somme only the officers were listed.

[13] A special issue of the *CRJ* (Pender 2018) addressed these and other questions; see Hardwick 2018, which discusses the attitude of some modern historians to evidence from poetry in general and that of WWI poets in particular. Vandiver 2010 discusses the privileging of the poetry of protest in the formation of the canon of WWI poetry.

explore in different ways some of the ironic implications of idealized conceptions of nature as a refuge for the mind in times of war.[14] Owen's 'Spring Offensive' (1918) turns on its head the trope of the comforting function of nature, painting a picture of when sky and earth themselves attack advancing soldiers (see commentary, pp. 163–73).

Making connections: how ancient and modern texts can be related to one another

Of course, Gallipoli is not Tomis or vice versa. But between these two poles, poetry can make its own connections

(Balmer 2009: xiv)

Thus Josephine Balmer wrote of how her receptions of Ovid's poetry of exile were folded into her own poetic response to the experience of a British soldier in the First World War, and his local associations. The capacity of writers and readers to 'make connections' provides the raw material for the commentaries on the WWI poems included in this book. The types of connection made by the different poets vary in range and character. Here, we give a list with brief explanations to show the range of possible 'connections' with Greek and Latin texts that can be mapped on to the texts of the WWI poems. More detailed explanation of the taxonomy developed by *OCRC* will be available in the larger scholarly edition (Hardwick, Harrison, and Vandiver 2024) and in its digital version. What is included here should be regarded as a handy glossary to illustrate the range of connections that might feature in the writings and readings of the poems. Different forms of agency come into play—some connections might be 'seeded' by the ancient author; some noticed and developed by subsequent writers; some brought in or activated by readers of either or both texts. Not all categories of connection will be equally applicable to all the authors and they may also vary across categories of reader. The differences and the reasons for these are illuminating and were significant influences on

---

[14] See further, Sassoon's prose account (Sassoon 1997 [1930]: 38), 'the larks and poppies that were so popular with war correspondents' and Rosenberg's poem 'Returning we hear the larks' (published in 1922 but composed in France, 1917, the same year as 'Dead Man's Dump', included in the commentary on Rosenberg, below, pp. 91–9. The 'stretched taxonomy' of classical receptions embedded in 'Returning we hear the larks' is discussed in the fuller scholarly edition of the commentaries on WWI poetry, Hardwick, Harrison, and Vandiver 2024).

the choice of poets for inclusion in this book. They include differences in education (in relation to classical texts and languages and to literature in English), differences in the ways in which classical material was encountered and in what circumstances and stage of life, and differences in how writers perceived Greek and Roman culture in relation to their own traditions. These are considered in detail in the commentaries on individual poems.[15] Comparable variants apply to readers/interpreters as well as writers and underscore the current developments in classical reception studies— developments that emphasize comparative analysis which recognizes connections and disjunctions, as well as the 'deep', even 'subterranean', patterns that permeate authorial, readerly, and critical interventions.[16]

Allusion: this term refers to a direct or oblique reference to a character (e.g. Penelope) or to a poem (e.g. an ode by Horace) or to a phrase or metaphor. An allusion might be embedded for the reader to notice or discover, or it might be signalled directly, by inclusion of a name, by a quotation in the ancient language, by a close translation of a maxim or by a description that is thought to be well known.

Historically, many classicists have adopted an approach to reading receptions of classical texts that is based on analysing allusions and their role in the relationships between different poems (ancient and modern). This approach tends to situate the ancient author as the main agent, implying that the formal and lexical aspects of a poem 'carry' a meaning that was in some sense intended and invokes more authority. More recently, however, scholars such as Stephen Hinds have emphasized that this type of analysis should not close down possibilities of pluralities of meaning (Hinds 1998: ch. 2). Allusion-based approaches also privilege the skills, education, and knowledge of the reader, who is expected to 'pick up' the allusions, whether they are openly signalled or whether they are subtly placed beneath the surface meaning (or both). Some allusions may have become part of the receivers' language to the extent that their origins have been submerged. For example, allusions in the English language to phrases from Shakespeare or to the Authorized translation into English of the Bible (AV; dating from the seventeenth century and frequently known as the 'King James

---

[15] This aspect also affects the extent to which the commentaries include quotations from the ancient languages. Original quotation will be greatest for Brooks and Sorley, who were classically educated, and least for Rosenberg, who did not read Greek or Latin.

[16] These 'deep' patterns of connection in the broad field of classical receptions are the subject of the essays in Butler ed. 2016, and see especially Butler's introduction, 1–19.

Bible') became absorbed into subsequent English-language culture, in which people use phrases from these sources in everyday discourse without knowing the original context.

Any allusion-based analysis has to operate with a number of possible relationships: direct allusion; allusion mediated through other texts and traditions (in the source language; in the language of the reception text; in other languages; through quotation in the original language or in translation); and indirect allusions, which can be seen as indirect either because they have travelled through multiple mediations and/or because they depend on a cultural emblem rather than literary wording that is specific to a particular text. These emblems are often referred to as 'hanging motifs' and are found in a variety of texts across time and place, so they are important for comparative analysis. They may be taken from the natural world, for example flora such as roses or poppies, or fauna such as eagles and other birds, or processes such as harvest, and are recontextualized in the new poem, often bringing with them multiple associations. Other kinds of cultural emblem include figures which may carry general associations (even stereotypes), for example, Achilles as hero; Homer as a poet of war; Dido as deserted lover; Aeneas as the founder of a new nation.[17]

Intertextuality: allusion that goes beyond the simple and conscious 'name-dropping' of a cultural figure or emblem is usually referred to as intertextuality, that is moving across and between the specifics of particular texts. Examples in this book include Sorley's authorially intended allusion to and use of material from *Odyssey* Book 4 in his poem 'I have not brought my Odyssey'. Intertextuality can also involve moving between and across ancient texts, and employing as vehicles mediating texts and texts that are not obviously classically orientated but which are part of the literary tradition of the new writer. There are many examples in the poetry of Wilfred Owen which will be discussed in the commentary on 'Strange Meeting', including how Owen moves between the *Iliad*, the *Odyssey*, and the *Aeneid*. Relationships with mediating writers in English are also significant, for instance in the work of Rosenberg, who creates connections between images from the poetry of William Blake and figures associated with the Trojan War.

Reader-response theory, for its part, has extended the agency of the reader in making inter-textual connections. Readers may bring to the poem echoes and interpretations that are grounded in other texts familiar to the reader

---

¹⁷ This is discussed in relation to different literary and cultural contexts in, for example, Graziosi and Greenwood 2007; Farrell and Putnam 2010; Harrison 2017; Burrow et al. 2020.

but not necessarily known to the original writer (including texts which may have been produced later). For example, twenty-first-century classicists would find it impossible to teach Horace *Odes* 3.2 without the intervention of Wilfred Owen's 'Dulce et Decorum Est' (discussed later in this book).[18]

Intratextuality: it is a term that refers to connections made by the poet, either within a poem or between it and other texts in the writer's oeuvre. Intratextuality often operates alongside intertextuality, enhancing the writer's self-referentiality. For instance, repeated or slightly altered phrases are a feature of the poetry of Rosenberg and sometimes serve to link classical and biblical allusions (see pp. 66–7 below on the ancient Near East as a site for cultural encounter).

The taxonomy used in this book is agile, reflecting the multiplicities of agency and the fact that writers are also readers and that readers may also be writers. In addition to the predominantly text-based relationships summarized above, there are other types of connection which may often overlap, enabling a poem to be experienced and interpreted through a number of different lenses. The balance in this 'thickness' or density of meanings may differ, not only between readers but in the same reader over time and context.[19]

Affinities: affinity contributes to connection. The writer helps readers to feel empathy for the text and for its antecedents, as well as for other readers, possibly through the use of familiar vernacular terms or situations. For example, Rosenberg discussed in his letters the affinity between Aeschylus and himself because as front-line soldiers both would have encountered lice. Readers are sometimes specifically steered towards noticing affinities between poets, an aspect articulated by Michael Longley (who in his poem 'A Poppy' aligns himself with Virgil in the poetic practice of 'stealing' from Homer).[20]

Associations: the writer can build associative triggers into a poem to create for the reader a means of bridging ancient and modern; equally the reader can bring associations that are activated by contemporary language and situations. Sometimes associations are derived from aspects that cross times and places (such as war, death, love, loss, trauma, and motifs or tropes that recur in many literatures). Sometimes apparently disparate experiences

---

[18] The scholarly hinterland to the interface between classical receptions and reader response theory is summarized and evaluated in Martindale 1993.

[19] Here the concepts of 'low' and 'high' intensity of classical awareness and the 'heightened receptivity' that may occur in situations of crisis and trauma come into play; see pp. 18–20 below for discussion.

[20] It is planned that future developments in *OCRC*, digitally and in print, will include studies of classical receptions by modern Irish poets, including Longley.

can be brought into association by a metaphor, simile, or key word that triggers an ongoing sequence of associations.

Associations of place are sometimes linked with the development of a sense of affinity. This is an important aspect of WWI poetry, especially found in writers immersed in Greek literature. It is evident in the links drawn by soldiers voyaging to Gallipoli with places in the Homeric poems and their location in the Greek islands and on the Trojan plain (discussed in the commentaries on Brooke and Sorley).

Glancing: this is a term used to point to a brief encounter in which neither text is absorbed into the other but they touch briefly, perhaps through a shared word or experience, and then go their separate ways, although readers' understanding of both may be affected. In creative terms, one analogy is with the tangent to a triangle—its velocity takes it away from the triangle but they nevertheless touch. Another analogy with glancing is with a sideways look that notices briefly, but quickly resumes its main focus. In poetic terms, 'glancing' can imply an apparently off-the-cuff reference that also involves a subtle steer to the reader or listener to notice something that might otherwise have passed them by. Alice Oswald's May Lecture 'Sidelong Glances' in her Oxford Professor of Poetry Series (27 May 2021) discussed how literature has 'a back door'. She identified aurality and orality (often exemplified by subaltern groups such as women and ethnically marginalized groups) as rich sources of unexpected ways into a poem. On the basis of her discussion of 'sidelong glances', Oswald also proposed that when poets sing, 'the dead will turn up and sing with you'—a suggestion relevant to epic in performance and therefore to the reception of Homer. Oswald's 'glancing' is a lateral and associative movement, allowing poetry to be made from a patchwork of remarks and voices, rather than relying on poetry being a link in a great chain of literary development. She also demonstrated how glancing sideways from poems can resonate with visual art. Such resonances are especially relevant for WWI poetry, in which writers such as Rosenberg and Jones were trained as artists. The commentary on Rosenberg's 'Dead Man's Dump' includes some examples.

Ghosting: this term is used to point to traces of an ancient text that survive into the subsequent reception but lie dormant, lurking beneath the surface and the readers' understanding until they rise, perhaps only to recede again. More formally, many receptions of Greek and Roman poetry use literary devices such as *katabasis* (descent to the Underworld) to activate these traces, both materially and metaphorically. Owen's 'Strange Meeting' is an example of both aspects.

Improvising and riffing: these are critical terms borrowed from music. They point to how a modern writer may take a theme or passage from an ancient author and work with it, exploring its creative possibilities and variations before returning to the base theme. Homer's performance poetry has been analysed for its improvisatory techniques (Bird 2018) and these are sometimes carried over into receptions. For example, Rosenberg's variations on the poppy motif from Homer's *Iliad* in 'Break of Day in the Trenches' show how improvisation can capture other perspectives and return these into the originating motif, enhancing understanding of the resonances of both.

Metalepsis: this is a term derived from ancient rhetoric that has been deployed in modern narratological scholarship to indicate how writers signal their own presence in the text and even directly highlight their intervention as narrators. The most obvious type of metalepsis is authorial, in which the writer is openly present as the narrator, shaping the plot rather than recounting a story in an apparently neutral or polyphonic way. Nevertheless, even if the author's agency is covert (hidden) the writer is nevertheless shaping the story (by selection, repression, emphasis, form, and language). For the same reasons metalepsis is also a useful lens for examining the presence and direct interpretative agency of the author in classical receptions of poetry that are not confined to extended narrative. Sometimes the author appears in person, for instance Isaac Rosenberg in 'Break of Day in the Trenches' implants himself and his perspective into the scene. However, metalepsis is not always indicated by the use of the first person 'I'—Christopher Logue in his *War Music: An Account of Homer's Iliad* apostrophizes, i.e. addresses the reader, as though he himself were a film director and in this way directs the reader's gaze and imagination (Logue 2015: 9). Once the reader is brought into a poem in this way, they can themselves have a role in shaping how the story is perceived (see further Matzner and Trimble 2020: ch. 1). Wilfred Owen's poem 'Dulce et Decorum Est' involves moves from 'we' to 'I' to 'you' that serve both to destabilize and enhance the narratological dynamics of the poem, prompting the reader to reconsider and then critique the cultural authority of the title phrase. Owen's use of the untranslated Latin for the title recognizes the prevalence of that particular phrase in the contemporary rhetoric of war and mourning. His manipulation of the pronouns for 'authorial' authority subverts the basis of the headline quote and thus undermines its status as a constituent of social belief.

Trace: this is a critical term used in two senses, as a verb and as a noun. As a verb it denotes ways in which a critic investigates and maps how a writer works and how connections are made. As a noun it denotes how the critic, or a new writer, or a new reader, identifies 'traces' (remnants and footprints) of other texts that persist into the new work. These residual elements may seem disconnected but also provide raw material for making new connections and questioning assumed ones. Examples of 'traces' include the indirect allusions to winds and their associations with the Trojan War and Agamemnon's daughter Iphigenia, mentioned elsewhere in this Introduction and discussed in the commentary on Brooke.

The format

The format used for the commentaries will be the same for digital and printed resources. Following a general introduction tailored to the subject matter of each volume, the material for individual authors will follow the same pattern:

Introduction to each poet: The purpose is to situate the individual writer, with special attention to their education and socio-cultural environment and the effects of these on how the ancient texts were accessed, read, and interpreted. A brief account of the writer's literary activities will point to their main works relevant to classical reception, with dates when these were composed and published, and to their literary, critical, and artistic contacts and networks. The important aspects of the writer's use of Greek and Roman material and implications for other areas of cultural analysis, ancient and modern, will be indicated. The selected poets provide significant comparative material for studies of English and American literature, visual culture, memory studies, and environmental and ecocriticism. Where relevant, key comparative aspects are indicated in the individual commentaries.

Paramaterial: This term is used for material external to the poems that is generated by the author, including letters, prefaces, interviews, and other creative work that is relevant to classical reception. Locations of the main archives and MSS repositories for this material will be indicated.[21]

Texts of poems: These are the poems selected for detailed commentary. For each poem information on its date of composition, form, content

---

[21] The digital archive at FWWPDA is of particular importance for texts, paramaterial, images, and facsimiles.

and publication information will be included, with comment on significant textual variations.

Reception Commentary: For each poem this will include identification and discussion of allusions, intertextualities, intratextualities, and other connections marked by the poet and/or noticed by readers.

Associated poems: Additional poems will be listed which help to clarify the use of classical material by this author or provide direct comparisons. These will mainly be poems by the same author but may occasionally be works by other authors that either directly engage with the poem under discussion or provide important comparative material.

Other classical interactions: Relevant poems by the selected author will also be listed but not discussed in detail (for example, passing references). These listings will be comprehensive in the fuller scholarly editions (print and digital).

Significant Themes

The inter-relationship between reception and comparison was emphasized above. In the case of WWI poetry there are a number of themes that recur in different ways across work by different writers. These provide points of comparison in the ways the poets work with classical material, and the effects of this on wider questions of interpretation and criticism. For the writers discussed in this volume, significant themes include: the poetry of unease; the poetry of survival; religious perspectives (cultural and faith-based); environment (including interactions between the human and natural worlds). Each of these themes seeps into and through the others.

The Poetry of Unease

This is a multi-faceted aspect. Nuancing the different elements helps to dispel the generalization that WWI poetry was primarily an anti-war enterprise. The unease expressed in poetry written at the beginning of the war ranges from forebodings about the future to troubled realization of the challenges and dangers ahead, the threats to survival, and also anxiety about ability to meet expectations of bravery and resilience. For example, Ivor Gurney's initial unease about the effects of war centred on whether poets could rise to the challenge of service in combat. In his sonnet 'To the Poet before Battle' (1915) he wrote, presciently, 'When mere noise numbs / The sense of being, the fearsick soul doth sway' (quoted and discussed in Kennedy 2021: 51).

Different kinds of unease and uncertainty are evident in the range of classical allusions, including Shaw-Stewart's identification of himself with the doomed Patroclus (who needs Achilles to shout for him).[22] For some poets identification with the classical tradition of heroism was problematic, and might be interpreted as justification for the slaughter.

In his more positive moments, Rosenberg hoped that, if he survived, war service would deepen and enhance his poetry. Yet already in 1914 his poem 'On Receiving News of the War: Cape Town' deployed images from the natural world to anticipate the uncertainty and disruption brought by war— 'Yet ice and frost and snow // From earth to sky / This summer land doth know. / No man knows why' (text in Noakes 2008: 71). Such poems are an important counterweight in the early poetry of the war to the less critical celebrations of heroism and sacrifice.

Poets voyaging to battle were aware that their *nostos* was problematic. Kathleen Riley has discussed the relationship between the desire for survival and returning home, the realization that the world they associated with home had changed, and the psychological condition of nostalgia (Riley 2021: 1–30). In terms of classical reception, the concept of *nostos* is closely allied to reception of Homer's *Odyssey*, the disruptions to Odysseus' ten-year return journey after the Greeks defeated the Trojans, and his eventual return to his home island, Ithaca, that had fundamentally changed. The ways in which desire for *nostos* and perceptions of home figure in WWI poetry are varied, ranging from Edward Thomas' exploration of the effects of absence on the English agricultural landscape to the sense that a different kind of *nostos* could be imagined. The latter is evident in Rupert Brooke's poem 'The Soldier' (1914) in which he accepts that his dead body cannot be repatriated but will transplant his nostalgia into foreign soil. Critics have called this a 'reverse *nostos*' (Riley 2021: 6, drawing on the insights in Vandiver 2010: 326–7). Paradoxically, Brooke's final resting place was in Greece, which might be said to be his cultural homeland (see further the commentary discussion pp. 33–6 below).

---

[22] Examples of this theme are discussed in Riley 2021: 5–8.

As the experiences of combat intensified, direct and robust criticism of the conduct of the war was expressed through poetry, especially of the high command (Sassoon), of the attitudes of people at home and of political decisions (Kipling).[23] Only Gurney seems to have criticized junior officers in the field, both in 'The Silent One' and in his June 1916 letter to Marion Scott—'everything went wrong...but everyone save the officers were doing what they ought to do' (Gurney 41.26). How to survive the awfulness of the moment, physically, mentally, and in hoping for luck, permeates the poetry and the 'coping strategies' it reveals.

Poetry of Survival

In the poems, the theme of unease is enmeshed with that of uncertainty about whether the writers, as serving soldiers, will live or die. The desire for survival was sometimes expressed as a yearning for the restoration of the world they previously knew. As the war progressed, the precariousness of survival was often explored through the poetics of chance or fate—for example, Rosenberg's poem 'Break of Day in the Trenches' (1916, discussed in the commentary pp. 89–90) conveys the temporary relief of survival.[24] A more concrete example of the poetry of survival is Ivor Gurney's 'The Silent One' (published 1925) in which he recounts an incident when he disobeyed a command that would have led to his death on the wire (text in Kendall 2013: 134).

Religious perspectives

Ancient ideas of 'chance' or 'luck' provided a religious and cultural contrast to the associations with Providence found in Christian theology. In antiquity

---

[23] Texts of some of Kipling's war poems are in Kendall 2013: 25–42. They reflect his growing sense of the sacrifice demanded of the young (intensified after the death of his only son). The two-line poem 'Common Form', 'If any question why we died, / Tell them, because our fathers lied', is a criticism of wrong political decisions rather than a reference to cosmic notions of ancestral guilt; see Vandiver 2010: 15–20.

[24] Rosenberg's 'Returning we hear the larks' (1917, discussed in the scholarly edition, Hardwick, Harrison, and Vandiver 2024 and in the digital commentary, combines elements from Aeschylus and Deuteronomy to evoke the uncertainty about the future and sense of impending catastrophe that is relieved by the temporary survival signalled by the song of the larks.

gods were powerful and mischievous but not associated with a systematic theology. The ancient associations in which humans might be playthings in power struggles between the gods (and by extension in struggles between powerful humans) allowed poets to voice uncertainty and foreboding as well as pain. Analogies with the sacrifices of humans made in the wars narrated in ancient Greek texts resonated with the imaginations of the poets embroiled in WWI. The socially and politically powerful religious order of the early twentieth century provides a backdrop for protest that was not primarily theological but instead directed against established socially embedded (Christian) religion and practices that were perceived as complicit in directing the war and sanctioning the suffering of the soldiers.[25] A mitigating figure found in the poetry of the war was that of Jesus Christ, represented as a symbol of the suffering servant, whose identity could be conflated with that of the soldiers.[26]

In the WWI poets discussed in this volume there are two main types of religious usage that stand out and are sometimes densely enmeshed with one another. These are: allusion to specific figures and rituals (sometimes via transplantation with the effective of transforming of poetic insights in writer and reader), and associations evoked through place and lived experience that may mix ancient and contemporary elements. Both have implications for discussions about the 'assumed reader' and the changing contexts of reading and understanding experienced by subsequent readers (and critics).

Allusion to gods, semi-divine heroes, and key figures such as prophets may take the form of naming (for example, Ares, Moses, Christ) or of a transplantation of rituals or symbolic actions that are re-enacted in the contexts of war. For example, the washing of feet is at one level good military practice (to facilitate the ability to march and to avoid conditions such as trench foot) but it also has metaphorical extensions in alluding to Jesus Christ's act of service in undertaking the menial task of washing of the disciples' feet (Matthew 26:14–39; John 13:1–17).[27] Gurney's poem

---

[25] For example, see the 'mockeries', 'prayers and bells' in Owen's 'Anthem for Doomed Youth' (see p. 144 below) and Sassoon's poems 'The Redeemer' (Sassoon's first 'front-line' poem, 1915–16), 'Christ and the Soldier' (1916, not published in his lifetime), 'They' (1916), 'How to Die' (1917). Texts in Kendall 2013: 88–100.

[26] The figure of the 'suffering servant' was adopted and adapted in early Christian texts from that in earlier Hebrew literature.

[27] A connection specifically made by Owen, in his letter to Osbert Sitwell, ?July 1918: 'For 14 hours yesterday I was at work—teaching Christ to lift his cross by numbers, and how to adjust his crown; and not to imagine he thirst till after the last halt; I attended his Supper to see that there were no complaints; and inspected his feet to see that they should be worthy of the nails.

'The Silent One' (1925) opens with the image of a soldier hanging on the wires. Gurney's phrase 'faithful to his stripes', merges the sacrifice made by the flagellated Christ with the loyalty and death of the non-commissioned officer.[28]

This interplay between Graeco-Roman and Judaeo-Christian religious associations is sometimes striking, suggesting displacement of current established beliefs and practices.[29] In addition, Rosenberg's poetry is distinctive for its deployment of Jewish textures, based on the texts, figures, and narratives of the Hebrew Bible. Across WWI poetry as a whole, geography as well as mythology plays a crucial role. Associations and disjunctions between place and religious resonances were acute for those participating in the funeral of Rupert Brooke on the island of Skyros. Frederick Kelly commented in his diary that 'the scent of the wild sage gave a strong classical tone which was so in harmony with the poet we were burying that for some of us the Christian ceremony seemed out of keeping'.[30] Brooke wrote in a letter dated 1915 from the troopship SS Grantully Castle that 'the winds of history will follow us all the way'.[31] He was ostensibly referring to reciting from Sappho and Homer on the voyage through the Cyclades, but with the advantage of hindsight the words may also be understood as a darkly ironic reflection on the 'fair winds for Troy' achieved by Agamemnon through the ritual sacrifice of his young child.[32]

Analysis of religious language and associations also has to take account of the additional complications carried by expectations of 'belief' or 'disbelief', whether attributed to the author, to readers, or to the grey area in the sometimes-overlapping spheres of cultural frameworks and

---

I see to it that he is dumb and stands to attention before his accusers. With a piece of silver I buy him every day, and with maps I make him familiar with the topography of Golgotha' (Potter 2023 pp. 380–1).

[28] Text in Kendall 2013: 134.

[29] The term 'Judaeo-Christian' is used here as shorthand to indicate the way in which the development of Christianity and its early twentieth-century forms included and appropriated some aspects of the religious texts, traditions, and thought of Jewish people in antiquity.

[30] Diary entry dated Friday, 23 April 1915, Hood Battalion SS Grantully Castle, Scyros by F. S. Kelly (Kelly 2004: 381, quoted in Riley 2021: 6).

[31] Letter to Jacques Raverat, dated 8 March 1915, quoted in Riley 2021: 5. Full text in Keynes 1968: 668.

[32] Owen explores this topic counter-factually in his poem 'The Parable of the Old Man and the Young' (July 1918), in which, contrary to Genesis 22:7–13, the ram caught in the bush is ignored and 'The old man slew his son / and half the seed of Europe one by one'. For detailed and sometimes angry and ironic comparison between ancient Israel and the Somme, see Mary Borden's 'Where is Jehovah?', part of her sequence 'At the Somme', composed 1916–17 while she was serving at a field hospital in Flanders (text in Kendall, 2013: 76–8).

confessional identities. Religious language may carry implications of a faith community or simply point to a shared cultural repository of allusions and metaphors, without implying that these bear the added freight of religious belief or theological orthodoxy. This 'soft', even 'passive' recognition of religious language and ritual is often referred to as 'low intensity' belief. Studies of 'implied belief' have also suggested that underlying perceptions of what shapes the external world can be a key element in populating the internal world of the individual. Research on the relationship between the body, the mind and the senses has, in Esther Eidinow's words, 'broadened our methodological palette' (Eidinow 2019a: 56). She uses the notion of enhanced 'palette' to question simplistic analyses in which 'low intensity' beliefs may tend to be described simply as 'unquestioned' or 'embedded in society'.[33] Cognitive theorists have tried to explain what they categorise as a universal instinct for humans to attribute agency to elements of their surroundings. Poets as cultural imaginaries absorb and refine this in their allusions, metaphors, and images (Eidinow 2019b: 115). This aspect is particularly evident in the WWI poets' exploration of the relationship between the natural environment, human sensibilities, and the polluting and destructive impact of war.

The distinction between 'low intensity' and 'high intensity' of religious belief also provides a useful way of categorising different levels of classical awareness and knowledge bases, both in the cultural profile and poetry of individual writers and in that of readers and critics (at the time and subsequently). The balance between low and high intensity of the classical knowledge base may shift over time and readership. It may also be conditioned by the socio-political circumstances of the time. The concept of 'heightened receptivity' points to contexts when classical images, figures, and texts may be seized on as a basis for exploring the crises and anxieties of the moment (see further Hardwick 2015). The commentaries will pinpoint particular poems when there seems to be a convergence of these elements, either in the texts of the poems or in what is brought to them by subsequent readers, or both. In Owen's 'The End', for instance, where for most readers the religious implications of the classically based personifications 'Life', 'Age', and 'Earth' would be low intensity, Owen's mother Susan Owen brought her own fervent evangelical Christian beliefs to bear on

---

[33] Eidinow 2019a also uses the ancient concept of *tyche* (chance) to highlight some of the problems surrounding the term 'belief'.

the poem when she chose a misquotation from it for her son's tombstone as an expression of Christian faith in the resurrection (see the discussion below, pp. 146–9).

Environment

Affinities of place (ancient and modern) and the agency of the environment, including its flora and fauna, form a significant thread in WWI poetry and prose, both in the lived experience of the war and in its symbolic reach.[34] In the poems analysed here, the environmental aspects include: the English countryside and its place in pre-war settings and poetry; the impact of the war on the English countryside and agriculture and on that of the war zone; the features of the war zone environment—at the front, behind the front lines, and in the phases between bombardment; the catastrophic destruction of the landscape and the possibilities of regeneration.[35] The poetic techniques range from observation and verbal description to recontextualization of motifs from the natural world that have been deployed in war poetry from antiquity to the twentieth century. In addition, there are important symbolic explorations of key motifs and images to create symbiosis between the material effects of war, the psychological response of writers and artists and the cosmic relationship between the spheres of the natural world and of humankind. Environmental experiences underlie the poetry of unease and of survival—for instance, Owen's 'Apologia pro Poemate Meo' (1917) includes the lines 'Whose world is but the trembling of a flare / And heaven but as the highway for a shell'. Siegfried Sassoon describes 'the brooding stillness' of the Flanders landscape, interrupted by the star shells that ominously made the sky sag' (Sassoon 1975 [1929]: 277).[36] Rosenberg's treatment of larks and poppies subverts the contemporary idealizations of these emblems. In her poem 'The Song of the Mud' (1916–17) Mary Borden gives Mud a visual, environmental, and catastrophic agency.[37]

---

[34] See further Lewis-Stemple 2016; Seldon 2022.

[35] The digital version will include more detailed commentary on this topic and a larger selection of poems and authors.

[36] Edmund Blunden's 'Vlamertinghe: Passing the Chateau, July 1917' (composed retrospectively between 1924 and 1927; text in Kendall 2013: 211) is a powerful example of the combination of recording the material effects of war and exploring the metaphorical relationship between the environment and war, including subversion of traditional associations.

[37] Borden's poem was composed while she was working in a field hospital in France. Further discussion in the Contemporaries section of the commentaries on Rosenberg's poems, pp. 106–9 below.

For the poets discussed in this book, this environmental thread can sometimes shade into poetic techniques that open the way to ecocriticism. Examples will be discussed in the commentaries. Images, motifs, and themes drawn from the impact of war on the environment are key aspects for the comparative and 'deep' aspects of classical reception outlined above. They form a bridge between the actualities of experience and its cosmic implications.[38]

Coda

As a coda to this Introduction, and as a poetic expression of the 'folding in' of possible connections that are discussed in the commentaries, we mention a poem by Michael Longley. Longley holds a leading place amongst modern poets who have worked at the interfaces between Greek and Roman literature, WWI poetry and lived experience, modern conflicts and associated places, material and imaginary. In his collection *The Candlelight Master* (2020), Longley included poems addressed to (William) Orpen, the society painter who was also a radical war artist, (Francis) Ledwidge, an Irish nationalist poet who died in the trenches fighting on the side of the British, and Wilfred Owen. Owen is the subject of the poem 'Ors', the location of the canal where he was killed in 1918, shortly before the armistice. Longley's poem works through creating a network of temporalities and locating himself at their nexus. Longley's metalepsis presents himself as an observer across and through time, experimenting with the possibilities of an impossible counter-factual outcome and yet embedding the possibilities of continuity through the experiences of associations with place.[39] Longley not only eavesdrops on the whispering of the war poets but also ghosts the foreshadowing and back-shadowing poetics of Homer, in which the listeners know the outcome, for the hero and for his parents, and can only watch the tragedy play itself out:

---

[38] Saunders 2008 discusses the development of an environmental literary tradition in relation to Virgil's *Eclogues*, identifying content and concepts such as Catasterisms, Cosmology, Geography, Topography, Landscape, Physics. His analysis provides examples of the 'deep classics' in the ancient texts that also underlies the 'thick' poetics of classical reception found in the WWI poets' emotional and aesthetic sensitivity to the clashes between the natural and man-made environments in times of conflict.

[39] For discussion of metalepsis as a category in the taxonomy of connections, see p. 12 above.

I

'I am standing on the canal bank at Ors
Willing Wilfred Owen to make it across
To the other side where his parents wait.
He and his men are constructing pontoons.
The German sniper doesn't know his poetry.

. . .

III

Last year I read my own poems at Craiglockhart
And eavesdropped on Robert, Siegfried, Wilfred
Whispering about poetry down the corridors.
If Wilfred can concentrate a little longer,
He might just make it to the other bank.' (Longley 2020: 5)[40]

---

[40] Owen did not make it to the other bank, but his poetry did.

Rupert Brooke (1887–1915)

Stephen Harrison

1. Poet—education, cultural context, output

Rupert Chawner Brooke (1887–1915) was the son of William Parker Brooke (1850–1910), a classical schoolmaster and housemaster at Rugby School (1879–1910), and Ruth Mary Brooke, a school matron. He received a traditional classical training at Rugby, a 'public' (i.e. elite private) secondary school in the English Midlands (Jones 2014: 40–2), and won a classical scholarship to King's College Cambridge, where he went in 1906 and was taught by several distinguished Greek scholars (Jones 2014: 51–2), including Walter Headlam, whom he admired and whose sudden death in 1908 he lamented (Keynes 1968: 142–3); his classical education was thus amongst the best available at the time. The authors he mentions later in his letters are Homer, Sappho, Sophocles, Ovid, and (with particular enthusiasm) Lucretius (Keynes 1968: 174, 668; 433, 668; 338–9; 361, 490; 90, 589).

At Cambridge he wrote poetry, acted, and engaged in left-wing politics, belonging to the Fabian Club along with his friend the future Labour Chancellor Hugh Dalton; after his Classical Tripos (second class, May 1909) he worked on a thesis in English literature on the Jacobean dramatist John Webster, and published his first volume of poetry (*Poems*, 1911). He was elected a Fellow of King's in 1913, and in 1913–14 (following an episode of ill health) travelled to North America, returning via the Pacific in an extended round-the-world trip, including a stay in Tahiti, where he may have fathered a daughter with a local woman (Jones 2014: 539).

In Cambridge he met some of the Bloomsbury Group of writers and artists such as Lytton Strachey and Virginia Woolf; he knew some of the Georgian poets (such as Lascelles Abercrombie and Edward Thomas; see Parker 1999), thus having links with two of the most significant literary groupings of his day. Famously hailed by his fellow poets Frances Cornford as 'the young Apollo, golden-haired' and W. B. Yeats (not in verse) as 'the

Greek and Roman Antiquity in First World War Poetry: Making Connections. Lorna Hardwick, Stephen Harrison, and Elizabeth Vandiver, Oxford University Press. © Lorna Hardwick, Stephen Harrison, and Elizabeth Vandiver 2024. DOI: 10.1093/oso/9780198907879.003.0002

handsomest young man in England' (Jones 2014: 269, 374), his charm and good looks brought him admirers of both sexes, but his emotional life was complicated and unhappy (for recent further information on this front see Beckett 2015).

He enlisted at the outbreak of war in August 1914 and was commissioned into the Royal Navy. In October he was part of a brief expedition to Belgium to assist the evacuation of Antwerp, his only real military experience, which he describes vividly in his letters; Brooke's unit came under shell-fire but was not otherwise engaged (Keynes 1968: 622–4). After further training in Britain he set off in early March for the Allied invasion of Gallipoli, sailing on the troopship Grantully Castle with a group of classically educated ex-public-school officers which included the poet Patrick Shaw-Stewart. They named themselves 'the Argonauts' (Jones 2014: 508), were known as 'the Latin Club' by their less privileged comrades (Delany 2015: 7), and used Homeric allusions in their letters to bypass the military censor (Jones 2014: 515–16); in one letter Brooke wrote of looking forward to seeing the Cyclades where he promised to recite Sappho and Homer (Keynes 1968: 668). He was never to reach Gallipoli: he died en route of an infected insect bite on 23 April 1915 and was buried on the Greek island of Skyros in the central Aegean.

Brooke, who had already achieved some prominence in literary and social circles before his death, became something of a posthumous celebrity, even if some of his fellow war poets found his work over-sentimental.[1] A number of obituaries and brief memoirs appeared, by e.g. Virginia Woolf, Edward Thomas, and Winston Churchill, many of them adulatory (for samples see Bloom 2003); later poems by other poets presented him as the modern equivalent of an ancient Greek hero (Vandiver 2010: 361–89). His *1914 and other Poems* was published in May 1915, and his *Collected Poems* (edited by his former patron Edward Marsh) came out in 1918 prefaced by an extensive memoir by the editor; both these volumes sold more than 100,000 copies in their various impressions. The standard edition of Brooke's poems was published a generation later by his friend and school contemporary Geoffrey Keynes (1946, 2nd edn. 1970), who also edited a selection of his correspondence (1968).

By the 1960s his war poems could seem politically naive alongside the darker perspectives of Siegfried Sassoon, Isaac Rosenberg, Wilfred Owen,

---

[1] e.g. Philip Bainbrigge and Charles Sorley: cf. Wilson 1985b: 175–6; Wilson 1990: 218–19; and Vandiver 2010: 328–31.

and Robert Graves, while Georgian poetry was also felt to be too formal and conventional, and his reputation suffered something of an eclipse (see e.g. Silkin 1972: 65–9, anticipated by Leavis 1932: 21–2 and Orwell 1940: 148). In the selection for this volume, the emphasis is on Brooke's war poems, but his 'The Old Vicarage, Grantchester' (1913) is also included as an indication of his earlier work and as a classically influenced poem; its Georgian evocation of the beauties of England is typical of the characterization of England from abroad found in much war poetry.

Only fifteen or so of Brooke's more than one hundred poems relate overtly to classical themes, but they include some of his most famous, especially 'The Soldier'. The authors, genres, and topics from Greek and Roman literature used or glanced at range on the Greek side from Homer and the Trojan War ('The Soldier' and the Gallipoli fragments [below], 'Menelaus and Helen', 'Mutability') to Greek tragedy ('The Old Vicarage, Grantchester' [below], 'Menelaus and Helen', 'The Goddess In The Wood'), Plato ('Mutability'), and Greek epigram ('The Soldier' [below]). This follows the taste of Brooke's generation for Greek rather than Roman culture, but there is also evidence of interest in Latin poetry: the Underworld of Vergil *Aeneid* 6 appears several times, with a particular interest in the meeting there of Dido and Aeneas ('Hauntings', 'It's Not Going to Happen Again', 'The Old Vicarage, Grantchester', and the sonnets of 1909 and 1913),[2] while 'Jealousy' is a reworking of an ode of Horace and 'One Day' looks to a poem of Catullus; the enthusiasm expressed by Brooke in his letters for Lucretius (see above) does not seem to be reflected by allusion in his poems. Classical literature is the most important non-English influence on Brooke in his more ambitious poems; the range of his reading is that of the conventional classical education of his time (see above); his poems make allusions which are to be noticed by appropriately trained readers.

Brooke's glamorous reputation, his complex emotional and sexual life, and his close links with some of the major literary figures of his time have ensured a continuing series of biographies, annotated correspondence, and contextual studies (see Jones 2014: 542–9). His war poems remain some of the best known of the 1914–18 conflict through anthologizing, especially 'The Soldier'; they have often been set to music, e.g. by John Ireland in his 'Two Songs' of 1917–18 ('The Soldier', 'Blow Out, You Bugles'); his early poem 'Dust', set by Danny Kirwan, was included by Fleetwood Mac on their

---

[2] Owen is also interested in the Homeric and Vergilian Underworld, especially in 'Strange Meeting': see pp. 155–63 in this volume.

1972 album *Bare Trees*. His pre-war emotional life has been the subject of a romantic novel (Jill Dawson's *The Great Lover*, 2009), while his wartime death has provided the plot for a thriller (Chris McKiernan's *Think Only This Of Me*, 2016); F. Scott Fitzgerald's first novel, *This Side of Paradise* (1920), derives its title from Brooke's 'Tiare Tahiti', cited in one of its epigraphs, while Brooke himself is a minor character in A. S. Byatt's novel *The Children's Book* (2009).

2. Paramaterial—letters, manuscripts

Keynes 1968 publishes a generous selection of Brooke's many letters. Some manuscripts of poems (including that of 'The Soldier') and of letters are in the British Library (https://www.bl.uk/collection-items/rupert-brooke), but the largest collection of material by and about Brooke (including many letters not in Keynes 1968) is now at King's College, Cambridge (https://cudl.lib.cam.ac.uk/view/MS-KINGS-RCB-S-00001/44); an earlier list of manuscripts and of Brooke's publications is to be found in Schroder 1970. Some recently rediscovered love letters are published in Beckett 2015; other correspondences printed selectively in Keynes 1968 appear complete in Harris 1991 and Hale 1998.

3. Poems

'The Old Vicarage, Grantchester' (1912)

(a) **Text of poem** [from Brooke 1918; Keynes 1970 has an unaltered text]
(*Café des Westens, Berlin, May 1912*)

> Just now the lilac is in bloom,
> All before my little room;
> And in my flower-beds, I think,
> Smile the carnation and the pink;
> And down the borders, well I know,   5
> The poppy and the pansy blow...
> Oh! there the chestnuts, summer through,
> Beside the river make for you

A tunnel of green gloom, and sleep
Deeply above; and green and deep   10
The stream mysterious glides beneath,
Green as a dream and deep as death.
—Oh, damn! I know it! and I know
How the May fields all golden show,
And when the day is young and sweet,   15
Gild gloriously the bare feet
That run to bathe...
                    'Du lieber Gott!'

Here am I, sweating, sick, and hot,
And there the shadowed waters fresh
Lean up to embrace the naked flesh.   20
Temperamentvoll German Jews
Drink beer around;—and *there* the dews
Are soft beneath a morn of gold.
Here tulips bloom as they are told;
Unkempt about those hedges blows   25
An English unofficial rose;
And there the unregulated sun
Slopes down to rest when day is done,
And wakes a vague unpunctual star,
A slippered Hesper; and there are   30
Meads towards Haslingfield and Coton
Where *das Betreten*'s not *verboten*.

εἴθε γενοίμην... would I were
In Grantchester, in Grantchester!—
Some, it may be, can get in touch   35
With Nature there, or Earth, or such.
And clever modern men have seen
A Faun a-peeping through the green,
And felt the Classics were not dead,
To glimpse a Naiad's reedy head,   40
Or hear the Goat-foot piping low:...
But these are things I do not know.
I only know that you may lie
Day long and watch the Cambridge sky,
And, flower-lulled in sleepy grass,   45

Hear the cool lapse of hours pass,
Until the centuries blend and blur
In Grantchester, in Grantchester...
Still in the dawnlit waters cool
His ghostly Lordship swims his pool,   50
And tries the strokes, essays the tricks,
Long learnt on Hellespont, or Styx.
Dan Chaucer hears his river still
Chatter beneath a phantom mill.
Tennyson notes, with studious eye,   55
How Cambridge waters hurry by...
And in that garden, black and white,
Creep whispers through the grass all night;
And spectral dance, before the dawn,
A hundred Vicars down the lawn;   60
Curates, long dust, will come and go
On lissom, clerical, printless toe;
And oft between the boughs is seen
The sly shade of a Rural Dean...
Till, at a shiver in the skies,   65
Vanishing with Satanic cries,
The prim ecclesiastic rout
Leaves but a startled sleeper-out,
Grey heavens, the first bird's drowsy calls,
The falling house that never falls.   70

God! I will pack, and take a train,
And get me to England once again!
For England's the one land, I know,
Where men with Splendid Hearts may go;
And Cambridgeshire, of all England,   75
The shire for Men who Understand;
And of *that* district I prefer
The lovely hamlet Grantchester.
For Cambridge people rarely smile,
Being urban, squat, and packed with guile;   80
And Royston men in the far South
Are black and fierce and strange of mouth;
At Over they fling oaths at one,
And worse than oaths at Trumpington,

And Ditton girls are mean and dirty,   85
And there's none in Harston under thirty,
And folks in Shelford and those parts
Have twisted lips and twisted hearts,
And Barton men make Cockney rhymes,
And Coton's full of nameless crimes,   90
And things are done you'd not believe
At Madingley on Christmas Eve.
Strong men have run for miles and miles,
When one from Cherry Hinton smiles;
Strong men have blanched, and shot their wives,   95
Rather than send them to St. Ives;
Strong men have cried like babes, bydam,
To hear what happened at Babraham.
But Grantchester! ah, Grantchester!
There's peace and holy quiet there,   100
Great clouds along pacific skies,
And men and women with straight eyes,
Lithe children lovelier than a dream,
A bosky wood, a slumbrous stream,
And little kindly winds that creep   105
Round twilight corners, half asleep.
In Grantchester their skins are white;
They bathe by day, they bathe by night;
The women there do all they ought;
The men observe the Rules of Thought.   110
They love the Good; they worship Truth;
They laugh uproariously in youth;
(And when they get to feeling old,
They up and shoot themselves, I'm told) ...

Ah God! to see the branches stir   115
Across the moon at Grantchester!
To smell the thrilling-sweet and rotten
Unforgettable, unforgotten
River-smell, and hear the breeze
Sobbing in the little trees.   120
Say, do the elm-clumps greatly stand
Still guardians of that holy land?
The chestnuts shade, in reverend dream,

The yet unacademic stream?
Is dawn a secret shy and cold   125
Anadyomene, silver-gold?
And sunset still a golden sea
From Haslingfield to Madingley?
And after, ere the night is born,
Do hares come out about the corn?   130
Oh, is the water sweet and cool,
Gentle and brown, above the pool?
And laughs the immortal river still
Under the mill, under the mill?
Say, is there Beauty yet to find?   135
And Certainty? and Quiet kind?
Deep meadows yet, for to forget
The lies, and truths, and pain?…Oh! yet
Stands the Church clock at ten to three?
And is there honey still for tea?   140

(b) Poem—date, form, and content

As its sub-title records, this famous poem, Brooke's longest apart from his early works written as school prize poems, was composed during his stay in Berlin in the spring of 1912 and published that June in the King's College magazine *Basileon* (with the title 'The Sentimental Exile'; the title was altered in Brooke 1915). It expresses nostalgia for the natural English world of Cambridgeshire he had left behind for a bustling foreign metropolitan environment, imagining the view from his rented room in the Old Vicarage, Grantchester, a pretty village a few miles down the River Cam from Cambridge. It echoes a similar famous poem of nostalgia for England from the Victorian era, Robert Browning's 'Home Thoughts, from Abroad', written from Italy in 1845, which begins with the lines 'Oh, to be in England / Now that April's there' (cf. 33–4 εἴθε γενοίμην…would I were / In Grantchester, in Grantchester!) and imagines the flowering of the poet's garden back home ('Hark, where my blossomed pear-tree in the hedge / Leans to the field and scatters on the clover / Blossoms and dewdrops'— cf. 1–2 'Just now the lilac is in bloom, / All before my little room)'. The rollicking iambic tetrameter couplets of Brooke's poem with their occasional feminine (two-syllable) rhymes (Coton/Verboten, rotten/unforgotten), recall Samuel Butler's anti-Puritan satire *Hudibras* of 1674–8, a suitable model for its content of comic invective, as well as colloquial epistles to friends and others by Jonathan Swift in the first half of the eighteenth century. Brooke's poem has indeed something of the letter-form, with an implied addressee and implied trajectory from home to abroad.

(c) Reception commentary

The main element of classical reception comes in the section where ancient Greek is cited in the original script (33–41):

> εἴθε γενοίμην . . . would I were
> In Grantchester, in Grantchester!—
> Some, it may be, can get in touch
> With Nature there, or Earth, or such.
> And clever modern men have seen
> A Faun a-peeping through the green,
> And felt the Classics were not dead,
> To glimpse a Naiad's reedy head,
> Or hear the Goat-foot piping low:...

The Greek phrase εἴθε γενοίμην (immediately translated in the text as 'would I were') looks back to a dramatic moment in Attic tragedy,[3] in Euripides' *Hippolytus*, where Phaedra, queen of Theseus, king of Athens, afflicted by Aphrodite with a passion for her hunting-mad stepson Hippolytus, wishes to be away from her palace and out in the country with him (228–31):

> δέσποιν' ἁλίας Ἄρτεμι Λίμνας
> καὶ γυμνασίων τῶν ἱπποκρότων,
> εἴθε γενοίμαν ἐν σοῖς δαπέδοις
> πώλους Ἐνετὰς δαμαλιζομένα.

> Artemis, mistress of the salt Lake
> And of the competitions where horses clatter,
> Would I were on your plains
> Mastering the colts of the Veneto!

[3] The Euripidean passage is usually printed with the Doric spelling γενοίμαν in modern texts such as the one quoted here, but in Brooke's time many editions had the Attic γενοίμην, the form he uses. The phrase εἴθε γενοίμην/γενοίμαν occurs only three times in classical Greek texts: the Euripidean passage and two epigrams in the *Greek Anthology*, neither of which seems to have a context which fits Brooke's poem (*AP* 7.699, 12.190).

Brooke thus represents himself as like Euripides' Phaedra, stifled by his current urban environment and longing to escape to the freedom of nature which he had enjoyed in the rural environment of Grantchester. Whether the poet saw himself as sharing the queen's forbidden erotic passion for one who is elsewhere is unclear.

The reference to 'clever modern men' concerned with perpetuating the classical figures of Fauns (half-human, half-goat), Naiads (water-nymphs), and Pan ('the Goat-foot') seems to refer to contemporary classical reception in the work of the sophisticated French symbolist poet Stéphane Mallarmé. In 1877 Mallarmé had published the final version of his substantial poem 'L'Après-midi d'un Faune'; it was later the subject of an orchestral piece by Debussy (1984) which in turn formed the basis for a ballet choreographed by Diaghilev which Brooke saw in 1911 (Jones 2014: 226). Mallarmé's poem concerns the story of Pan and Syrinx (from Ovid *Metamorphoses* 1) and is essentially a meditation by a Faun (Mallarmé's equivalent of Pan) on the invention of the Pan-pipes as a result of the metamorphosis into the reed of the Naiad Syrinx, details which seem to underlie Brooke's lines here. The detail that Pan is 'goat-footed' (not in Mallarmé) may come from the *Homeric Hymn to Pan*, where the matching Greek term αἰγιπόδης is twice used of the god (2, 37).[4]

Otherwise there are only a few details. Lines 49–52, referring to Byron's Pool on the river Cam at Grantchester where both the earlier poet and Brooke had bathed (Jones 2014: 112, 162), evoke both Byron's famous swim in 180 across the Hellespont imitating the Greek hero Leander (MacCarthy 2002: 118–19) and the Styx, the river of the classical Underworld, a theme in Brooke's 1913 poem 'It's not going to Happen Again'. The capitalized 'Good' in line 111, like 'Truth' in the same line, 'Beauty' in 135, and 'Certainty' and 'Quiet' in 136, looks like a version of a Platonic abstract Form (see Sedley 2016), a theme of Brooke's 1913 poem 'Mutability' (3 'Where Faith and Good, Wisdom and Truth abide'). At line 126 the comparison of the dawn to Venus Anadyomene (Greek for 'Venus emerging [from the sea]'), a famous work of the Greek painter Apelles (Pliny *Natural History* 35.87, 91), looks like a variation of the common Homeric personification of the Dawn-goddess in formulas for the break of day (cf. e.g. *Iliad* 1.477).

---

[4] Otherwise this epithet is found in classical Greek only in two epigrams in the Greek Anthology, neither of which seems to have similar concerns (*AP* 6.57, 9.330).

(d) Associated works

The evocation of Euripides' *Hippolytus* is shared with 'The Goddess in the Wood' (1910), which also takes up a theme from Ovid's *Metamorphoses*.

'The Soldier' (1914)

(a) **Text of poem** [from Brooke 1918; Keynes 1970 has an unaltered text]

> If I should die, think only this of me:
>   That there's some corner of a foreign field
> That is for ever England. There shall be
>   In that rich earth a richer dust concealed;
> A dust whom England bore, shaped, made aware,
>   Gave, once, her flowers to love, her ways to roam,
> A body of England's, breathing English air,
>   Washed by the rivers, blest by suns of home.
>
> And think, this heart, all evil shed away,
>   A pulse in the eternal mind, no less
> Gives somewhere back the thoughts by England given;
> Her sights and sounds; dreams happy as her day;
>   And laughter, learnt of friends; and gentleness,
> In hearts at peace, under an English heaven.

(b) Poem—date, form, and content

'The Soldier' is the last and most celebrated of the series of five war sonnets entitled '1914',[5] written by Brooke in naval training camp in Blandford, Dorset, and at Walmer Castle, Kent, in November–December 1914, and first published in the short-lived literary periodical *New Numbers* (issue 4) in December. It was republished together with the fourth, 'The Dead', in *The Times Literary Supplement* in March 1915, and read aloud by Dean Inge at St. Paul's Cathedral on Easter Sunday, 4 April, less than three weeks before Brooke's death on 23 April, something Brooke learned from friends before his death (Jones 2014: 514, 518). The sonnet sequence was placed at the head of the first posthumous collection *1914 and other Poems* (Brooke 1915) and

---

[5] The previous four are entitled 'Peace', 'Safety', 'The Dead', and 'The Dead' (again).

in all subsequent editions of Brooke's poems. In form, 'The Soldier' is a Petrarchan sonnet in iambic pentameters, consisting of an initial octave with rhyming scheme ABABCDCD, followed by a sestet with rhyming scheme EFGEFG. The sonnet is not a classical form (it originated in Italian in the thirteenth century CE), but its length might suggest a link with Greek epigrams, which could be as long as twelve or sixteen lines; this becomes more likely given its initial topic of imagined death, since the epitaph is a standard epigram form (see next section).

(c) Reception commentary

J. W. Mackail's anthology of Greek epigrams, first published in 1890 and much read in English schools (see Vandiver 2010: 43; Nisbet 2013: 237–56), has a section of sixty-three epitaphs. Some of these are presented as spoken in the first person by the dead, including warriors slain in battle; an example is the famous terse epigram by Simonides on the three hundred Spartans dead far from home at Thermopylae (*AP* 7.249 'Stranger, report to the Spartans that here we lie, obeying their instructions', Ὦ ξεῖν᾽, ἄγγειλον Λακεδαιμονίοις ὅτι τῇδε / κείμεθα, τοῖς κείνων ῥήμασι πειθόμενοι). None of these matches Brooke's poem in imagining the speaker's own future death, 'proleptic mourning', in Elizabeth Vandiver's felicitous phrase (2010: 325).

The general idea of the poet-speaker envisaging his own end may come from another classical genre, Latin love-elegy; there anticipating one's own future death and funeral is found as a theme, sometimes with similar details: e.g. Tibullus 1.3.55–6, where the poet pictures himself dying on military service, or Propertius 2.13.35–8, where the poet imagines being turned to dust in death and compares his tomb to that of Achilles at Troy. Latin love-elegy would have formed part of Brooke's schoolboy reading, and such an allusion fits with the prominence of first-person love-poetry in his own work.

The poem's central idea of the soldier falling and being buried in a foreign environment is a key notion in the Trojan War as narrated in Homer's *Iliad*, where many Greeks and Trojan allies from other regions die and are laid to rest far from home; Brooke knew the poem, central to his education (Keynes 1968: 668). The 'foreign field' might look to the 'Flanders fields' of the contemporary Western Front that he had visited briefly in October 1914, but he could well have already been aware in November/December 1914 of plans to open up an Eastern front at Gallipoli in the Dardanelles campaign, proposed by his acquaintance Winston Churchill (the First Lord of the Admiralty) at around that time, especially since his patron and London landlord Edward Marsh was then Churchill's private secretary and his friend Violet Asquith (daughter of the then Prime Minister H. H. Asquith) reported some of her father's military discussions to him in her letters (Jones 2014: 490). Gallipoli provided not only an alternative foreign field but one associated with Homer and the Trojan War, as this Turkish peninsula faced the site of ancient Troy, a feature noted and explored by classically educated poets sent to fight there, including Brooke himself in other poems (see pp. 38–9 below and Vandiver 2010: 241–80).

In the *Iliad*, the pathos of death far from home is repeatedly emphasized in the many obituaries of warriors on both sides (see e.g. Griffin 1980: 106–12). Brooke's central conceit in 'The Soldier', that an element of the foreign country becomes perpetually a part of England via the dead man's burial in it, inverts Thomas Hardy's similar Boer War obituary of 'Drummer Hodge' (1899), where an Englishman's body is absorbed into the alien landscape of southern Africa (see Vandiver 2010: 327–8). It has been noted as an inverted *nostos* (return): instead of returning home, the soldier finds a substitute permanent residence in the land of the enemy (see Vandiver 2010: 326–7; Riley 2021: 6–7; on the general theme of *nostos* in WWI poetry see the Introduction to this volume, pp. 15–16). But it also reverses the pathos of those Homeric moments where the dead man's home country is movingly evoked by name as somewhere to which he will never return. Achilles taunts the dead Trojan ally Iphition by saying 'here is your death, but your birth was on the Gygaean lake' (*Iliad* 20.390–1), while we find an extended account of the death of the brothers Crethon and Orsilochus, born in Phere in Greece but killed by Aeneas at Troy (*Iliad* 5.541–53); in both these cases the key idea is that the land of Troy takes possession of the foreign dead. The detail of 'a body' 'washed by the rivers' might also be an ironical inversion of the rivers of Troy which are several times mentioned as washing over corpses, especially the river Scamander which complains to Achilles that he has blocked it with the dead bodies of his victims (*Iliad* 21.214–21).

The line 'In that rich earth a richer dust concealed' evokes another literary version of the Trojan War, that presented in the *Agamemnon* of Aeschylus.[6] In that key Athenian tragedy from the fifth century BCE, the chorus of Greek elders at Argos lament the fate of their younger compatriots who died far from home at Troy (452–5): 'And there, about the wall, they, fair in

---

[6] Brooke had acted in the *Eumenides* of Aeschylus (part of the same trilogy as *Agamemnon*) at Cambridge in November 1906 (Jones 2014: 56).

form, occupy tombs of the land of Troy, and the enemy land concealed its possessors' (οἱ δ' αὐτοῦ περὶ τεῖχος / θήκας Ἰλιάδος γᾶς / εὔμορφοι κατέχουσιν, ἐχ-/θρὰ δ' ἔχοντας ἔκρυψεν). Here we find the same idea of the foreign land hiding the soldier's remains. The same chorus in the same play also plays on the dust of the warrior that (alternatively) returns home not alive but as ashes (435–6): 'And instead of men urns and dust arrive at each man's house' (ἀντὶ δὲ φωτῶν / τεύχη καὶ σποδὸς εἰς ἑκάσ-/του δόμους ἀφικνεῖται).

The conceit of the 'richer dust' might also look to the common classical idea that the bodies of the slain contribute to the later fertility of battlefields; this is famously exploited by Vergil in his description of the Roman civil war battlefields of his own time in Greece (*Georgics* 1.491–2, in Dryden's translation, which Brooke may well have known): 'For this, the Emathian plains once more were strewed / With Roman bodies, and just heaven thought good / To fatten twice those fields with Roman blood' (*nec fuit indignum superis bis sanguine nostro / Emathiam et latos Haemi pinguescere campos*). Virgil's conceit is echoed by Horace at *Odes* 2.1.29–31, 'What field is not enriched by Latin blood, bearing witness to impious battles by its burials?' (*quis non Latino sanguine pinguior / campus sepulcris impia proelia/testatur... ?*), another poem which Brooke is very likely to have read as a standard school text.

The poem could be complete at the end of the octave, and the classical colouring seems to cease then. An apparent closure at this point might not be coincidental, since eight lines is a regular length for a Greek epigram. The final sestet seems to have little classical resonance: 'eternal mind' is drawn from Wordsworth's 'Ode on Intimations of Immortality' (114) and may look back distantly to Neoplatonic ideas about the all-encompassing eternal divine mind (*nous*). Neoplatonism and its relation to Christianity had recently been popularized in the UK by Dean Inge (Inge 1900), who in 1915 ordered this sonnet to be read in St Paul's Cathedral (see above).

(d) Associated works

Three late fragments by Brooke look forward to the Gallipoli campaign as a repeat of the Trojan War (see below) in specific recall of the *Iliad* (for the fragments and some reception discussion see Vandiver 2010: 241–3 and the commentary below).

Brooke's poem was much imitated by other war poets, both in admiration and in subversion (see Vandiver 2010: 328–30, especially on Philip Bainbrigge's ironic sonnet which begins with the same words 'If I should die').

One famous poem which seems to respond to Brooke on several levels is W. B. Yeats' 'An Irish Airman foresees his Death' (1918):

> I know that I shall meet my fate
> Somewhere among the clouds above;
> Those that I fight I do not hate,
> Those that I guard I do not love;
>
> My country is Kiltartan Cross,
> My countrymen Kiltartan's poor,
> No likely end could bring them loss
> Or leave them happier than before.
>
> Nor law, nor duty bade me fight,
> Nor public men, nor cheering crowds,
> A lonely impulse of delight
> Drove to this tumult in the clouds;
>
> I balanced all, brought all to mind,
> The years to come seemed waste of breath,
> A waste of breath the years behind
> In balance with this life, this death.

Yeats and Brooke had met in 1913, when the older poet had been much impressed by the younger's good looks (Jones 2014: 374), and Brooke's sonnet was well known by 1918. Yeats' poem, in four-quatrain stanzas two lines longer than a sonnet, is imagined as spoken by his close friend Major Robert Gregory, who had been killed in February 1918 in a Royal Flying Corps mission over Italy. It looks back to 'The Soldier' with its opening prophecy of the speaker's own end, already fulfilled for Gregory, only hypothetical for Brooke at the time of writing, and specifically reverses Brooke's patriotic commitment; the Anglo-Irish Gregory (perhaps unrealistically—see Foster 2014: 119) is presented as indifferent to the British war effort in which he is engaged; he is following his own inclinations in serving as a pilot, not a nationalistic imperative, and the focus on the moment, with past and future both irrelevant, contrasts fundamentally with Brooke's notion of perpetual commemoration. Both speakers specify their distant home with emphatic anaphoric naming ('England…England…English', 'Kiltartan…Kiltartan's' [referring to County Galway]), and both poems make effective use of multiple repetitions striking in such short poems (Brooke: 'rich…richer', 'dust… dust', 'her' [four times]; Yeats: 'those that…those that', 'my country…my countrymen', 'nor' [four times], 'waste of breath…waste of breath'). Both share the idea that death and life are in some sense equivalent: for Brooke death on campaign is a form of eternal existence, for Yeats existence and non-existence are indifferent in the moment of meditation.

'Fragments written on the voyage to Gallipoli' (1915)

[from Brooke 1918; Keynes 1970 has an unaltered text]

1

They say Achilles in the darkness stirred,
And Hector, his old enemy,
Moved the great shades that were his limbs. They heard
More than Olympian thunder on the sea.

2

                      Death and Sleep
Bear many a young Sarpedon home.

3

And Priam and his fifty sons
Wake all amazed, and hear the guns,
And shake for Troy again.

These three classical fragments (which I have numbered for convenience) were found with others in Brooke's notebooks after his death in April 1915 (Jones 2014: 530). Like a number of other classically educated officers on the Gallipoli campaign (see Vandiver 2010: 228–20), Brooke was understandably struck by the proximity of the Gallipoli peninsula to the traditional site of the city of Troy, just on the opposite side of the narrow channel of the Dardanelles, and naturally recalled his reading of Homer (see Jones 2014: 515–16). The three fragments may have been intended for a single poem pointing to the waking of the Homeric dead by new war activity in their locality and the general idea of a modern repetition of the Trojan War.

Fragments 1 and 3 refer to the noise of the guns; Fragment 3 is headed 'Queen Elizabeth' in a notebook, suggesting that the guns are those of the dreadnought battleship Queen Elizabeth, launched 1913 and flagship of the Gallipoli expedition (see Burt 1986).

Fragment 1 alludes to the tombs of Achilles and Hector close to Troy: the establishment of the latter is the final event of the *Iliad*, while the tomb of Achilles does not occur in Homer but in a famous passage of Cicero which records a visit to it by Alexander the Great (Cicero *Pro Archia* 24), while 'Olympian thunder' refers to the thunder of Zeus which is described several times in the *Iliad*.

Fragment 2 compares modern casualties on the battlefield and their rescue to the episode in the *Iliad* where Apollo is told by Zeus to remove the body of Zeus' son Sarpedon, slain by Patroclus, from the battlefield and hand it over for transport home for burial in Lycia (*Iliad* 16.665–85). Given that Lycia is not too far away in Asia Minor, Brooke may be thinking of local Turkish casualties rather than the British and Anzac dead who were not taken home but buried in more than thirty cemeteries nearby (see e.g. Taylor and Cupper 2000).

Fragment 3 refers to the Trojan king Priam and his fifty sons (*Iliad* 24.495), almost all of whom died at Troy (the only one spared according to some sources was the prophet Helenus, who appears in Vergil's *Aeneid*).

4. Other classical interactions

'III: The Dead' (1914). The third of the five war sonnets of late 1914 deploys the image of the 'rich Dead', which recalls the claim of Solon in Herodotus (1.31) that only the dead can be called truly *olbios* (Greek = 'rich, happy'), while its idea that 'Honour has come back, as a king, to earth' looks back to the return of Justice to earth at Vergil *Eclogue* 4.6–7 (on these echoes see further Vandiver 2010: 285–7).

Charles Sorley (1895–1915)

Stephen Harrison

1. Poet—education, cultural context, output

Charles Hamilton Sorley (1895–1915), was the son of William Ritchie Sorley (1855–1935), Professor of Moral Philosophy at the University of Cambridge 1900–33,[1] and his wife Janetta Colquhoun Smith (d. 1957), author of the collective historical biography *Kings' Daughters* (1937). He received a traditional classical education at his public (i.e. elite private) secondary school, Marlborough College in the south-west of England (attended by Siegfried Sassoon a decade before), where one of the classics teachers was his fellow-Scot John Bain, the addressee of 'I have not brought my Odyssey' (see below).[2] Though he planned to read classics at university, was clearly an able scholar in the subject and read Homer and Greek tragedy for pleasure,[3] his correspondence shows that he viewed his classical studies mainly as a passport to an Oxford degree and to a potential career in social work.[4]

He began publishing poetry while still at school, and won a classical scholarship to University College, Oxford, in December 1913. In the first half of 1914, before his planned start at Oxford in October, he went to Germany, first to study German in Schwerin and then to attend a term of lectures at the University of Jena. At the outbreak of war in August he was briefly interned at Trier on the Moselle while on a walking holiday;[5] on his return to the UK soon afterwards, he joined the Suffolk Regiment as a second lieutenant. He arrived on the Western Front in late May 1915; promoted to captain in August, he was shot in the head by a sniper and

---

[1] See *ODNB*, 'Sorley, William Ritchie, (1855–1935)', F. R. Tennant, revised by S. M. den Otter (2007), https://doi.org/10.1093/ref:odnb/36197.

[2] Sorley was never taught by Bain but appreciated him as a character, fellow-Scot, and poet: see Wilson 1985b: 64.

[3] Wilson 1990: 105.   [4] Wilson 1985b: 92; Wilson 1990: 44, 76.

[5] His own narrative of this episode is to be found in Wilson 1990: 263–8.

Greek and Roman Antiquity in First World War Poetry: Making Connections. Lorna Hardwick, Stephen Harrison, and Elizabeth Vandiver, Oxford University Press. © Lorna Hardwick, Stephen Harrison, and Elizabeth Vandiver 2024. DOI: 10.1093/oso/9780198907879.003.0003

killed during the last stages of the Battle of Loos on 13 October 1915 at the age of 20. His body was not found; he is commemorated in an inscription on Sir Herbert Baker's memorial at Dud Corner Cemetery, Loos, and as one of the sixteen Great War poets commemorated on a collective tablet in Poets' Corner in Westminster Abbey in 1985.[6]

The year after Sorley's death, his family published a collection of his poems in *Marlborough and Other Poems* (1916a). More recently, the scholar Jean Moorcroft Wilson, biographer of Rosenberg and Sassoon, has produced complete editions of the poems (1985a) and letters (1990) and written a full biography (1985b), which have cemented Sorley's status as a significant poet of the First World War. Classical material appears in only a small number of his poems (six out of forty-five), but is central to his two most important war pieces, 'I have not brought my Odyssey' and 'When you see millions of the mouthless dead' (see below). Homeric epic and the Trojan War are prominent in his work (see the two poems just mentioned along with 'To Germany' and 'The Song of the Ungirt Runners' and 'All the hills and vales along'), as for many poets of WWI (see Vandiver 2010), while the Horatian elements in 'I have not brought my Odyssey' are reflected in the early Horace translation 'Quis Desiderio'.[7] These two authors were central to the contemporary school curriculum in classics which Sorley had recently completed. His favourite text seems to have been the *Odyssey*, which is regularly quoted in his correspondence and provides the basis for his poem 'I have not brought my Odyssey' (see further below). The poems examined here reflect his detailed classical reading, and make allusions which are to be picked up by his original readers of similar background such as the classics teacher John Bain.

Sorley's correspondence makes it clear that knew he knew the poetry of Rupert Brooke, whom he viewed as 'undoubtedly a poet, though a slight and lyrical one';[8] he seems to have liked 'The Old Vicarage, Grantchester' which he read while still at school and later imitated,[9] but reacted strongly against the war sonnets which he read while training to go to France at Aldershot in April 1915. These he regarded as self-dramatizing and sentimental, commenting that 'he [Brooke] is far too obsessed with his own sacrifice . . . he has clothed his attitude in fine words: but he has taken the sentimental

---

[6] See https://www.westminster-abbey.org/abbey-commemorations/commemorations/poets-of-the-first-world-war.

[7] For Sorley's perceived prowess in verse translation at school see Wilson 1985b: 73.

[8] Wilson 1990: 47.   [9] See Wilson 1985b: 104; Wilson 1990: 47–8, 218.

attitude'.[10] Sorley's own more resigned and stoical approach to the war is clear from the sonnet 'When you see millions of the mouthless dead' (see below).

Robert Graves enthused in his correspondence about Sorley's poetry which he discovered in 1916, after the latter's death, and described Sorley in his memoir *Goodbye to All That* (1929) as 'one of the three poets of importance killed during the war' (Graves 1960: 141, the others being Wilfred Owen and Isaac Rosenberg); he also dedicated a poem to Sorley's memory in 1918, 'Sorley's Weather'. The future Poet Laureate John Masefield also regarded him as a key poetic loss of the conflict.[11] Sorley's sonnet 'When you see millions of the mouthless dead' has been much anthologized, and has been set as part of his orchestrated song-cycle *The Torn Fields* by the English composer Mark-Anthony Turnage (2000–2) and as a part-song by the Scottish composer Sir James Macmillan (2017). Sorley's life and work have been the subject of the Olivier Award-nominated play *It Is Easy to Be Dead* by Neil McPherson (2016); his sonnet is also quoted in the title and as the epigraph of Robert Goddard's *In Pale Battalions* (1988), a detective novel which unravels a World War I mystery two generations later. A line from the sonnet is also quoted by Sorley's fictional contemporary General Gamart in Penelope Fitzgerald's 1978 novel *The Bookshop* (Chapter 2).

2. Paramaterial—letters, manuscripts

The manuscripts of twelve poems are held in the archives at Marlborough College; that of 'I have not brought my Odyssey' is owned by the family of its addressee John Bain.[12] Sorley's *Letters from Germany and from the army* (1916b), and *The letters of Charles Sorley*, with a chapter of biography (1919) were published early on by his family; a complete edition was produced by Jean Moorcroft Wilson (1990); almost all the originals held by the family were destroyed by his father after their first publication.[13] The letters are well written and often highly entertaining, and provide a valuable source for Sorley's life, reading, and views in the period 1911–15.

---

[10] Wilson 1990: 218–19, with comment in Wilson 1985b: 175–6.
[11] Wilson 1985b: 213.   [12] Wilson 1985a: 35.   [13] Wilson 1990: 32.

3. Poems

These are presented in the edition of Jean Moorcroft Wilson (1985, hereafter referred to as MW, with its numeration of poems and pages), but reordered in more or less reverse chronological sequence.[14]

'I have not brought my Odyssey' (1915)

(a) **Text of poem** [= MW 41, pp. 129–33]

I have not brought my Odyssey
With me here across the sea;
But you'll remember, when I say
How, when they went down Sparta way,
To sandy Sparta, long ere dawn
Horses were harnessed, rations drawn,
Equipment polished sparkling bright,
And breakfasts swallowed (as the white
Of Eastern heavens turned to gold)—
The dogs barked, swift farewells were told. 10
The sun springs up, the horses neigh,
Crackles the whip thrice—then away!
From sun-go-up to sun-go-down
All day across the sandy down
The gallant horses galloped, till
The wind across the downs more chill
Blew, the sun. sank and all the road
Was darkened, that it only showed
Right at the end the town's red light
And twilight glimmering into night. 20
The horses never slackened till
They reached the doorway and stood still.
Then came the knock, the unlading; then
The honey-sweet converse of men,
The splendid bath, the change of dress,

[14] We are most grateful to Jean Moorcroft Wilson for her kind permission to use her text and her support for this project.

Then—O the grandeur of their Mess,
The henchmen, the prim stewardess!
And O the breaking of old ground,
The tales, after the port went round!
(The wondrous wiles of old Odysseus,   30
Old Agamemnon and his misuse
Of his command, and that young chit
Paris—who didn't care a bit
For Helen—only to annoy Pa
He did it really, κ.τ.λ.)
But soon they led amidst the din
The honey-sweet ἀοιδός in,
Whose eyes were blind, whose soul had sight,
Who knew the fame of men in fight—
Bard of white hair and trembling foot,   40
Who sang whatever God might put
Into his heart. And there he sung,
Those war-worn veterans among,
Tales of great war and strong hearts wrung,
Of clash of arms, of council's brawl,
Of beauty that must early fall,
Of battle hate and battle joy
By the old windy walls of Troy.
They felt that they were unreal then,
Visions and shadow-forms, not men.   50
But those the Bard did sing and say
(Some were their comrades, some were they)
Took shape and loomed and strengthened more
Greatly than they had guessed of yore.
And now the fight begins again,
The old war-joy, the old war-pain.
Sons of one school across the sea
We have no fear to fight, for we
Have echo of our deeds in you
We have our ἀοιδός too.   60

And soon, O soon, I do not doubt it,
With the body or without it,
We shall all come tumbling down

To our old wrinkled red-capped town.
Perhaps the road up Ilsley way,
The old ridge-track, will be my way.
High up among the sheep and sky,
Look down on Wantage, passing by,
And see the smoke from Swindon town
And then full left at Liddington,   70
Where the four winds of heaven meet
The earth-blest traveller to greet.
And then my face is toward the south,
There is a singing on my mouth:
Away to rightward I descry
My Barbury ensconced in sky,
Far underneath the Ogbourne twins,
And at my feet the thyme and whins,
The grasses with their little crowns
Of gold, the lovely Aldbourne downs,   80
And that old signpost (well I knew
That crazy signpost, arms askew,
Old mother of the four grass ways).
And then my mouth is dumb with praise,
For, past the wood and chalkpit tiny,
A glimpse of Marlborough ἐρατεινή!
So I descend beneath the rail
To warmth and welcome and wassail,
And you, our minstrel, you our bard,
Who makes war's grievous things and hard,   90
Lightsome and glorious and fair
Will be, at least in spirit, there.
We'll read your rhymes, and we will sing
The toun o' touns till the roofs ring.
And if you'll come among us, then
We shall be most blest of men,
We shall forget the old old pain,
Remember Marlborough again
And hearken all the tales you tell
And bless our old ἀοιδός. Well,   100
This for the future. Now we stand
Stronger through you, to guard our land,

I do but give the thanks of each
(Thanks far far greater than my speech)
Of those who knew or did not know
(For all knew you) not long ago
In places that we see in sleep
Our eyes are dry but our hearts weep
Warm living tears that memory dear
Calls up the moment that we hear   110
(For we do hear it) your kind voice
Who understood us, men and boys.
So now and for the ages through
We are all dead and living too.
Our common life lies on your tongue
For as the bards sang, you have sung.
This from the battered trenches—rough,
Jingling and tedious enough.
And so I sign myself to you:
One, who some crooked pathways knew   120
Round Bedwyn: who could scarcely leave
The Downs on a December eve:
Was at his happiest in shorts,
And got—not many good reports!
Small skill of rhyming in his hand—
But you'll forgive—you'll understand.

(b) Poem—date, form, and content

'I have not brought my Odyssey', at 126 lines in its full version, is one of the longer preserved poems in English from the First World War and is dated 12 July 1915, three months before the author's death.[15] It is written in iambic tetrameter couplets (with occasional triplets), as used for Samuel Butler's anti-Puritan satire *Hudibras* (1674–8), but more importantly for similar colloquial epistles to friends and others by Jonathan Swift in the first half of the eighteenth century; it is also the metre of Rupert Brooke's contemporary 'The Old Vicarage, Grantchester', a poem which Sorley certainly knew (see above) and which like Sorley's poem expresses nostalgia for England from abroad.[16] The poem's Homeric affinities are evident from its

---

[15] For a brief account see Wilson 1985b: 193–5.
[16] See the treatment of Brooke's poem in this volume.

title and are detailed (see below), but this metrical link with the tradition of English poetic epistles also has classical implications, since at its end the poem alludes to the closures of two of Horace's hexameter *Epistles* to friends (1.10 and 1.20, see below), and its overall framework scenario of writing to a friend on a Homeric topic may also echo the opening of another poem from the same epistolary book. In *Epistles* 1.2 Horace addresses his friend Lollius in Rome, saying that he has been reading both Homeric epics when away from Rome and retailing moral lessons he draws from their texts. Though Sorley paraphrases only the *Odyssey* and does not moralize, the element of epistolary sharing of a love for Homer between like-minded separated literary friends, addressed from one in a peripheral location to one in a cultural centre the two have shared, is clearly common to the two texts.

Structurally, the poem falls into clear sections: the opening paraphrase of episodes from the *Odyssey* (1–54), a transition passage (55–60) in which the appearance of the Homeric bard provides a link to the addressee, the classics master and poet John Bain, whom the author regards as the Marlborough bard of the First World War,[17] and an imagined return journey of Sorley himself to Marlborough, clearly seen as parallel to Ithaca as the yearned-for home destination of Odysseus, for a joyful reunion with the addressee as tale-telling bard (61–101). The penultimate section (101–16) expands on Bain's function as the local bard of those former Marlborough pupils at war who are celebrated in his verse, again stressing his parallel role to that of the bards of the *Odyssey* in commemorating warriors, while the final section (117–26) presents an Horatian epistolary sign-off and ironic autobiographical sketch by the poet.

(c) Reception commentary

The title suggests that Sorley had not taken his copy of the *Odyssey* to the trenches;[18] he did take it with him to Germany in the first half of 1914 (see above). His letters from Germany show not only that he was reading the *Odyssey* in Greek there,[19] but also that he was already comparing the hospitality of Helen and Menelaus in Sparta to the visiting Telemachus to his own boarding abroad: 'I could write a brilliant book comparing life in Ithaca, Sparta and holy Pylos with life in Mecklenburg-Schwerin in the time

---

[17] For a sample of Bain's memorial verse and Sorley's admiration for it see Vandiver 2010: 82–5.

[18] His memory of the poem was still strong there in June 1915; see Wilson 1990: 229.

[19] For pleasure as opposed to the Demosthenes and Cicero recommended by his future tutor at Oxford, A. B. Poynton: see Wilson 1990: 105, 124, 135, 151.

of Herr Dr Beutin'.[20] He was also already thinking of the analogy between the hilly landscape of Marlborough and that of Sparta as described by Homer.[21] Both these elements emerge together a year later in 'I have not brought my Odyssey'.

After the opening address to John Bain, lines 4–22 provide a fairly close paraphrase of the brief Odyssean narrative of the last leg of the two-day journey of Telemachus and Peisistratus across the Peloponnese from the court of Peisistratus' father Nestor at Pylos to that of Menelaus and Helen at Sparta (*Odyssey* 3.481–97): 'So soon as early Dawn appeared, the rosy-fingered, they yoked the horses and mounted the inlaid car, and drove forth from the gateway and the echoing portico. Then Peisistratus touched the horses with the whip to start them, and nothing loath the pair sped onward. So they came to the wheat-bearing plain, and thereafter pressed on toward their journey's end, so well did their swift horses bear them on. And the sun set and all the ways grew dark'. The elements of bathing and changing (25) are elements of the pair's warm reception when they arrive at the court at Sparta (*Odyssey* 4.47–51), while the 'prim stewardess' translates the Homeric αἰδοίη ταμίη (4.55) and 'henchmen' reflects the activities of (mostly female) servants in the original (4.49–58).

In lines 36–54 this Homeric episode is combined with another court scene when the local blind bard appears and sings of the war at Troy (which does not happen at Sparta, where it is Menelaus himself who recalls earlier events): this is *Odyssey* 8.62–82 at the court of Alcinous in Phaeacia, where the similarly blind Demodocus, whom the Muse had deprived of sight but given the gift of song (picked up in line 37), sings of the quarrel of Agamemnon and Achilles (also recalled in the after-dinner talk of lines 31–2 as well as in the bard's song of lines 45–8). But the topic of the 'wiles of old Odysseus' recalls not a bardic song but Helen's post-dinner narrative to Telemachus in Sparta, where she tells of Odysseus' cunning infiltration of Troy in disguise (*Odyssey* 4.240–58); the story of Paris and Helen (lines 32–5) is never narrated in Homer.

The abbreviation κ.τ.λ. in line 35 for καὶ τὰ λοιπά (*kai ta loipa*, not a Homeric phrase) is a shared in-joke between an elite author and his classics teacher who understand that the Greek abbreviation (meaning 'and what remains', i.e. 'etc.') has to be expanded to make the (comic) rhyme with

---

[20] Wilson 1990: 105; see further 107 and 123 (the latter is in a letter to Sorley's former headmaster, full of Odyssean quotations in Greek).

[21] See Wilson 1990: 85–6 (a letter to a former Marlborough friend).

'annoy Pa' , while the repeated use of the Greek word ἀοιδός (*a-oidos*, used of Demodocus, *Odyssey* 8.62), points to the poem's central parallel between the Homeric bard who sings of war's sufferings and heroism and his modern analogue John Bain, a theme especially stressed in lines 55–60. Engagements with Homeric language can be playful: the compound adjective in 'honey-sweet ἀοιδός' of line 37 translates the epithet μελιηδής which is usually used not of people but of things to eat and drink, while 'the windy walls of Troy' varies the standard phrase 'windy Troy' (Ἴλιον ἠνεμόεσσαν, *Iliad* 18.174).

This first half of the poem shows some effective conflations between ancient and modern settings. 'Rations drawn, / Equipment polished sparkling bright' (6–7) and 'the town's red light' (19) suggest a modern, war-time scenario, while 'sandy down' (14) looks not just to 'sandy Sparta' (5: in fact neatly applying the normal epithet of 'sandy' Pylos, the pair's starting-point [cf. *Odyssey* 1.93 Πύλον ἠμαθόεντα] to Sparta, their destination) but also to the Wiltshire Downs near Marlborough evoked at the poem's end (122 'The Downs'). Likewise, the court of Menelaus and Helen is likened to a modern officers' mess (26) with the circulation of port and accompanying anecdotes of the past (29), evoking the moment at Sparta where Helen serves up her famous drugged drink after dinner to alleviate the company's sad recollections of Troy (4.220–8).

The imagined return of the poet to Marlborough in lines 61–101 seems to take us away from Homer, but a couple of allusions suggest that this longed-for journey reflects the equally longed-for homecoming of Odysseus to Ithaca: the 'smoke from Swindon town' befits the home of the railway industry in south-west England, but also recalls Odysseus' longing when with Calypso to see even the smoke of his home on Ithaca (*Odyssey* 1.58–9). This is cleverly conflated with the journey to Sparta already described: the use of the Homeric epithet ἐρατεινή, 'lovely' (line 86) of Marlborough (rhyming with 'tiny' in the different Greek pronunciation of the time) recalls its use of Sparta (Lacedaemon) at *Iliad* 3.443 Λακεδαίμονος ἐξ ἐρατεινῆς, suggesting the warm welcome available in both places ('warmth and welcome and wassail'). Both places are also set in attractive hills, another reason for the classical analogy which is also found in Sorley's letters (see above).

In the concluding section, as suggested above, we move back to the framework of the Horatian epistle. Here two letter-endings from Horace are merged, that of *Epistles* 1.10 (49), appropriately Horace's letter to his friend Fuscus, another teacher, where he says 'This I am dictating to you behind the shrine of Vacuna' (*Haec tibi dictabam post fanum putre Vacunae*), giving a similar address-location commencing with a pronoun referring to the letter itself (117 'This from the battered trenches'), and that of 1.20, an ironic self-description (23–5): 'You (i.e. the personified book of the *Epistles*) will say that I pleased the leaders of the city both in war and at home, that I was of slender body, early greying, sun-seeking, swift to anger, but so as to be easily placated'; the reference to a 'December eve' (122) may even pick up Horace's recording in the lines immediately afterwards, the very end of his poem (1.20.27–8), that he passed 'forty-four Decembers' in the year of Lollius' consulship (21 BCE). Sorley's overtly Homeric narrative is thus rounded off with recognizably Horatian ironic self-deprecation.

(d) Associated works

'J.B.' (MW 40, 127), written in October 1913 in Sorley's last term at school, is a tribute to John Bain, the addressee of this poem, who had left Marlborough that summer, and shows their warm relationship (both were literary-minded Scots) as well as quoting Bain's description of Marlborough in the lyrics of a song as 'toun of touns'[22] which reappears in this poem (line 94). Sorley's interest in Homer also emerges in his 1914 poems 'The Song of the Ungirt Runners', 'To Germany', and his 1915 sonnet 'When you see millions of the mouthless dead' (see below), while his 1911 poem 'Quis Desiderio' is a translation of Horace *Odes* 1.24. Sorley writes with similar affection about the town of Marlborough in his 1914 'Marlborough' (MW 10, pp. 62–4), the title poem of *Marlborough and Other Poems* (1916a).

'When you see millions of the mouthless dead' (1915)

(a) **Text of poem** [= MW 26, p. 91]

> When you see millions of the mouthless dead
> Across your dreams in pale battalions go,
> Say not soft things as other men have said,
> That you'll remember. For you need not so.
> Give them not praise. For, deaf, how should they know
> It is not curses heaped on each gashed head?
> Nor tears. Their blind eyes see not your tears flow.
> Nor honour. It is easy to be dead.

---

[22] See Wilson 1990: 49–50, and for the text of the song see Wilson 1985b: 66.

> Say only this, "They are dead." Then add thereto,
> "Yet many a better one has died before."
> Then, scanning all the o'ercrowded mass, should you
> Perceive one face that you loved heretofore,
> It is a spook. None wears the face you knew.
> Great death has made all his for evermore.

(b) Poem—date, form, and content

This Petrarchan sonnet, with rhyme-scheme ABABBABA (octet) and
ABABAB (sestet), was found in Sorley's army kit after his death in
October 1915 and first published in Sorley 1916a. It is a reaction to the
slaughter Sorley witnessed on the Western Front, and a meditation on how
a poet should react to the mass death of comrades.[23] It has been plausibly
seen as a reaction against the ardent 1914 war sonnets of Rupert Brooke
with their lavish lauding of the war dead (see above in this volume),[24] which
Sorley described (see above) as sentimental, over-optimistic, and over-
praised (cf. line 3 'Say not soft things as other men have said'). Its sombre
presentation of the world of the dead, viewed in a dream, has much more in
common with Wilfred Owen's 'Strange Meeting' (not printed until 1919)—
see Vandiver 1999 and her treatment of that poem in this volume—and like
Owen's poem it draws on the Homeric description of the Underworld and
on the classical idea of *katabasis*, the descent of a living individual into the
realm of the departed, as well as on the meeting of Achilles and Lycaon in
the *Iliad* (see below).

Sorley's sonnet also engages polemically with comforting Christian traditions of the afterlife, in particular with J. H. Newman's celebrated 1833
hymn, 'Lead, kindly light', which presents a positive picture of eventual
posthumous reunion with loved ones in heaven (lines 13–18):

> So long Thy power hath blest me, sure it still
> Will lead me on.
> O'er moor and fen, o'er crag and torrent, till
> The night is gone,
> And with the morn those angel faces smile,
> Which I have loved long since, and lost awhile!

---

[23] For a brief account see Wilson 1985b: 211–12.
[24] See Wilson 1985b: 212 and Vandiver 2010: 82–3, 295–6.

Note the shared details of 'faces' (Newman's familiar 'angel faces' become the indistinct face of the sinister 'spook') and of 'loved long since' (for Sorley the loss of loved ones is permanent not temporary). For Sorley there is no resurrection and death has conquered, an inversion of Christian doctrine; the poem's bleak and stoical consolation for death, that better men have died before, echoes not Christian reassurance but the uncompromising words and views of Achilles in the *Iliad* (see below). The Underworld of the poet's dream reproduces his waking nightmare world of the dense horrors of mass warfare and the oppressive congestion of the trenches: the souls of the dead move in millions in 'pale battalions' (2), some of them have a 'gashed head' (6), and they form an 'o'ercrowded mass' (11).

(c) Reception commentary

The Homeric elements in this poem have been fully studied by Elizabeth Vandiver (Vandiver 1999 and 2010: 292–7), who shows clearly that the poem draws on the description of the Underworld in Book 11 of the *Odyssey* where Odysseus encounters the world of the dead. There too the ghosts at least initially have no sentience or speech, until this is revived in them by drinking the blood of a sacrifice, and there too the dead are an 'o'ercrowded mass' as they crowd around the hero (cf. *Odyssey* 11.42); but the whole subsequent focus of Odysseus' meeting with them is recognition of and conversation with his former comrades and late mother, while in Sorley's poem no communication is possible with the 'mouthless dead'; his nightmare Underworld lacks even the limited emotional comfort of Homer's.

As scholars have long pointed out (cf. Wilson 1985a: 91 and Vandiver 2010: 293–4), these Odyssean echoes are supplemented by quotation of the famous Iliadic line of Achilles in the midst of battle to his just-taken Trojan prisoner and previous acquaintance Lycaon, who asks to be spared death but receives the answer ἀλλὰ φίλος θάνε καὶ σύ· τί ἦ ὀλοφύρεαι οὕτως; / κάτθανε καὶ Πάτροκλος, ὅ περ σέο πολλὸν ἀμείνων, 'but, my friend, die yourself too: why do you lament in vain? / Patroclus too died, a much better man than you' (*Iliad* 20.106–7).[25] This uncompromising reply (swiftly followed by Lycaon's killing) is a version of a traditional mode of consolation that even the great have to die and so death should be accepted by others without

---

[25] Sorley quotes *Iliad* 20.107 in Greek in a letter written from military training in November 1914 to his former headmaster concerning the death of a school contemporary, commenting that 'no saner and splendider comment on death has been made' (Wilson 1990: 203–4). The contemporary was Harold William Roseveare, who died of wounds on 20 September 1914 after the Battle of the Aisne (Vandiver 2010: 293–4).

complaint; Achilles articulates this again at *Iliad* 18.117–20, saying that even the mighty Heracles died and that he himself is prepared to suffer the same fate.

(d) Associated works

Sorley's knowledge of Homer is clear from 'I have not brought my Odyssey' (above), written a few months earlier, 'The Song of the Ungirt Runners' (1914), and 'To Germany' (both below). His memorial poem for his Marlborough contemporary Sidney Woodroffe, V.C. (MW 27, p. 92) shows a much more conventional attitude to memorializing the war dead, talking Homerically of 'A glory that can never die' (κλέος ἄφθιτον, *Iliad* 9.413, of Achilles, similarly doomed to an early end); this seems to be aimed primarily at consoling the living rather than at dialogue with the dead.

4. Other classical interactions

'To Germany' (1914, MW 14, p. 70). This sonnet seems to have been stimulated by the outbreak of war in August 1914. Its lines 'When it is peace, then we may view again / With new-won eyes each other's truer form / And wonder' look back to the meeting of the Trojan War enemies Achilles and Priam, when they wonder at each other's appearance (*Iliad* 24.629–32 ἤτοι Δαρδανίδης Πρίαμος θαύμαζ' Ἀχιλῆα / ὅσσος ἔην οἷός τε· θεοῖσι γὰρ ἄντα ἐῴκει· / αὐτὰρ ὃ Δαρδανίδην Πρίαμον θαύμαζεν Ἀχιλλεὺς / εἰσορόων ὄψίν τ' ἀγαθὴν καὶ μῦθον ἀκούων, 'And Priam the son of Dardanus wondered at Achilles, his size and appearance, for he seemed equal to the gods; but Achilles wondered at Priam the son of Dardanus, seeing his fine looks and hearing his speech'). Both passages suggest reconciliation, unsurprising for Sorley who had just spent seven months in Germany and made a number of friends there, though his poem sees this as only a future post-war prospect.[26]

'The Song of the Ungirt Runners' (1914, MW 11, p. 65). This poem refers to cross-country running during Sorley's military training in England in late 1914 (cf. Owen's 'Training' [1918] which treats the same topic).[27] It contains the emphatically repeated line 'we do not run for prize': this looks like an allusion to the description of Achilles chasing Hector in *Iliad* 22, a pursuit that will end in the latter's death (159–61): ἐπεὶ οὐχ ἱερήιον οὐδὲ

---

[26] For Sorley's attitude to Germany see further Wilson 1985b: 127, 168, 203–4.
[27] For Sorley's running in training see Wilson 1985b: 172–3.

βοείην / ἀρνύσθην, ἅ τε ποσσὶν ἀέθλια γίγνεται ἀνδρῶν, / ἀλλὰ περὶ ψυχῆς θέον Ἕκτορος ἱπποδάμοιο, 'for it was not for beast of sacrifice or for bull's hide that they strove, such as are men's prizes for swiftness of foot, but it was for the life of horse-taming Hector that they ran'. This tragic context is inverted in Sorley's poem, where running is not for competition (whether mortal or otherwise) but on instructions ('we run because we must') and for the pleasure of it ('we run because we like it');[28] both poets exploit the tragic contrast between a peacetime festival and the deadly context of war (Sorley and his fellow-runners are training for the trenches).

'**All the hills and vales along**' (1914, MW 13, pp. 68–9). This poem, an ironic marching song, also from the period of 1914 military training, includes the phrase 'hemlock for Socrates', an allusion to the drug with which the philosopher was forced to commit suicide according to Plato (*Phaedo* 117a–e). The strong personification of Earth perhaps recalls Sophocles *Antigone* 338–9 τὰν ὑπερτάταν, Γᾶν / ἄφθιτον, ἀκαμάταν ('Earth the supreme, the immortal, the unwearying') as well as biblical language (cf. Isaiah 35:1 KJV 'The wilderness and the solitary place shall be glad for them; and the desert shall rejoice, and blossom as the rose').

---

[28] Sorley had already enjoyed cross-country running at school; see Wilson 1985b: 45.

Isaac Rosenberg (1890–1918)

Lorna Hardwick

1. Poet—educational and cultural context

Isaac Rosenberg (1890–1918) was killed in France on the night of 31 March /
1 April 1918. Of the major war poets, his background was the most socially
alienated and economically deprived. He was born in Bristol to an immigrant family from Lithuania. They were poor Jewish refugees who moved to
the East End of London in 1897, partly in the hope of improving his
educational chances, although it turned out that no place was available for
him in the Jews' Free School at Spitalfields. Rosenberg's father had a
Rabbinic education and Rosenberg's early poetry shows that he was steeped
in the images and poetry of the Hebrew Bible. Rosenberg probably read
this in the translation of the Old Testament in the English Authorized
Version, which was published in 1611 (Noakes 2008: xii). The translators
of the Authorized Version (often referred to as the King James Bible) used
the Hebrew Rabbinic Bible (Daniel Bomberg, 1524/5) as well as the Greek
Septuagint, the Latin Vulgate, and earlier English versions (Campbell 2010).[1]
The Rabbinic background of Rosenberg's family is an important counterweight to perceptions of him as uneducated. His family were poor immigrants
and English was not their first language, but they were not illiterate or
culturally ignorant. Rosenberg's first language was Yiddish and in 1911 he
was described by a friend as being 'semi-literate' (sc. in English). Furthermore,
his grounding in Hebrew poetry provides significant comparative insights in
analysis of the Greek and Roman material that he threads into his war poetry.

Rosenberg received a basic formal education at the Board School in Baker
Street, leaving at the age of 14 to be apprenticed to an engraver. The family's

---

[1] An external reader made the additional point that some translations of the Hebrew Bible
into English made by Jewish scholars were influenced by the language of the Authorized Version
(AV), so there are interesting implications for reciprocity.

Greek and Roman Antiquity in First World War Poetry: Making Connections. Lorna Hardwick,
Stephen Harrison, and Elizabeth Vandiver, Oxford University Press. © Lorna Hardwick, Stephen Harrison,
and Elizabeth Vandiver 2024. DOI: 10.1093/oso/9780198907879.003.0004

poverty meant that his first efforts at drawing were with chalk on the pavements. However, he quickly developed educational and literary contacts. He was associated with the Whitechapel Boys' Group which was one element in what came to be known as the 'University of the Ghetto' in the East End of London that centred on the Passmore Edwards Library in Whitechapel High Street, one of the first free public libraries.[2] Rosenberg enrolled for classes at the Arts and Crafts School in Stepney Green and at Birkbeck College, where a teacher, Alice Wright, gave him books of poetry. These included copies of Shelley and Blake, both of whom were to influence his work. Blake's influence was visual as well as verbal.

After his initial education, Rosenberg subsequently received financial support from a group of Jewish women patrons and from the Jewish Educational Aid Society to study at the Slade School of Fine Art (Liddiard 2003: 10; Vandiver 2010: 136). His prose writing includes detailed and sometimes ironic comments on his experience of the buildings and people at the Slade ('promiscuous obscurity' in Bloomsbury) and its place in the history of art ('The Slade and its Relations to the Universe' and 'The Slade and Modern Culture', written 1911 or 1912; Noakes 2008: 204–6). Rosenberg became an assiduous networker and actively developed contacts with literary figures. His correspondence with Gordon Bottomley and Edward Marsh in particular gives significant insight into his literary views as well as his financial and personal problems. His correspondence with Laurence Binyon reveals that he hoped that war service would enhance his poetic sensibilities and achievements (Noakes 2008: 320–1).[3]

Rosenberg's educational and class background is importantly different from that of the other poets treated in this printed volume.[4] Discussion of the classical themes and resonances in his poetry and their relationship with the other literary and cultural traditions on which he drew requires a full range of analytic tools, from 'allusion' and 'code switching' to 'hanging motifs' and readerly 'associations' (see discussion of the taxonomy in the Introduction, pp. 7–13 above). Of all the poems included in this volume. Rosenberg's work requires the most 'stretched' taxonomy. This is partly because his engagement with the classical material is mediated via translations, literary traditions in English, and 'low intensity' cultural awareness of

---

[2] For fuller discussion of the Whitechapel context, see Dickson et al. 2009.

[3] That aspiration provides an interesting comparison with the view of May Sinclair that the war would provide excitement and challenge to personal development (see Introduction, p.3n5 above, and Sinclair's poem 'Dedication'; text in Kendall 2013: 19–20).

[4] See further the discussion in Vandiver 2010: 95, 110–13, and 136–44, with references.

figures and myths. Equally important, however, is that his deployment of classical material, especially in the Trench poems, is in interaction with oral and written literature from the Hebrew tradition and from the ancient Near East. In that sense his work mirrors ancient cultural interactions, especially those in Homer. Furthermore, analysis of Rosenberg's work can contribute distinctively to current debates in classical reception research theory and methodology concerning issues of 'erasure', that is how an exclusive focus on classical threads can (unwittingly) lead to the erasure of other elements, including those from the writer's own traditions and cultural hinterland.[5] The taxonomies and 'thick' analysis in the commentaries on Rosenberg's poems reflect all the three aspects summarized here: range of mediations in English including translations of the ancient texts; interaction with Hebrew literature; resistance to the risks of erasure that might be the result if classical material dominated to the exclusion of other cultural agencies.

Rosenberg had no formal classical training, but there is persuasive evidence from his letters as well as in his poetry that he read Greek poetry and tragedy in translation, including material that was sent to him in the trenches. In a letter to Bottomley postmarked 5 January 1917, Rosenberg comments that Aeschylus was 'a private in the army' and wonders whether he was, like himself 'bothered by lice'.[6] Rosenberg's poem 'Louse Hunting' (summer 1916–February 1917) gives this a surreal setting (Noakes 2008: 110). Two other references to classical authors are important. A letter to R. C. Trevelyan sends thanks for Trevelyan's 1917 translation of Lucretius' *De Rerum Natura* (undated letter, probably late October or early November 1917; Noakes 2008: 354). A letter to Edward Marsh refers to the need for 'a Homer for this war' and aligns Homer with Walt Whitman's 'Drum Taps' (undated letter, December 1916; Noakes 2008: 324–5). Apart from the evidence of Whitman's influence, the letter is significant because it demonstrates Rosenberg's conception of Homer as a 'poet of war'.

Although Rosenberg's formal education did not include classical languages, classical receptions in his poetry provide evidence about the perceptions of ancient literature and mythology that he developed through his study of art and his later reading. These feature in his poetry in visual images as well as in verbal allusions and motifs. Examples of his portraiture,

---

[5] Erasure is an important aspect of current research on Black classicisms in the USA and elsewhere, on classical receptions by and about indigenous peoples in Australasia, and on classics and class.

[6] This resonates with the Herald's speech at Aeschylus *Agamemnon* 562. Rosenberg seems to have been aware that Aeschylus served as a hoplite soldier.

landscape painting, and drawings are reproduced in the study by Parsons (Parsons 1979) and some are held by the Imperial War Museum, the Carlisle Art Gallery, the Joseph Cohen Collection at the University of South Carolina, and the Cape Town Art Gallery. Development of Rosenberg's career as a writer depended on mentoring and patronage from funders, publishers, and manuscript preservers, hence the importance of biographical and documentary information about his networks. He never ceased to be an autodidact and the (sometimes patchy) evidence about his reading and discussions is, alongside his reflections on his life experiences, a revealing element in the paramaterial that helps in tracking his development. Formally and stylistically, his work is important for consideration of receptions of classical material that are mediated, allusive, associative, and often not directly intertextual. His work is a good example of what Vandiver terms 'intermediate reception', that is where 'it is often impossible to know if a working-class poet had read translations of ancient texts or had encountered classics only at a second remove through an earlier English author's refigurations and adaptations' (Vandiver 2010: 95).

Rosenberg's prose writings, although often rough drafts and even fragmentary, demonstrate his awareness of major figures in the history of art and literature. He wrote that while poetry and painting both express emotional truth, painting captures the visual aspect of the moment while poetry *suggests* (emphasis added): 'Painting is stationary while poetry is motion' ('Thoughts on Beauty', date unknown; Noakes 2008: 222). He elaborated on this in his reflection that 'the poet is not so because he is weak but because he is *perverse*' (emphasis added; 'Thoughts on Words and Writing', probably written between June 1914 and February 1915, Noakes 2008: 223–4). The distinctive combination in Rosenberg's oeuvre of poetry, art, letters, and prose also challenges some of the judgements that have been made about the unsophisticated effects of his lack of formal education.

Rosenberg's social and intellectual hinterland and the content and critical reception of his work inform the topic of class and education in interesting and sometimes unexpected ways. The authors of the Introduction to *Three Poets of the First World War* (Stallworthy and Potter 2011) are surely mistaken on all counts to refer to Gurney, Rosenberg, and Owen collectively as 'three young men of the English underclass' (p. xxxi). The comment is inaccurate. In fact, the three poets mentioned differed very much in their education and socio-economic backgrounds. Ivor Gurney was the son of a tailor and, helped by his godfather who was a clergyman, became a choral scholar at the King's School in Gloucester before winning a scholarship to the Royal College of Music in London.[7] Wilfred Owen, the only commissioned officer amongst the three, might best be described as from a 'lower middle-class' family (his father had started his career as a railway clerk, although he progressed to assistant superintendent). Owen had an education typical of his class, although it was definitely not comparable with a public-school education, as is wrongly implied by some critics, and he did not complete a university degree (for more detail on his aspirations, see Vandiver's account in ch. 4 below).

Although Isaac Rosenberg was the most socially and economically deprived of the war poets, the poverty of his family did not amount to the destitution, exclusion, and even potential criminality associated with the anachronistic term 'underclass'. His immigrant family was poor but demonstrably valued education. Although his Jewish identity was a source of literary and artistic sensibility it also made him a target for anti-Semitism. Stallworthy's and Potter's observation seems in this context to label anyone not educated in the elite public-school system as 'underclass'. Not only does their use of this term lump together three poets with very different backgrounds, it anachronistically imports late twentieth- and twenty-first-century connotations of the term to indicate rootless, unemployed, ill-educated people who have no identifiable place or opportunities in society and who are deemed to have failed to attain 'working-class respectability'.[8]

Rosenberg's letters and prose writing emphasize that he wanted his poetry to be individual, even quirky, and that he wanted his creative energy to survive the rigours of war. In the Trench poems this aspiration is fulfilled and has two very significant outcomes. He avoids the trap (identified by Fussell and Poole—see Poole 2013: 150) of invoking canonical poetics and motifs that could serve to sanction the war by placing it in a tradition of past poetry that glorifies heroism (an accusation sometimes levied at Rupert Brooke, see p. 101 below and pp. 24 and 34–6 above). Rosenberg's poetry transplants and transforms motifs and associations, changing their significance and often subverting idealization. The same is true of the ways in which he moves away from the idealized pastoral of some Georgian poetry and towards a more ecocritical perspective. His treatment of the relationship between poetic tradition and

---

[7] The King's School was, in effect, a public school and included classics in its curriculum. Gurney's letters include Latin tags and poems such as 'The Iliad and Badminton' allude to classical figures (see further Kennedy 2021: 304–6).

[8] On class, see further the discussion in the Introduction to this p. 5 (including reference to Poole's discussion of David Jones and others in Poole 2013: 144–55).

the experiences of the present is rarely didactic but is layered, opening up deep echoes and changes of key. This represents a 'thick' poetics in which reception of classical motifs and associations plays a crucial role, especially when expressed via the sardonic persona he adopts in his narrative and reflective voice (his expression of the 'perversity' of the poet). The Greek associations are often associated with the literature and tropes of the ancient Near East and the points at which Greek resonances become dominant are pivotal. These aspects will be discussed in more detail in the commentaries on individual poems.[9] A major element in Rosenberg's Trench poems is the treatment of the relationship between the natural environment, including flora and fauna, and the making and unmaking of the physical and psychological conditions in war. In these aspects of his work, Rosenberg's blend of allusions and resonances from Greek and Hebrew literature is crucial and will be discussed in the commentary on individual poems.

The poems selected for discussion in this volume are predominantly from the third phase of Rosenberg's work. I use the term 'phase' not in a strictly chronological sense (there are instructive overlaps) but rather to indicate the predominant tones and trajectory of his work. In the initial and largely pre-war phase, Rosenberg was experimenting with the subject matter and poetic techniques that he valued in the Romantic and Georgian traditions in English. However, he was already setting himself beyond being identified with any specific tradition. Even at this early stage there are already signs of the 'poetry of unease', which is a feature of the second phase. 'Unease' has two aspects: poems that carry open and underlying evocations of the impact of cultural apartness and of anti-Semitism; pre-enlistment poems that embed his forebodings about the war. The third phase of his work culminates in the Trench poems, in which his variations on classical material are pivotal, and in which the poetry of survival combines with the poetry of unease to take on a distinctive stance and tone.[10]

Analysis of Rosenberg's use of classical material highlights three key aspects of his work which also carry implications for the study of ideas and texts beyond WWI poetry. The first area of importance is the demands made on readerly and scholarly approaches, especially in relation to conceptual tools and the taxonomies outlined in the Introduction to this

---

[9] None of Rosenberg's fragments are particularly relevant for his classical receptions and so are not included here.

[10] For discussion of the terms 'poetry of unease' and 'poetry of survival' see the Introduction to this volume, pp. 14–16 above.

volume. Intertextual allusions to poetry in English (especially to Blake, Donne, and Milton) are significant drivers of Rosenberg's selection of motifs and of the improvisations and variation he creates. The same is true of his allusions to episodes, figures, and imagery from Homeric epic and from Aeschylus, as well as his allusions to passages in the Hebrew Bible and to the Christian New Testament.

Intratextuality is also a significant element in his favoured motifs, metaphors, and figures. Tracking Rosenberg's intratextuality is helpful in making judgements about the development and variation of his techniques and in discerning the impact of the increasingly tightly focused lens of his Trench poems. These provide a rich field, usually with multiple resonances that morph according to the time and place of reception, permitting readers to see the poems as activating new and different networks of allusion, association, and suggestion.[11] Rosenberg's allusions to classical texts are not usually overtly signalled as such. They include transferred and masked motifs, intertextual seizure of 'hanging' motifs (often from agriculture, fauna, and flora that are receptive to transplantation into different contexts), recontextualization of images to transform fields of reference, especially in the light of his insistence that the poet should be 'perverse'. The poems work in and for themselves. For the 'innocent' reader they are self-standing, but they are also sites for the convergence of material from different codes and spheres of reference—classical, biblical, literary, visual. They therefore offer a range of 'entry points' for readers with different knowledge bases. Glancing, ghosting, and tracing are all important aspects of reading and responding to Rosenberg and will be discussed ad loc. (for a survey of critical concepts and brief explanations, see the Introduction pp. 7–13 above). In this taxonomy, improvising and riffing are key terms in arts criticism that help with analysis of Rosenberg's formal, aural, and rhythmic energy, especially when his poetics take and develop a theme or motif and then return to its starting point, which is then subtly altered by the process.[12] The range of personal and communal voices deployed by Rosenberg (sometimes amounting to metalepsis) offer ways into appreciation of the density and depth of classical and biblical receptions in his reflections on the war.

---

[11] This includes insights that readers may bring from their knowledge of the work of subsequent poets. Reading Rosenberg yields many examples of how the dynamics of reception operate forwards as well as backwards.

[12] For a detailed discussion of improvisation in Homeric epic, see Bird 2018.

Rosenberg's work is also characterized by close relationships between visual, aural, and lexical aesthetics.[13] His oeuvre as a whole contributes to analysis of writerly/painterly interactions in response to the lived experiences of the war. Rosenberg's extant art from the pre- and early war period is largely portrait and landscape based, perhaps reflecting the training that he received at the Slade. The self-portraits suggest that his self-image changed as the war progressed. In addition, there are core images in Rosenberg's poetry that resonate with those in WWI art—e.g. William Roberts RA, 'Burying the Dead after a Battle' (1919, black crayon on paper IWM ART 15594) and 'Study for "Crucifixion"', 1922 (chalk, watercolour on paper IWM ART 17435), both of which offer dialogue with 'Dead Man's Dump'.[14] These and other cross-genre affinities, such as those with paintings by William Orpen, will be discussed ad loc.

The second main feature of Rosenberg's work derives from the oblique challenges and provocations it offers. These include the ways in which he thinks and writes about the war. The complaints about his personal sufferings, as set out in his letters, inform his choice of subject and diction but they do not dominate or limit the tonal quality and imaginative range of the poems. His work is distinctive for the sardonic situating of his own experiences and the sometimes ironic transformation of the resonances in the 'hanging motifs' of harvest, poppies, rats, birds, and wheels that were central to much war poetry and prose. Amongst WWI poets, Rosenberg is one who provides examples of how changes in soldier-writers' perspectives on the war are not merely evident in the poetry but are arguably worked out in and through the poetry, which was not composed retrospectively.

In his poems Rosenberg employs several types of narrative voice, for example, the 'I' of the narrator, often sliding into 'we'; the use of direct address to the reader; the imperative commands to look and listen. In addition, there is the verbal self-portrait, which is used as an indicator of survival (psychological and physical). In this persona he stands aside, sometimes sardonically (e.g. in 'Break of Day in the Trenches'), and survives for the moment (in that poem and in 'Returning we hear the larks'). Rosenberg's treatment of the war is never sentimental, idealized, or patronizing, nor does he direct anger explicitly against those at home, senior officers, or politicians (in contrast with Owen and Sassoon). He uses lived

---

[13] Although not a trained musician like Gurney, much of Rosenberg's Trench poetry has a pervasive aural timbre.

[14] Roberts had been a member of the avant-garde Vorticist group before the war and a soldier-artist during it. There are further illustrations in the Imperial War Museum's publication *Art from the First World War* (Anon. 2014: 32–3).

experience both to communicate vignettes and to provide a springboard for reflecting on huge questions of human existence (chance, luck, death, catastrophe, humankind, and the ecosphere). The fact that he was not formally educated in 'the classical tradition' but absorbed various aspects of Greek and Roman mythology and literature through his own reading enabled him to escape the anxieties found in some other poets, who might see contemporary inheritance of ancient heroic values, in which they were steeped through their education and class affiliation, both as a defining feature of their world-view and as in some sense responsible for the destruction of young men's lives.[15] Rosenberg is rarely directly didactic. His poetics grow the huge questions of life and death from the scenes of experience and enable him to be a poet of quirky survival and imagination as well as a poet of unease. His changes of view are highlighted by variations in his use of classical motifs and referents and hence this element of Rosenberg scholarship depends to a high degree on the taxonomies outlined in the Introduction.

There are rewarding comparisons to be made with Wilfred Owen's challenges to the pastoral verse tradition in English and with Edward Thomas' focus on the impact of war on place and activity in the English countryside. Rosenberg's aspiration that poets should be perverse and his determination that the war should not destroy his creativity led him both to outflank the approaches to the natural world that characterized much Romantic and Georgian poetry, and to present his own persona and agency through a double consciousness refined by the traumas associated with imminent death. The poetry of unease and the poetry of survival play off one another.

A third distinctive aspect of Rosenberg's work will be discussed in the commentaries. This focuses on *how* he achieved the characteristics outlined in the preceding paragraphs and what the further implications might be. In particular, the commentaries discuss his creation of an additional and different dimension to how the natural world is perceived in a war environment, and it will be suggested that this opens the way to ecocritical readings, in which natural history and the history of humans are intertwined.[16] The eco-aesthetic dimension of Rosenberg's work frequently emerges from the encounter between classical and Hebraic in the Trench

---

[15] For discussion of different aspects of the poetry of unease, see Introduction pp. 14–16 above. Vandiver 2010: 225 comments on the concomitant denunciation of the classical tradition in Owen and (later) in Pound.

[16] In this respect there are significant comparisons to be made with Edward Thomas' poems on the effects of the war on the English landscape.

poems. This enables Rosenberg's poetry to communicate at the interfaces between catastrophe literature, war, the poetry of the grotesque and the images and processes associated with agriculture and cropping (Maggioni 2016; De Graef 2017). In particular, the poems contribute a distinctive strand in cross-cultural developments in catastrophe literature, bridging the convergence of the everyday harsh realities and complex temporalities to presage different kinds of catastrophe literature, an aspect that has been seen as foreshadowing the later events of the twentieth century.[17]

1.1 Critical readings and 'thick' receptions

Intertextualities with Homer and with Hebrew poetry open up possible relationships with other texts of the ancient Near East—in M. L. West's judgement, 'Greek literature is a Near Eastern literature' (West 1966: 31). The affinities between the Hebrew Bible's agricultural imagery and that in other texts of the ancient Near East are well recognized and have suggested a three-fold parallelism between second millennium Sumerian forerunners and first millennium Akkadian and biblical sequels, traces of which can be found in Rosenberg's poetry. For example, common phrases in Sumerian literature describe mass killing as 'to pile up [sc. corpses] like sheaves' (Samet 2012: 4).[18] In *Ninurta's Exploits* 6 the god is said to 'reap like barley the necks of the insubordinates'. In *Ninisima* A 116–17, the goddess Ninisima boasts that she has 'grabbed the shepherd of the enemy band as the threshing sledge grabs barley' (sc. the shepherd is the king; cf. the Homeric epithet of Agamemnon as 'shepherd of the people'). *Letter from Sin-iddinan to the God Uta* 15 says 'your young men have been harvested like barley at the due time; they have been picked, they have been plucked like first fruits'. A neo-Assyrian source identifies killed enemies with cut trees. In the Hebrew Bible human corpses are like dung in the open fields, like grain stalks after the reaper (Jeremiah 9:21). So far as subsequent readings and literary refigurations are concerned, theoretical models for analysing the Hebrew texts have explored the latent potential of their 'sub-surface' culture which may be retrieved and directly or indirectly redeployed in subsequent receptions (discussed in Fishbane 1985). The cultural tropes identified in the ancient Near East have strong affinities with those of the

---

[17] See e.g. the discussion of Michael Longley's response to Rosenberg, pp. 110–111 below.
[18] Samet's article also lists extensive examples from texts in the Hebrew Bible.

culture of the Homeric poems, reflecting the myths and histories which have been connected in studies such as Johannes Haubold's *Greece and Mesopotamia: Dialogues in Literature* (Haubold 2013). These in turn are echoed in Rosenberg's Trench poems.[19]

Engaging with Rosenberg's poetry, its rich hinterland, and its ongoing implications is an exercise in 'thick' reception. As the commentary indicates, Rosenberg's 'Autumn 1914' is enriched by reading not only Homer (where there is a possible direct allusion) but also the imagery of harvest and iron in the cultures of the ancient Near East, including the Hebrew Bible, which provides a bridge between the other ancient Near East material and that in Homer. Rosenberg's poetry can be read both alongside Homer and also alongside the prophetic literature of the Hebrew Bible, which is in its turn read alongside ancient Near East imagery. Readers might use any of these as an entry point into the poem. The outcome is a multi-directional poetics that also serves to give his war poetry extensive resonances with catastrophe literature, ancient and modern.

1.2 Rosenberg's experiences before and during WWI

Rosenberg was in South Africa at the outbreak of WWI, probably to improve his health and in search of better opportunities for his painting and writing as well as to visit his sister. His uncle was a rabbi in Cape Town at that time and also served as a rabbi in Johannesburg. An early portrait of him by Rosenberg is illustrated in Parsons 1979 (plate 1a), but the current whereabouts of the portrait is unknown. Rosenberg returned to England in February 1915, overseeing his second privately published volume of poems and then enlisting in the army in October 1915. He was not a conscript; his motives for voluntary enlistment seem to have been primarily economic (an allowance for his mother, which she did not immediately receive). His poor health and limited physique were a constant problem. There were special arrangements for undersized recruits to serve in 'bantam' battalions, but shortage of men soon led to them being posted to the front line. In January 1917 Edward Marsh tried to get him transferred to a clerical post, but the attempt failed. Marsh's War Office contact said he was sorry for the 'Hebrew bard', but could do very little (Noakes 2008: 434).

---

[19] Currie 2016 (ch. 5) discusses, with some caution, transferred motifs in relation to Homeric epic and the cultural contexts of the ancient Near East.

The vast majority of Rosenberg's poems are not directly about war, although some presage themes that he developed in his war poems. The war poems were not written in recollection but on active service. Rosenberg was conscious at an early stage of the impact that experience of the war would have on his poetic development and in a letter to Binyon (probably dating from autumn 1916) emphasizes that 'I am determined that this war with all its powers of devastation, shall not master my poeting: that is if I am lucky enough to come through all right, I will not leave a corner of my consciousness covered up but saturate myself with the strange and extra-ordinary new conditions of this life, and it will all refine itself into poetry later on' (Noakes 2008: 320–1). Rosenberg also says in this letter that 'If I get the chance I'll write a sequence of poems of trench life that I mean to be a startler.…I won't worry you with my experiences now, but they [sc. the poems] will be psychological and individual, and I hope interesting'. The major poems analysed in this commentary are the result of this intent. However, war conditions made creative thinking and writing difficult. Rosenberg frequently lacked access to paper and some of his drafts are on notepaper with Salvation Army or YMCA headers. Many of the pencilled manuscripts are mud-stained (Liddiard 2003: 38 and the information relating to Rosenberg at FWWPDA, search under Rosenberg). The poet commented in a letter to his patron Edward Marsh, postmarked 26 January 1918, that 'we spend most of the time pulling each other out of the mud.…I am not strong.…Christ never endured what I endure. It is breaking me completely' (Noakes 2008: 356). The censor redacted the last two sentences. After periods of sickness and hospitalization (possibly for treatment for VD, although most biographers refer to 'flu'; Noakes 2008: 36), Rosenberg moved with his unit to Arras in March 1918 and then to the front line, where he was killed on the night of 31 March / 1 April. In 1926 he was reburied at a military cemetery near Arras. The words 'Artist and Poet' were engraved at the foot of his headstone. This entailed a charge to his family of three shillings and threepence, levied by the Imperial War Graves Commission (Noakes 2008: 18n16).

Rosenberg's name is included with those of fifteen other poets on the WWI stone in Westminster Abbey. In 2014 a public subscription was supported by the Jewish East End Celebration Society to fund a statue of Rosenberg to be situated in Torrington Square, Bloomsbury, near Birkbeck College and the Slade (*Camden New Journal*). That project appears not to have come to fruition.

1.3 Publication and literary and artistic contacts

Some of Rosenberg's poems were published in his lifetime in the small pamphlet collections *Night and Day* (1912) and *Youth* (1915), with fifty and one hundred copies printed respectively. In 1915 the magazine *Colour*, edited by T. M. Wood, published 'Heart's First Word' (June), 'A Girl's Thoughts' (July), and 'Wedded' (August). *Moses*, a pamphlet containing poems and a verse play, was offered for sale to friends in 1916. In December of the same year, the Chicago magazine *Poetry*, edited by Harriet Monroe, published 'Marching' and 'Break of Day in the Trenches'. The first edition of Rosenberg's collected poems was not published until 1937 (Bottomley and Harding 1937). His patrons and other network contacts were vital in the preservation and publication of his work. This was already the case with his earliest poems but became especially important for the poems and plays written in difficult conditions during his war service.

Rosenberg's literary and artistic contacts were extensive (*indicates fellow members of the Whitechapel Boys group). They included Lascelles Abercrombie, poet; J. H. Amschewitz, artist; Laurence Binyon, Keeper of Prints and Drawings, British Museum; David Bomberg*, painter; Gordon Bottomley, poet; Morley Dainow, librarian, Whitechapel Library and Art Gallery; Mark Gertler*, painter and conscientious objector; T. E. Hulme, poet and critic; Joseph Leftwich*, poet; Edward Marsh, civil servant (including private secretary to Winston Churchill), editor of *Georgian Poetry*, patron of Rosenberg and of Rupert Brooke; Ezra Pound, poet; John Rodker*, poet, imprisoned as conscientious objector; Winifreda Seaton, schoolteacher, who introduced him to the metaphysical poets; Sydney Schiff, novelist and mentor; Alice Wright, tutor on William Blake at Birkbeck College; W. B. Yeats, poet.

1.4 Anti-Semitism, readings, and critical judgements

Rosenberg's cultural range and the anti-Semitic and class-based attitudes expressed towards him (at the time and subsequently) are intertwined: 'Every critic sees him in terms of dichotomies, but each sees a different dichotomy. He is English but [sic] Jewish; he is from London's East End yet also from the Slade School and the café Royal; his work reveals Hebrew elements as well as his relationship with the English Romantic tradition; he is orthodox and unorthodox in his religious vision; from a pacifist background, he is nonetheless obsessed with the creative destructive energy of power … he and his poetry became the touchstone of cultural conflicts that revealed themselves only after his death' (Liddiard 2003: 38).

Rosenberg's letters attest to the difficulties he encountered, not only in coping with the conditions of the war but also with the anti-Semitism and bullying he experienced. Anti-Semitism, endemic at the time, is also a dark presence in some of his earlier art and writing. Examples include his sketch 'The Wharf', 1912 (which shows three threatening men against a docklands background). His poem 'The Jew' (?1917) refers to the place of the Ten Commandments in non-Jewish as well as Jewish religion and culture and ends despairingly: 'Then why do they sneer at me?' (Noakes 2008: 119). Rosenberg commented that his verse-play *Moses* (one Act 1915; two Acts 1916) was written in barracks 'in rotten conditions … I suppose you know what an ordinary soldier's life is like … [Moses] symbolises the fierce desire for virility and original action in contrast to slavery of the most abject kind' (Letter to R. C. Trevelyan, post-marked 15 June 1916; Noakes 2008: 298).

Paradoxically, Rosenberg's relationship with the notorious anti-Semite Ezra Pound had positive results. He was recommended to Pound by W. B. Yeats. Pound did not think highly of Rosenberg's poetry but nevertheless forwarded his work to Harriet Monroe, publisher of the Chicago magazine *Poetry* which in 1916 printed 'Break of Day in the Trenches' and 'Marching'. The terms of Pound's comment to Monroe combine class prejudice with anti-Semitism: 'he has something in him, horribly rough but then "Stepney East". We ought to have a real burglar – ma che!!!'[20] A draft letter from Rosenberg to Pound in late summer or autumn 1915 laments the loss of poets 'sacrificed in this stupid business' but acknowledges, apparently in response to Pound's suggestion, that enlisting is tempting 'if you are making no money' (Noakes 2008: 275).[21]

Rosenberg undoubtedly suffered both materially and psychologically as a result of anti-Semitism. Sometimes this was overt abuse; sometimes it expressed the casual anti-Semitism of the time (and is evident in the language used even by those who tried to support his career). Those attitudes are well documented with a further unfortunate effect in that they have formed the

---

[20] The nature of Pound's anti-Semitism and that of T. S. Eliot have provoked considerable scholarly debate. This will be discussed in more detail in Hardwick, Harrison, and Vandiver 2024. For overviews of the evidence (covering Eliot's poetry and prose) see Julius 2003; Schucard 2003; and Goldman 2021. See also the analysis of Rosenberg's deployment of the image of the rat in 'Break of Day in the Trenches' (pp. 84–90 below).

[21] A facsimile is available at FWWPDA.

basis for a false polarity to be perceived between his Jewish heritage and the culture and language in which he was writing (unwittingly evidenced by Liddiard's description of him as 'English but Jewish'). On the contrary, analysis of the registers and convergences in Rosenberg's poems of Jewish and Hellenic images and metaphors with those derived from literature in English suggests rather that 'Jewish *and* English' is a better description of his war poetry, in which Hellenic texts and images provided a site through which English and Hebrew literatures could interact creatively. This interaction between Hebrew and English was recognized by the poet Siegfried Sassoon (who subsequently became a Jewish convert to Catholicism). In his Foreword to Rosenberg's *Collected Works* (1937), Sassoon referred to Rosenberg's 'fruitful fusion between English and Hebrew culture' (quoted by Parsons 1979: ix). A major aim of this commentary is to pinpoint and evaluate the contribution of Rosenberg's classical referents to the development of that aesthetic. Sassoon's concept of 'fusion' is perhaps not the best choice of metaphor, but it does point to the dynamic cultural interactions discussed in the commentaries on the Trench poems. In those interactions neither Jewish nor Graeco-Roman referents are erased; both retain their distinctive elements as well as the combined energy generated by their encounter.

It was Rosenberg's energy that prompted the strongest appreciations of his work. Edith Sitwell wrote of his poems: 'they terrify by their crouch and spring; the fire in them is acrid and terrible...Isaac Rosenberg is one of the greatest poets we have had in this or the last generation, and I do not understand why the critics are preserving this strange silence on the subject' (Sitwell 1922). Sitwell's observation points to the neglect suffered by Rosenberg's work. T. S. Eliot made this point as early as 1920 when remarking that 'the disease of contemporary reviewing is only a form of the radical malady of journalism'. Eliot suggests the public should 'ask itself why it has never heard of the poems of T. E. Hulme [the poet and critic] or of Isaac Rosenberg' (Eliot 1920a). Although Eliot also described Rosenberg as 'the most remarkable of the British poets killed in that war' (discussed in Corcoran 2013), the 1937 collection was the first posthumous edition of Rosenberg's poetry. This was evidently immediately influential—Keith Douglas the WWII poet alluded to Rosenberg in 'Desert Flowers': 'Rosenberg, I only repeat what you were saying' (see further, p. 110 below).

All the poems by Rosenberg that are considered in detail below are from the third phase of his work. These are 'Trench poems' in which the interactions between classical and biblical material are crucial in the content, diction, and the thickly layered response to the war. The section on associated poems includes some examples from the second phase of his writing.

2. Paramaterial—letters, manuscripts, art

In 1953 Rosenberg's sister Annie offered her collection of his papers to the British Museum. The offer was declined (apart from a few items) but in 1979 the papers and manuscripts that had been in her possession and those held by Bottomley's literary executors were donated to the Imperial War Museum. Rosenberg's letters (in Noakes 2008) are an important source for the writing and transmission of the texts of the poems. Rosenberg's letters and prose writings also include his comments on style and his attitude to other traditions and writers (ranging from William Blake to Rupert Brooke). The letters are an important source of information about the conditions under which he wrote and the difficulty he had in sending poems back to England from France, as the censors did not want to be bothered by having to read them. There is a significant difference between Rosenberg's comments in his letters about his experiences in his military training and in France and the way in which he uses those experiences in his poetry. The letters provide detail—and complaints—about food, boots, attitudes of other soldiers and officers, mud, exhaustion, and despair. In the poems, these personal experiences are rarely alluded to. Although they can be traced in the poetic diction, this is usually generalized as an experience of all combatants (e.g. in 'Dead Man's Dump'). Where Rosenberg does refer to himself in the poems, this is usually to focus, sometimes sardonically, on his survival and its precariousness (e.g. in 'Break of Day in the Trenches'. Only occasionally (as in 'The Jew') does he rail against his own situation. The poems move the lens from the personal to the universal without the distraction of invective against policy and practice in the military. This subtlety not only makes comparison between Rosenberg's poetry and letters particularly valuable. It also makes him an important comparator with other Trench poets when consideration is being given to the status of poetry as a source for study of WWI.

Rosenberg's art is also helpful for study of his life and poetry. His landscape painting, mainly from his pre-war period when he visited Epping Forest and Hampstead Heath, provides some unexpected comparisons with his poetic treatment of the environment. There is a triangular relationship between the experiences of the poet and his visualization in war and in peace of the landscape and the animals and birds that inhabit it. Rosenberg's portraiture is also important, both his images of others and, especially, his self-portraits. How Rosenberg saw himself is a theme for which the Trench poems provide another dimension. Poems such as 'Break of Day in the Trenches' show the poet creating his own identity. There are strong contrasts between the composition, colour, and materials used in his pre-war art and those of his later art. Although his self-portrait of 1915 (National Portrait Gallery 4129) is oil on panel, most of the materials used in his war-time sketches consist of charcoal, black chalk, and pencil. Combined with the lack of availability of high-quality paper, these create colour-neutral, shaded images that resonate with the tonalities in his poetry.

Rosenberg's landscape paintings include: *Sea and Beach*, 1910 (Imperial War Museum ART 6365), *Landscape with River*, 1911–12 (IWM ART 6360), *The Fountain*, 1911 (IWM ART 6366), *Landscape with Flowering Trees* (IWM ART 6361), 1911–12, *Trees* 1912 (IWM ART 6363), *The Road*, 1911 (IWM ART 6359). Self-portraits include the well-known oil on panel, 1915 (National Portrait Gallery 4129). There is also a bromide print mounted on a postcard showing Rosenberg in military uniform, *c.*1915, with a handwritten inscription 'Kind regards Rosenberg 1917' (NPG P230). Major archive collections with relevant material include: the Berg Collection at the New York Public Library (which holds Edward Marsh's collection of correspondence, including Rosenberg's letters to him), the British Museum Prints and Drawings Department in London, and the Imperial War Museum in London (which has MSS of poems and letters, paintings and photographs). The IWM collection includes a pencilled self-portrait, wearing a helmet inscribed in Rosenberg's hand 'I.R. France July 1917', IWM HU59126 and 'Self Portrait in a Pink Tie' (1914: IWM ART 6372). Tate Britain, the National Portrait Gallery in London, and the Ben Uri Gallery each hold a self-portrait, and more paintings can be found at the Slade School of Fine Art, London, and the Carlisle Art Gallery. The Oxford WWI poetry archive has a section devoted to Rosenberg's poems and paramaterial (FWWPDA).

3. Poems

'August 1914' (composed summer 1916, published 1937)

(a) **Text of poem**
[from Noakes 2008: 106–8; reprinted in Kendall 2013: 138]

What in our lives is burnt
In the fire of this?
The heart's dear granary?
The much we shall miss?

Three lives hath one life—
Iron, honey, gold.
The gold, the honey gone—
Left is the hard and cold.

Iron are the lives
Molten through our youth.   10
A burnt space through ripe fields,
A fair mouth's broken tooth.

(b) Poem—date, form, and content

The text has been dated to summer 1916. It was enclosed in an undated letter to Mrs Cohen, his patron and frequent correspondent (Noakes 2008: 304). It was not published until 1937.

'August 1914' is one of a number of poems that show different aspects of how 'the summer of 1914' became a literary as well as an artistic image, a touchstone for nostalgia as well as for a growing sense of horror at the slaughter taking place in the war. 1914 was a 'golden' summer that in cultural memory became symbolic of loss (Britain entered the war on 4 August).

Rosenberg's twelve-line poem is divided into three four-line stanzas with the rhyme scheme ABCB. In each stanza there is an enjambement between lines one and two (problematized by a hiatus in the second stanza). The third stanza transfers to the first line the rhythm used in the second lines of the two previous stanzas, hardening the impact ('Iron are the lives') and opening the way to the extended and inter-related images of the closing three lines of the poem. The effect is to jolt the reader into a change of perspective and a transformation of understanding.

The poem is important for two reasons: firstly, because of the combination of embedded allusion to a simile in Homer and its play on motifs found in Hebrew and Near Eastern literature (which in turn link to the receptions and improvisations in Homeric poetics). Secondly, it is a proto-imagist poem that has affinities with the poetry of Ezra Pound and H.D. Pound had in 1912 given the description 'Imagiste' to H.D. when he read her poem 'Hermes of the Ways'. Imagist poetry represented an early wave of Modernism, avoiding abstraction and emphasizing the visual and concrete. This approach was exploited by H.D. and Richard Aldington for its affinities with Greek lyric.

In 'August 1914' the first stanza's emphasis on fire subverts conventional images associated with harvest and plenty, and by extension those of fulfilment ('The heart's dear granary'). The alliteration in 'the much we shall miss' conveys with a quasi-military beat the remorseless truncation of assumptions about the future. The references to iron, honey, and gold interrupt the expected sequence of 'ages' (a paradigm in antiquity, underlying the revisionist approach in Hesiod's *Works and Days* 106–201) and signal a reversion away from the progression from iron to gold that readers might expect. Rosenberg follows Hesiod in substituting movement back towards iron (as in Hesiod's account of human decline). The violence involved in the forging (which links allusion to Vulcan's forging with Mars as the god of war in order to intensify the image) is not only destructive but persistent ('Molten right through'). Rosenberg's line 'Left is the hard and cold' is perhaps a tactile expression of the wish, expressed in his letters, to move to a more sculptured and concentrated poetics as well as a comment on the effects of the war.

(c) Reception commentary

'Autumn 1914' exemplifies the multiple trajectories of the classical resonances in Rosenberg's poetry. Its allusions and intertextualities point to a cluster of images that feed off one another.

Allusions: Iron is associated with the forge of Mars as God of war; honey is aligned with nectar and with the ambrosia of the gods which was associated with immortality.[22] This could also be read as an ironic riff on Brooke's notion of nostalgia for gilded youth. Rosenberg had initially admired Brooke but as the war progressed he rejected Brooke's poetics, commenting in his letter to Mrs Cohen that he did not like 'Brooke's begloried sonnets' (?summer 1916, Noakes 2008: 304). In the same letter he criticized the recently published poetry of some soldiers, berating it as 'commonplace'. He also referred to the poem he enclosed with his letter as, in contrast,

---

[22] For discussion of the evidence for the many aspects of Mars, see the *OCD* ad loc. For ambrosia and nectar, the food and drink of the gods and links with immortality, see *Odyssey* 5.92–3. The allusion to honey also aligns with the associations between milk and honey in Hebrew literature (*Exodus* 3:8 refers to the Jews being led from slavery into a land flowing with milk and honey).

freshly written and 'red from the anvil'. That poem was 'August 1914'. The visceral image created in that poem was also important for its challenge to the idealizing tendencies of Georgian pastoral and hence for its subversion of the 'for the landscape of England' rationale for the war.

Intertextualities: The devastating closing lines of the poem draw on the simile in Homer *Iliad* 11.67–71, in which the Trojans and the Achaeans cut each other down like two lines of reapers harvesting wheat or barley. Rosenberg stretches the Homeric simile into an image that links the violations of both nature and humanity:

> A burnt space through ripe fields
> A fair mouth's broken tooth.

Rosenberg, unlike Homer, does not complicate the image of the destroyed fields by commenting on how the reapers/killers are all working on behalf of the rich and powerful. He adds the association with fire as a marker of destruction. The Homeric simile does not link cutting with burning, although at *Iliad* 20.588ff. Achilles' killing of Trojans is likened to fire in a wood. Virgil in *Aeneid* 2.304–5 does image the fall of Troy as fire in a cornfield. Rosenberg's poem is drawing on and contributing to a cluster of associations and comparisons between harvest and war. However, it does not envisage the restoration of agriculture as a mark of peace, hence its importance for revision of the poetics of Virgilian georgic and for its resonances with paintings by the war artists (see Hardwick 2018). The poem is a key text for the immediacy of the relationship between visual and verbal responses to experience of the war. It also points forward to the post-WWI work of Ezra Pound and T. S. Eliot on the desolation of Europe (desolation which led to the rise of Fascism and to WWII).

Equally significant are the poem's intertextualities with key motifs in the poetry of the Hebrew Bible. The most important of these relate to the motif of harvest and its multiple associations, for example with the judgement of God (Isaiah 18:4–6; Jeremiah 12:13) and with destruction by an enemy (Jeremiah 51:33). In the Hebrew Bible destruction of crops is also an emblem for the destruction of a nation; the notion of reaping can represent either benefit or suffering as the result of past actions. Thus harvest can be associated with catastrophe, which may be caused not only by natural disasters such as drought, excessive heat, or flood, but also by war and other forms of desecration and affliction (Job 5:5; Isaiah 16:9, 17:11;

Jeremiah 5:17, 50:16, 51:33; Hosea 6:11; Joel 3:13). Harvest imagery in the Hebrew Bible also deploys words associated with threshing and the treading and trampling of vines. Those textual associations are echoed by Rosenberg in poems such as 'Dead Man's Dump' (see below pp. 91–99).

There are also intertextualities that cross creative genres and are activated by experiences in the war. This is evident in the treatment of the topic in painting, especially William Orpen's *Harvest 1918* (Imperial War Museum ART 4663). In that painting three peasant women bend over as if harvesting but are actually tending graves that are encircled by stakes and barbed wire.

Intratextualities: As with a number of Rosenberg's poems there are in 'August 1914' overlaps with and allusions to his other work, notably with lines 7–8 'The gold, the honey gone…cold' which are echoed in 'Dead Man's Dump' lines 30–1, 'When the swift iron burning bee / Drained the wild honey of their youth' and 'Death', line 5: 'even the honey on life's lips is curst'. Intratextuality is an important marker in analysing Rosenberg's poetics and his response to the experience of war.

'[A Worm fed on the heart of Corinth]' ?Composed May or June 1916 in England, published 1937

(a) **Text of poem** [from Noakes 2008: 104–5; also in Kendall 2013: 137]

A worm fed on the heart of Corinth,
Babylon and Rome.
Not Paris raped tall Helen,
But this incestuous worm,
Who lured her vivid beauty   5
To his amorphous sleep.
England! Famous as Helen
Is thy betrothal sung.
To him the shadowless,
More amorous than Solomon.   10

(b) Poem—date, form, and content

The poem was composed in England (May or June 1916), but was not published until 1937. As indicated by the square brackets, the title was added by later editors. The ten lines are structured in the form of sentences with a loose rhyme scheme that benefits from being heard rather than read silently. Half rhymes and alliteration also serve to link the sections of the poem and to advance the idea—'Rome/worm' and 'sung/Solomon'. The first two lines introduce the image of the worm and set it in the ancient historical context of the cities of Corinth, Babylon, and Rome, all of which are associated with great wealth and power and eventual decadence.[23] Corinth was particularly associated with debauchery. Rosenberg elaborates on this aspect in his poem 'Destruction of Jerusalem by the Babylonian Hordes' (composed early 1916; text in Noakes 2008: 112).[24] In the poem under discussion, the figure of the worm is carried into the next four lines, which expand the historical frame of reference to include the legend of the Trojan war. Elsewhere, Rosenberg uses the sexualised image of the worm as a metaphor for persistent and insidious penetration that taints sensibilities: 'My thoughts are worms that suck my softness all away' (*The Amulet*, line 103; text in Noakes 2008: 179).[25] In this poem, these associations of the image of the worm are further extended, deploying the worm to project a sexualized vision of the rapacities of war and the mutual destruction of fellow humans. Rosenberg uses an inverted syntax, possibly reflecting the influence of biblical style ('not Paris raped') to convey an anonymous authorial imperative that challenges the accepted narrative, which was that Paris abducted Helen (the wife of Menelaus, ruler of Sparta). In myth and in the poems of the Epic Cycle and the Homeric epics this resulted in the Trojan War, in which the great city of Troy, a symbol of the great wealth of the cities of Asia Minor, was eventually razed to the ground by the Greeks, after a siege of ten years.

In Rosenberg's poem the rapist was not Paris, the son of the Trojan king Priam, but the worm, the symbol of sexual depravity. The 'amorphous sleep' of the worm perhaps indicates its all-embracing persistence through the

---

[23] Babylon was a standard cultural allusion to signify decadence—Wilfred Owen wrote in a letter to his mother of 'Babylon the fallen' (letter dated 19 January 1917; Potter 2023: 244–246: 429). The rise and fall of ancient cities was an established trope in poetry in English, e.g. Kipling's remarkably prescient poem on the decline of empire, 'Recessional 1897' (published 1897), includes the lines: 'Far-called, our navies melt away: / On dune and headland sinks the fire: / Lo, all our pomp of yesterday / Is one with Nineveh and Tyre!'

[24] Jerusalem was destroyed by the Babylonian king Nebuchadnezzar in 597 BCE, followed by the exile of the people of Judah. In 'Destruction of Jerusalem by the Babylonian Hordes', Rosenberg deploys imagery that also infuses his poem 'August 1914', e.g. 'And shadowy sowers went / Before their spears to sow / The fruit whose taste is ash'.

[25] A pencil draft of the text of *The Amulet*, written on the Salvation Army paper supplied to troops at the Front, is in the Imperial War Museum (fig. 8 in Noakes 2008: 178). The MS bears the traces of water and mud.

centuries, opening up the frame of reference to include social and political behaviours and attitudes. The emphasis is on seduction rather than rape. Lines 7 and 8 are pivotal, turning the frame of reference from the figure of Helen to the present state of England. The term 'England', rather than Britain, was in general use at the time, even in contexts that referred to the British Empire—for instance, 'the King of England' was also the King Emperor of India. The 'betrothal' of England is not an abduction, let alone a rape, but a mysterious alliance expressed here in a comparison with the biblical figure of Solomon, King of Israel (*c*.965–931 BCE), but also echoing Blake's poem 'London' (1784, in the collection *Songs of Experience*, which also included 'The Rose'). Blake likened the sexual corruption and social exploitation of London to a plague that 'blights the Marriage hearse'. King Solomon was renowned/notorious for his many wives and concubines (the biblical book Song of Solomon (or Song of Songs) is primarily a series of poems about erotic love). The Old Testament/Hebrew Bible text in 1 *Kings* 11:3 refers to Solomon's seven hundred wives and three hundred concubines, so to say that England's betrothed is more amorous than Solomon suggests huge rapaciousness. Solomon was also famous for his relationship with the Queen of Sheba who, in the narrative in 1 Kings 10–12 visited Solomon on account of his great wisdom, bringing with her a vast retinue, spices, and gold, which he used to build a great temple. According to the fourteenth-century Ethiopian national epic *The Glory of the Kings* (*Kebra Nugast*) ch. 29, Solomon tricked the Queen of Sheba on the last night of her visit and fathered a son with her, Menilek. I *Kings* 10:23 says that Solomon exceeded all the rulers of the world for his riches and wisdom and that he accrued great wealth (in the form of tribute) from other nations, so the imperial resonances are powerful.

(c) Reception commentary

This poem ushers in Rosenberg's second, or transitional phase, in which he experiments with the transfer of motifs across time, place, and situation and classical material begins to take on a pivotal role. In this poem Rosenberg alludes to William Blake's poem 'The Sick Rose' (1794), which used the emblem of the polluted rose to signify corruption and venereal disease ('the invisible worm.... does thy life destroy').[26] Rosenberg introduces the

---

[26] In the poetry of the Second World War, the image of the worm recurs in the poem by Edith Sitwell (1887–1964) about the air raids of 1940, 'Still Falls the Rain', subtitled '*The raids, 1940. Night and Dawn*' (first published in the *Times Literary Supplement* in 1941). Sitwell's lines

ancient cities of Babylon, Rome, and Corinth, also associated with corruption, and transfers the image of the worm to the rape of Helen, problematizing associations with the Trojan War. In a parallel swerve, Rosenberg also transfers the agency in the rape from the individual Paris onto endemic historic corruptions. By associating these with the modern age, Rosenberg creates a vehicle for switching the focus to England. The image of the worm carries associations of deep-seated burrowing, incestuous corruption, and unceasing rapacious demands of an unnamed shadowless menace.

This is a muddled poem, both in its syntax and in its melange of images and named figures and cities, but it does provide an example of how Rosenberg was beginning to use classical allusions as a hinge between multivalent motifs (Blake's worm, Helen, Troy, England) that he could develop in different contexts. The poem also provides an example of Rosenberg's interest in how phenomena from the natural world touch otherwise unconnected people and situations and are material and metaphorical carriers of associations and continuities.

'In the Trenches', composed in France, June or early July 1916

Included as a preliminary draft of 'Break of Day' in a letter sent to Bottomley, postmarked 12 July 1916 (Noakes 2008: 300–2). Published 1937.

(a) **Text of poem** [Noakes 2008: 105]

> I snatched two poppies
> From the parapet's edge,
> Two bright red poppies
> That winked on the ledge.
> Behind my ear   5
> I stuck one through,
> One blood red poppy
> I gave to you.

extend the reach of the metaphor with an allusion to the Old Testament figure of Cain, who killed his brother: 'Still falls the Rain / In the Field of Blood where the small hopes breed and the human brain / Nurtures its greed, that worm with the brow of Cain'.

The sandbags narrowed
And screwed out our jest   10
And tore the poppy
You had on your breast...
Down—a shell—O! Christ
I am choked...safe...dust blind—I
See trench floor poppies   15
Strewn. Smashed you lie.

(b) Poem—date, form, and content

'In the Trenches' was composed in France, probably in June or July 1916, and published in 1937. An undated letter to Sonia Rodker, thought to be from late 1916, includes the sentence 'Here's a little poem, a bit common-place I'm afraid'. The MS of the poem is in the Imperial War Museum (facsimile in Liddiard 2003: 160). There is also a letter to Bottomley, postmarked 22 October 1917, in which Rosenberg says that 'It happened to one of our chaps, poor fellow—and I've tried to write it' (Noakes 2008: 352). The poem represents a more visceral treatment of an experience used in the sequel 'Break of Day in the Trenches' and is a preliminary site for Rosenberg's deepening exploration of the image and cultural significance of the poppy.[27] The poem, together with 'Break of Day in the Trenches', 'Returning we hear the larks' and 'Dead Man's Dump', marks a phase of development in Rosenberg's treatment of the war, when classical material takes a more fully integrated and pivotal role in his poetics.

The poem consists of two eight-line stanzas. The first stanza is in quasi-ballad form, with a strong regular rhythm in the first four lines. The content is focused on two poppies, picked from the edge where the trench meets the exposed face of the defences. In lines 1 and 3 'poppies' is repeated at the end of the line, emphasizing the driving image of the poem. In lines 2 and 4 'edge' and 'ledge' provide an echoing rhyme, adding tonal elements to the aurality of the poem. The narrative presents the narrator as 'I'. There is a sharpness and urgency in the diction—'snatched', 'bright-red', 'winked'. The red poppies winking on the ledge suggest a warning light on the ledge to

---

[27] Rosenberg's emphasis is on the association of the poppy and the visual indications of slaughter, as opposed to the warning signal presented by the association of the poppy with red traffic lights. There is an interesting comparison with Wilfred Owen's visualization of blood and wounds in 'I saw his round mouth crimson' which uses colour as the main indicator (compare the discussion of that poem in ch. 4 below and the discussion of Rosenberg's monochrome techniques, p. 94).

indicate danger, like that of signals and traffic-lights.[28] 'Winking' also carries undertones of signalling a bizarre joke. The second quatrain in the first stanza further interrupts the narrative flow, with its inverted syntax— 'Behind my ear / I stuck one through'. The poppy given to the narrator's comrade becomes 'blood-red', not 'bright-red' as in line 2. The opening lines of the second stanza appear to continue the narrative, resetting the scene to turn the lens on the sandbag defences but the protection they give has been 'narrowed' (it turns out, by bombardment), appearing to mock the soldiers who joked about picking the poppies. The first quatrain of the second stanza holds its structure—'jest' not only picks up the associations of 'winks' but also changes the tone by rhyming with 'breast'—the poppy is 'torn' (with the breast). The rhythm then fragments as the narrator struggles to survive the onslaught. The tense moves from past to present—'I am choked', 'I see'. 'See' implies the clearing of dust from the mouth and eyes, understanding of what has happened, and the changed material and metaphorical symbolism of the poppy. The effect of the poem on the page is intensified by hiatus, by the visual effect of '…', in which the dots resemble tracer bullets, as well as by the single word expostulation, until the narrator realizes that he has survived although initially blinded by dust. The disjunctions in syntax reflect the disrupted experience and the destruction of joking. The narrator then sees that the floor of the trench appears to be carpeted with the blood red poppies—'strewn' in an image that merges destruction, the laying of flowers and the shattered remains of his friend. The shift of emphasis in the poem is marked by the move from the 'I' of the opening sequence to the 'you' of the final line. The two poppies that were picked have different fates. The one that Rosenberg tucked behind his ear survives, the 'blood red' poppy given to his friend merges with the smashed body. Rosenberg tightly controls his material, using multiple associations of words and changes in rhythm to build up the hints of menace to a crescendo that progressively darkens the joke of the opening lines. The forceful alliterations, the obscenity carried with the word 'screwed' in addition to the image of the trajectory of a bullet, and the double insinuations of the word 'lie' make this a poem that is carefully crafted to carry a meaning that goes beyond the actual episode. The poem is both self-contained and can be read as a kind of prequel to 'Break of Day in the Trenches'.

---

[28] Traffic lights were used to control passage through the trenches and light narrow-gauge railways were built to move ammunition and building materials from the main depots up to the front line (Stevenson 2014).

(c) Reception commentary

John McCrae's poem 'In Flanders Fields' was published anonymously in 1915 (6 December, in *Punch*, which ensured wide circulation; text in Silkin 1981: 75). Is emblematic of the immediate inscription of the image of the poppy to a general readership as well as in the experience of those serving on the front line. McCrae's poem subsequently became a vehicle for absorbing the emblem of the poppy into the public imagination and memorial traditions that have persisted right up to the present day. Readers of Rosenberg (when the poem was published and later) would inevitably be aware that the poppy was both a visual part of the battle environment itself and a symbol of remembrance.

The intertextuality and intratextuality with Homer's deployment of the image of the poppy as a representation of the bodily destruction of death in battle is discussed below in the analysis of 'Break of Day in the Trenches'. 'In the Trenches' provides another example of the importance of intratextuality in Rosenberg's work. It also attests the importance for his poetry, and for its wider readership across many years, of taxonomies of association, glancing and improvisation as poetic techniques.

'In the Trenches' and its sequel 'Break of Day in the Trenches' both resonate with the Homeric image of a poppy as the symbol of destroyed youth, *Iliad* 8.306–8. Homer's lines refer to a son of Priam, Gorgythion, whose formulaic epithet was 'the blameless'. He was hit in the chest by an arrow from Teucer's bow and died 'drooping his head to one side, as a garden poppy bends beneath the weight of its yield and the rains of springtime'. Like Gorgythion, Rosenberg's comrade was wounded in the chest and did nothing to deserve his fate. The poppy itself was torn down from his breast (an echo of how Gorgythion collapsed), and the images of the narrowing sandbags and the hail of bullets and shrapnel resonate visually and lexically with how Gorgythion was targeted by the arrow from the bow of Teucer. 'In the Trenches' begins with word play and jest and ends in death and dawning comprehension. 'Break of Day in the Trenches' explores sardonically the effects of this experience. It also uses the image and associative dynamic of the poppy to explore wider issues and experiences. Thus 'In the Trenches' combines intertextuality with Homer and intratextuality with 'Break of Day in the Trenches'. The intertextuality with Homer is perhaps best characterized as ghosting (see Introduction, p. 11 above), in which traces of the ancient text initially lie beneath the surface and are then activated in the reader's understanding by the multiple resonances of the images and diction deployed by the poet.[29] The ways in which the Homeric resonances are threaded into the poem recall Alice Oswald's categorization of 'glancing' as a 'back door' in literature (see Introduction, p. 11 above), an entry process that often hinges on aurality and orality and gives a voice to the experience of subaltern figures, such as Rosenberg's fellow-soldier, who has no name and no direct voice. Rosenberg's control of the narrative and his shift from the overt narrative of the metaleptic 'I' to the direct address 'You', presage how he broadens perspectives in the sequel poem.

'Break of Day in the Trenches', composed in France, June or July 1916

Published December 1916 in *Poetry: A Magazine of Verse*, vol. 9, no. 3, 128–9. Text in Noakes 2008: 106; also in Kendall 2013: 137–8. Noakes 2008: 106 points out the textual variants and the difficulties of identifying the precise point at which Rosenberg made changes. The text in Noakes differs from that in *Poetry* 9.3, especially in the last eight lines, where 'Poppies whose roots are in men's veins' was not included. The addition of that connection intensifies the intratextual relationship with 'In the Trenches'.

(a) **Text of poem** [from Noakes 2008: 106]

The darkness crumbles away.
It is the same old Druid Time as ever.
Only a live thing leaps my hand,
A queer sardonic rat,
As I pull the parapet's poppy
To stick behind my ear.   5
Droll rat, they would shoot you if they knew
Your cosmopolitan sympathies.
Now you have touched this English hand
You will do the same to a German
Soon, no doubt, if it be your pleasure   10
To cross the sleeping green between.

---

[29] There is a long history of reception within antiquity of the image of the poppy in various contexts, e.g. in Catullus 11.22–4, where the cutting down of the poppy at the edge of the field signifies the death of love.

It seems, odd thing, you grin as you pass
Strong limbs, fine eyes, haughty athletes,
Less chanced than you for life,   15
Bonds to the whims of murder,
Sprawled in the bowels of the earth,
The torn fields of France.
What do you see in our eyes
At the shrieking iron and flame   20
Hurl'd through still heavens?
What quaver—what heart aghast?
Poppies whose roots are in man's veins
Drop, and are ever dropping,
But mine in my ear is safe—   25
Just a little white with the dust.

(b) Poem—date, form, and content

The poem was composed in France, June or July 1916 and published December 1916 in the Chicago journal *Poetry: A Magazine of Verse*, vol. 9, no. 3, 128–9, at the instigation of Ezra Pound. The title possibly alludes to John Donne's aubade 'Break of Day' (Kendall 2013: 268). Rosenberg admired Donne and carried a text of Donne's poems with him while serving in France. Rosenberg's ironic play on the format of the lover's scene in Donne substitutes rat for lover and war for the bedroom. The poem is one of the few by Rosenberg that were available to the wider reading public during the war. The content, including some phrases, is closely related to 'In the Trenches', and they can be read as poems that complement each other.

Rosenberg enclosed the poem in a letter to Edward Marsh, dated 4 August [1916] (Noakes 2008: 308). He refers to it as 'a poem I wrote in the trenches, which is surely as simple as ordinary talk. You might object to the second line as vague, but that was the best way I could express the sense of dawn' ['It is the same old Druid time as ever'].[30] There is some confusion with the title of a poem that he sent to Bottomley in a letter postmarked 12 July 1916. He entitled this 'In the Trenches' but the text is that of 'Break of Day in the Trenches' (see further Noakes 2008: 283–4, which also identifies and discusses variants). There is a further reference to the poem in an undated letter to Trevelyan (thought to be from late July 1916) in which Rosenberg wrote

---

[30] Druids were priests in pre-Roman and Celtic Britain for whom sunrise was of particular religious significance.

'I have asked my sister to send you a poem that Bottomley liked—"Break of Day in the Trenches"' (Noakes 2008: 306–7). That letter also provides evidence that Rosenberg 'had an idea for a book of war poems', which included plans for '[a] few longish dramatic poems'. In his forward to the 1937 edition of Rosenberg's poems, Siegfried Sassoon commented on the poem's 'poignant and nostalgic quality which eliminated critical analysis' and emphasised its authenticity—'Sensuous front-line existence is there, hateful and repellent, unforgettable and inescapable' (Noakes 2008: 384). Sassoon's use of the term 'nostalgic' needs probing in the context of modern literary theory. He probably meant that the poem was evocative of past experience rather than that it encoded a desire for the past that could not be fulfilled.

The poem has twenty-six lines and is not divided into stanzas. A typescript, with pencil alterations and bearing Rosenberg's signature, is in the British Library (Noakes 2008: 107, fig. 3). The lines vary in length and there is no consistent rhyme scheme. An important element in the poet's technique is the use of enjambement to carry forward associations and to develop and deepen pivotal lines of thought, for example in lines 7–8 where he makes the link between the rat (described by Poole as a 'totem figure'; Poole 2013: 126) and the stereotypical use of the rat to signal anti-Semitic assumptions (in this case 'cosmopolitan sympathies' implies lack of national loyalties).[31] In lines 9–12 this is made specific, with the rat associated with crossing no man's land to the German lines. The effect is of a discursive meditation that also conveys the poet's delight in contemplating the promiscuous movements of the rat.[32] The rat is directly addressed as 'droll' and becomes an actor in the poem, credited with taking pleasure from its ability to move across boundaries and grinning at the [Aryan] figures it passes who are 'less chanced than you for

---

[31] In poems dating from the immediate post-WWI period such as 'Burbank with a Baedeker: Bleistein with a Cigar', 'Gerontion', and 'Sweeney Among the Nightingales', T. S. Eliot's anti-Semitism is infused with the image of the rat. Bleistein is described as a 'Chicago Semite Viennese' tourist viewing the Rialto Bridge in Venice. The poem contains the lines: 'A lustrous protrusive eye / Stares from the protozoic slime. / The rats are underneath the pile / The jew is underneath the lot' (Eliot 1920b).

[32] See above pp. 69–71 for the importance of the extensive evidence in Rosenberg's letters that he encountered anti-Semitism in civilian and military life. This found expression in his poem 'The Jew' (possibly composed in the summer of 1917, published 1922; text in Noakes 2008: 119, with discussion 392–3). The poem celebrates the diversity of Jewish heritage and ends 'Why do they sneer at me'. It corresponds with information included in Rosenberg's letters to Schiff (from the Bantam Regiment training depot in Bury St Edmunds, early November 1915, 'my being a Jew makes it bad among these wretches') and to Bottomley (postmarked 11 July 1917). Texts in Noakes 2008: 279 and 337–8.

life'. The play on the word 'chanced' combines suggestions of uncertainty and less likelihood of survival—an example of the delight in wordplay that Rosenberg admired in Donne but which he here exploits for sardonic effect.

The rhythm and phrasing contrasts with the orality, ballad rhythm, and form of 'In the Trenches'. In lines 22–6 the syntax is interrupted, as was the case in the previous poem, conveying a comparable sense of urgency and intensity, but through a prism that in a flash-back recreates recent experience rather than communicating it as a present scene. Bottomley commented that this made the poem 'fall away a little at the end', but an alternative view could be that this intensifies the poet's determination not to crumble in response to the awful sight of the bloodied remains in the trench. The poem ends with a positive evocation of the survival of the poppy in the poet's ear 'just a little white with the dust'—dust which in the previous poem had come close to choking him. In another inversion that contrasts with the prequel poem, it is the poppy that is named as safe, rather than the poet-narrator, but the identities of the poppy and the poet merge in the image. Thus the movement of the poem as a whole shifts the lens from the opening reference to past time (Druids), to the figure of the poet himself, then to the rat which becomes the active agent in the narrative, moving across the lines and observing the reactions amongst combatants on both sides. This is followed by the intense experience of fear and its bodily effects and the image of death represented by the red poppies but subverted by the ironic change in the appearance of the white-tinged poppy behind the poet's ear.

(c) Reception commentary

This is a densely constructed poem which to create its effects draws on direct and indirect allusions to a number of precedents in English literature. These function as stepping-stones to the most dynamic and 'thick' allusions, which are to Homer and the Hebrew Bible. The promiscuous rat echoes John Donne's poem 'The Flea' (see discussion on p. 104 below) in which the insect bites the poet and his lover, mingling their blood. This provides an analogy with the rat as a cosmopolitan trope, to which Rosenberg adds a play on anti-Semitism, nationalism, and the all-seeing aspects of the rat's travels, which grounds the allusion in his own day.[33] The urgent questioning

---

[33] The rat's ability to move across and between the ravages of conflict and to symbolize the inversion of conventional world views is also implicit in David Jones' reference to the rat's 'amphibian paradise' (*IP* 54).

and images in line 22, 'What quaver—what heart aghast?' resonate with William Blake's 'The Tyger' (published in Blake's *Songs of Experience*, 1794), in which there is rhythmic reiteration of questions such as 'What immortal hand or eye / Could frame thy fearful symmetry' (lines 3–4). The questions are about the agency of design and also about the agencies of destruction so that by the end of the poem the question mutates into 'dare frame'. Lines 23–4 recall George Herbert's 'Virtue' (published in *The Temple*, 1633)—'Sweet rose.../ Thy root is ever in its grave / And thou must die' (quoted with comment by Noakes 2008: 385). Rosenberg transplants and reworks an image to make Homer's use of the poppy as an image of destroyed innocent youth in the death of Gorgythion in *Iliad* 8.306–8 resonate with the contemporary situation—'Poppies, whose roots are in man's veins / Drop, and are ever dropping' (see discussion of 'In the Trenches', pp. 80–84 above). The references to athletes and their limbs in line 14 echo the Homeric association between the warrior and athletic prowess (e.g. *Iliad* 8.337 and 6.27–8 which refers to limbs). The convergence of the images of flowers, roots, blood, and death was a trope in the literature of conflict in various contexts, for example W. B. Yeats' poem 'The Rose Tree' recounts an exchange between Pearse and Connolly, the executed leaders of the 1916 Easter Rising in Ireland: 'There's nothing but our own red blood / Can make a right Rose Tree' (published 1921).[34] Rosenberg, however, is not complicit with the sacrifice/memorial associations and instead offers an independent and idiosyncratic variation on the theme.[35]

In the rat sequence in the poem, Rosenberg played on the dual implications of the word 'chanced'. In the same sequence he also executes a skilful and multi-layered play on the 'sleeping green' that is crossed by the rat. At one level this indicates no man's land, which remained still and quiet at night and at dawn and is not yet a site of conflict and bloodshed. The image of the 'green' as a site for enjoyment has a long literary history. For example, William Blake's poem 'The Echoing Green' (in *Songs of Innocence*, 1789) pictures children playing on the green, evoking sunrise, sports, and youth. Only at the end of Blake's poem, at sunset, does it become 'the darkening

[34] Yeats' collection *Michael Robartes and the Dancer* (Yeats 1921) also included the poems 'Easter 1916', 'Sixteen Dead Men', 'The Second Coming', 'A Meditation in the Time of War', 'The Leaders of the Crowd', and 'Towards Break of Day'.

[35] The multiple resonances of the omni-presence of the poppy in the landscape of war are sometimes overlooked because of its dominant association in the cultural memory with death and memorial. Ivor Gurney commented in a letter to Marion Scott, 29 June 1916, that 'There is a bunch of glorious poppies, perched as if they meant to astonish and delight one, on a little green knoll just back of the firing line' (Gurney Archive 41.27).

green'. Rosenberg's 'sleeping green' also has an ominous resonance. In Psalms 37:2, which is a Psalm of David, the psalmist sings 'for they shall soon be cut down like the grass and wither as the green herb'. Rosenberg read the English translation of the Old Testament in the King James Bible version and so would have been familiar with the diction used in this passage. Psalm 37:1 makes clear that those who will be killed are the evil people whereas in Rosenberg's poem the location is no man's land which is accessible to both sides in the conflict (as symbolized by the rat). Psalm 103:14–16 brings together the images of dust and grass—'he remembereth that we are dust. / As for man, his days are as grass: as a flower of the fields so he flourisheth. / For the wind passeth over it and it is gone; and the place thereof shall know it no more.'

There is a further layer of meaning in Rosenberg's phrase, as green is also associated with green shoots of regeneration in nature and in agriculture. There is evidence in other poems by Rosenberg that he was familiar with the main figures in a number of Greek myths (for examples, see below pp. 100–103, under associated poems). Here, there may also be a trace element of the Greek myth of Persephone and Demeter. Persephone, daughter of Demeter, was allowed to emerge each spring from captivity in Hades. This aspect of the myth has been a touchstone for poets concerned with catastrophic death and regeneration. A similar trace element of Persephone's myth appears in Owen's 'Exposure' and the myth also figures in the fragmentary 'Perseus' (both discussed in ch. 4 below). Seamus Heaney's 1966 poem 'Requiem for the Croppies' mirrors the myth—the corn carried in the pockets of the agricultural labourers killed in conflict in Ireland in 1798 provided the seed for future growth on the land where they died (see further Hardwick 2019). The paintings of World War I war artists also depict and problematize the regeneration of the landscape. For example, in 'View from the old British Trenches at La Boisette' by William Orpen (1917), a gradual regreening of the fields of Flanders is painted showing patches of grass growing out of the mud. However, heavy clouds above cast their shadow on a field in the distance, and there are grotesque shapes embedded in the scarred patches of ground, suggesting it is underpinned by the skulls of the dead.[36] The word-play in 'sleeping green' is an example of

---

[36] Imperial War Museum ART 2966. Sir William Orpen RA (1878–1931) was an official war artist who had been a society painter before the war. His many war paintings reflect the scenes of desolation and suffering that he witnessed. Subsequently, Orpen was commissioned to produce three paintings of the Peace Conference in 1919. The final work 'To the Unknown British

Rosenberg's poetic resourcefulness in layering meanings that challenge easy assumptions and closures and instead open up a range of possibilities.

In contrast to the companion poem 'In the Trenches', the trajectory in 'Break of Day in the Trenches' is towards a focus on the poet, but the ending then further subverts the reader's expectation by turning the lens on the associations between the poppy and some kind of safety. The poppy becomes an emblem of survival rather than death, its appearance changed from the red that when plucked from the edge of the trench represented the blood that flows through men's veins (a contrast perhaps with the ichor, or ambrosia, that he refers to in 'Dead Man's Dump'). The redness of a poppy signifies bloodshed and death (as depicted on the floor of the trench in the prequel poem). In 'Break of Day in the Trenches', the appearance of the relatively undamaged poppy changes after the bombardment and it is tinged with white dust, a residue of the bombardment as well as a symbol of the human condition. Rosenberg's diction reflects his sense of irony and of the contingencies of survival.[37] It exemplifies his commitment to be 'perverse', in that he allows Homer's simile to bubble beneath the surface but then denies it the power to dictate the outcome for him. Both Homer's poppy and those in Flanders are initially part of the natural landscape; Homer's droops because of the rain, WWI's because of the man-made fusillades of bombardment. In 'In the Trenches' the poppy morphs into a bloodied mass of the remains of a soldier on the floor of the trench.[38] In 'Break of Day', Rosenberg's fragile survival is exemplified by the changed appearance of the poppy behind his ear. Fringed with the dust (of the season and of conflict) Rosenberg's poppy is both material and ephemeral, signalling the experience of the moment and a survival that, although it may not last, preserves his sardonic independence.[39]

Soldier in France' caused controversy because he painted over the politicians and military leaders who had originally been included as part of the neo-classical monumental structure and replaced them with a flag-draped coffin, with two semi-nude soldiers guarding the tomb. Orpen commented that 'After all the negotiations and discussions, the Armistice and Peace, the only tangible result is the ragged unemployed soldiers and the Dead'. The Imperial War Museum only accepted the painting (1923) after the figures of the soldiers were removed.

[37] The contingencies of survival is an under-researched topic in the analysis of WWI poetry. Ivor Gurney's poem 'The Silent One' (published 1925) narrates the poet's avoidance of an officer's request to advance through a dangerous gap in the wire, where the body of a comrade already hung: 'I smiled as politely replied – / "I'm afraid not Sir". There was no hole, no way to be seen / Nothing but chance of death, after tearing of clothes' (text in Kendall 2013: 134).

[38] There is an analogous image in Gurney's 1918 poem 'To his Love' ('that red wet / Thing I must somehow forget'; text in Kendall 2013: 121).

[39] See further the extended discussion in Vandiver 2010: 142–4. The protean quality that Rosenberg accorded to the motif of the poppy contrasts with the overt embedding of the

'Dead Man's Dump' (composed by May 1917, published 1922)

(a) **Text of poem** [Noakes 2008: 113–16; also in Kendall 2013: 140–2]

The plunging limbers over the shattered track
Racketed with their rusty freight,
Stuck out like many crowns of thorns
And the rusty stakes like sceptres old
To stay the flood of brutish men   5
Upon our brothers dear.

The wheels lurched over sprawled dead
But pained them not, though their bones crunched,
Their shut mouths made no moan,
They lie there huddled, friend and foeman,   10
Man born of man, and born of woman,
And shells go crying over them
From night till night and now.

Earth has waited for them
All the time of their growth   15
Fretting for their decay:
Now she has them at last!
In the strength of their strength
Suspended—stopped and held.

What fierce imaginings their dark souls lit   20
Earth! Have they gone into you?
Somewhere they must have gone,
And flung on your hard back
Is their soul's sack,
Emptied of God-ancestralled essences.   25
Who hurled them out? Who hurled?

None saw their spirits' shadow shake the grass
Or stood aside for the half used life to pass
Out of those doomed nostrils and the doomed mouth,

Homeric simile that was practised by Michael Longley in his response to the death of Gorgythion in *Iliad* 8 (his 2000 poem 'A Poppy'; text in Longley 2006; 255—see p. 110 below).

When the swift iron burning bee   30
Drained the wild honey of their youth.

What of us, who flung on the shrieking pyre,
Walk, our usual thoughts untouched,
Our lucky limbs as on ichor fed,
Immortal seeming ever?   35
Perhaps when the flames beat loud on us,
A fear may choke in our veins
And the startled blood may stop.

The air is loud with death,
The dark air spurts with fire   40
The explosions ceaseless are.

Timelessly now, some minutes past,
These dead strode time with vigorous life,
Till the shrapnel called 'an end!'
But not to all. In bleeding pangs   45
Some borne on stretchers dreamed of home,
Dear things, war-blotted from their hearts.

A man's brains splattered on
A stretcher-bearer's face;
His shook shoulders slipped their load,   50
But when they bent to look again
That drowning soul was sunk too deep
For human tenderness.

They left this dead with the older dead,
Stretched at the cross-roads.   55

Burnt black by strange decay
Their sinister faces lie
The lid over each eye,
The grass and coloured clay,
More motion have than they,   60
Joined to the great sunk silences.

Here is one not long dead;
His dark hearing caught our far wheels,
And the choked soul stretched weak hands
To reach the living word the far wheels said,   65
The blood-dazed intelligence beating for light,

Crying through the suspense of the far-torturing
      wheels
Swift for the end to break,
Cried as the tide of the world broke over his sight.   70

Will they come? Will they ever come?
Even as the mixed hooves of the mules,
The quivering-bellied mules,
And the rushing wheels all mixed
With his tortured upturned sight,   75
So we crashed round the bend,
We heard his weak scream,
We heard his very last sound,
And our wheels grazed his dead face.

(b) Poem—date, form, and content

The poem was composed by May 1917 and published in 1922 (text in Noakes 2008: 113–16, who includes a facsimile of a pencil draft of an earlier poem with elements incorporated into 'Dead Man's Dump'). It describes the experiences of soldiers who have to take wire up to the front line at night and whose wagons (limbers) then return on a rough track that is littered with the dead and dying. Rosenberg had been transferred to the Royal Engineers in January 1917 and wiring was amongst their duties. He sets the context to the poem in a letter to Marsh postmarked 8 May 1917: 'I've written some lines suggested by going out wiring, or rather carrying wire up the line on limbers and running over dead bodies lying about' (text in Noakes 2008: 331–2). The poem has seventy-nine lines, which makes it long in comparison with Rosenberg's other Trench poems. It is divided into stanzas which are uneven in length, but that irregularity also contains a certain pattern in the poem, nesting short scenes amongst more extended reflections. Rosenberg commented in a later letter to Marsh postmarked 27 May 1917 that he did not agree with Marsh's criticism of the poem's combination of rhyme and free verse—'I know how it spoils the unity of a poem. But if I couldn't before, I can now, I am sure, plead the absolute necessity of fixing an idea before it is lost, because of the situation it's conceived in. Regular rhythms I do not like much ... if Andrew Marvell had broken up his rhythms more he would have been considered a terrific poet' (text in Noakes 2008: 332).[40]

---

[40] The letter continues with a discussion of flooded tents, diarrhoea, and 'the poor chap's discoloured pants hanging on a bough nearby, and I thought after all I had the best of it'.

The poem is strikingly aural and should ideally be read aloud before it is analysed. This 'poem of sounds' is redolent with alliteration, repetition of key words, long vowels, and hard consonants. Working with its timbre is a palette that is devoid of vivid colours, depending on the grey of metal, leaden tints, rust, and pallor. Even the reference to flames (line 36) is not accompanied by words of colour and the 'spurting with fire' (line 40) is just contrasted with the 'dark air'. The poem's lack of vivid colour is itself a reflection of Rosenberg's painterly insights. Artworks from this time depict the dark, metallic environment created by the war. For example, Paul Nash, 'The Ypres Salient at Night' (1918: IWM ART 1145), presents visually the timber and wire with curved corrugated iron that compares with Rosenberg's verbal images. In 'Wire' (1919, IWM ART 2705) Nash depicted the choking effect of wire on trees.[41] Vorticist Percy Wyndham Lewis in 'A Battery Shelled' (1919, IWM ART 2747) deploys metallic shades, including for the faces of the troops, and David Bomberg, an associate of Rosenberg, created shades of darkness in the figures of men and material in a charcoal on paper study for 'Sappers at Work: Canadian Tunnelling Company, R 14, St Eloi' (1918–19, IWM ART 2708).

The first stanza of 'Dead Man's Dump' is of six lines. Its immediate impact is carried by the alliteration in line 2 ('racketed … rusty') and the hard consonants of words ending in 't'. The second stanza has seven lines, with half rhymes ending the central three lines ('moan', 'foeman', 'woman'). 'Foeman' is paired with 'friend', the alliteration drawing attention to the move away from the opposition in the first stanza between 'brutish men' and 'brothers dear'. In line 12, 'crying' has double significance, carrying associations of grief and lament as well as the noise made by the shells. The onomatopoeia in 'crunched' and the repetition of the 'n' sound in line 13 supply a sound-track to 'moan'. The third stanza reverts to six lines, with half rhymes in the second and fifth lines, 'growth' and 'strength' and a further use of repetition and alliteration in 'strength' and 'suspended—stopped'. The fourth stanza has seven lines with rhymes in lines 23 and 24 ('back' and 'sack', in an alliterative pairing with 'soul's'). The repetition of 'hurled' in line 26 increases the tempo to convey violence. Also important in

---

[41] Nash commented that he was in a barn studio in Buckinghamshire when starting on his great work 'The Menin Road' (1919) and that it was difficult to put aside the luxuriant green countryside and brood on the destruction in Flanders, to 'rob the war of the last shine of glamour' (Anon. 2014: 34). In that painting streams of sunlight are painted as though they were gun barrels and the reflections of destroyed trees in the stagnant water resemble derelict iron columns.

this stanza is the epithet 'hard' that is applied to the earth, subverting any idealized notion that the earth is benign and welcoming.[42]

The fifth stanza (beginning at line 27) has five lines with rhymes at lines 27 and 28 and half rhymes at lines 29 and 31. The sibilants in line 27 carry menace and the repetition of the echoing vowels in 'doomed' (line 29) anticipate the finality in lines 30–1. The 'iron burning bee' in line 30 (with double associations depending on the part of speech represented by 'burning') opens the way to the associations of the pyre (line 32). This next stanza (the sixth) has seven lines, with half rhymes at lines 33 and 34. The 'shrieking pyre' carries the sounds of those burned alive as well as of the hissing of the wood. It is the springboard for Rosenberg's introduction of the torment represented by the flames (line 36). The (funeral) pyre is also a dynamic link in the thread of classical allusions (see below in the Reception commentary). This is followed at line 39 by the three-line stanza 7 (with half rhymes at lines 40 and 41), which verbalizes the aural—the air is 'loud with death'. Stanzas 8 and 9 have six lines each. Stanza 8 has half rhymes framing its opening and closing lines (42 and 47) and resumes a mini-narrative to give the context for the 'freeze-frame' scene in stanza 9, which has half rhymes at lines 49 and 53 that link 'face' and 'tenderness'. In line 50, 'shook shoulders slipped their load' has an almost Hopkinsian verbal and rhythmic texture.

Stanza 10, beginning at line 54, has two lines, with the repetition of 'dead' and the half rhyme with 'roads' intensifying the hardness and finality communicated in the lapidary couplet. Stanza 11 has six short lines, closely connected and intensified by rhymes—('decay', 'clay', 'they' and 'lie', 'eye') and ends with the compound 'sunk silences'. The faces 'burnt black by strange decay' pick up the images of death and flames from stanzas 6 and 7.[43] The double resonance of 'black' also anticipates 'sinister' in line 57. The two remaining stanzas are more expansive, of nine lines each. Stanza 12 (lines 62–70) is characterized by repetition of key words ('wheels', 'break', 'broke') and by startling combinations of adjectives and nouns ('dark hearing', 'choked soul', 'blood-dazed intelligence'). The final stanza, stanza 13

---

[42] The earth has been trampled and beaten down by the traffic and bombardments of the war, cf. G. M. Hopkins: 'Generations have trod, have trod, have trod' ('God's Grandeur'). Unlike Hopkins, Rosenberg did not look for divine deliverance.

[43] The image is recalled by Tony Harrison's visualization of the burnt face of the Iraqi soldier in his Gulf War poem 'A Cold Coming' (Harrison 2007: 313–20), which begins 'I saw the charred Iraqi lean'. The poem includes the couplet 'I doubt victorious Greeks let Hector / Join their feast as spoiling spectre'. The relationship between the Rosenberg and Harrison poems provides yet another example of how 'reception' can resonate both forwards and backwards, for authors and for readers.

(lines 71–9) also has repetitions—'Will they come? Will they ever come?', 'mules', 'wheels' and urgent compound, almost formulaic nouns—'mixed hooves', 'quivering bellies'. The aural diction builds excruciatingly to the climax—'hoofs', 'crashed', 'weak scream', 'very last sound', 'grazed'.

In this poem, the irregular lengths of the lines, the movement between free verse and the internal repetitions, half rhymes and changing rhyme schemes combine to contain and frame the development of scenes within the poem. This enables the narrative voice to be supported and interrupted by detailed description, which at times corresponds to 'freeze-framing', for example in the opening description of the limbers and in the short stanzas at lines 39–41 (the sounds and visual impact of bombardment) and lines 48–53 (the brains that splattered the stretcher-bearer's face). The scenes function as milestones for the reflective sequences and provide a scaffolding for the multi-valency of the key words.

(c) Reception commentary

This poem is a fine example of the 'thick' reception and 'deep classics' that characterize Rosenberg's Trench poems. The receptions are in the warp and weft of the poem, threaded through by the rhyme schemes, rhythms, and nuanced verbal and aural poetics described in section (b) above. The receptions (both writerly and readerly) have intertextual, intratextual, and associative dimensions. The specifically classical referents (mainly Homeric), some of which are mediated, occur at pivotal points in the narrative and in the shifts of narrative voice in the poem (for comment on the Homeric intertexts, see Vandiver 2010: 297–302).

The intertextualities in the poem are of three main kinds: biblical, Homeric, and with literature in English (predecessors and contemporary). Because of the density of imagination and composition in the poem, intertextualities and intratextualities interact at key points and are energized by the pivotal motifs—ambrosia, wheels, [funeral] pyre, grass/earth.

There are biblical intratextualities with Rosenberg's recurrent references to images of Christ, especially in stanza 1 line 3 where the rusty wire that protrudes from the limber is likened to the crown of thorns placed on the head of Jesus Christ before his execution, the intention being to mock him for being called King of the Jews (Matthew 27:29). Rosenberg's letters show that he compared the suffering of the soldiers (including himself) with that of Christ, but in this instance the emphasis is on the mockery—the protruding wires seems to mock both the living and the dead by mimicking a spurious crown. The mockery here takes a step further from the 'winking' suggested by the image of the poppy in 'In the Trenches'. Lines 27–9 thread into the poem an image from the Hebrew Bible, the reference in Psalms 103:15–16 to the days of man as 'days of grass', 'as the flower of the field', but when the wind shakes the grass 'it is gone and the place whereof shall know it no more'. Rosenberg then adds a cultural swerve, alluding in the phrase 'the half-used life' to Homeric imaginings of the moment of death, for example at the deaths of Patroclus (*Iliad* 16.856–7) and Hector (*Iliad* 22.362–3).[44]

Lines 30–1 ('the swift iron burning bee / Drained the wild honey of their youth') pick up the allusion in 'August 1914' and this is intensified with the use of 'ichor' in line 34 (to point to the fluid that flows in the veins of the gods in Greek mythology). 'Dead Man's Dump' line 25 duplicates the 'God-ancestralled essences' of line 153 of *The Amulet* (Noakes 2008: 180), with the technical term 'ichor' following in line 34 (as in *Iliad* 5.340). The effect is to undermine equivalence with the heroes of Greek mythology and Homeric epic by drawing attention to the differences. The soldiers' limbs may be lucky so long as they are not hit by the bombardment, but the 'as on ichor fed' immediately makes their survival provisional, their immortality questionable. The 'may' in the image of the choking veins and the ceasing of the 'startled blood' appears to signal a future that is likely rather than remote.

The dominant allusion in the motif of the wheels driving over the dead is a variation (even an improvisation) based on the sequence in Homer's *Iliad* when the body of the Trojan hero Hector is defiled by being attached to the wheels of Achilles' chariot and dragged round the battlefield outside the walls of Troy in the sight of his mother (*Iliad* 22.395–440). In contrast with the lumbering wagon in Rosenberg's poem, Hector's body was not driven over by Achilles' chariot but attached to it so that when Achilles' horses were whipped into a run and 'A cloud of dust rose where Hektor was dragged, his dark hair was falling / about him and all that head that was once so handsome was tumbled / in the dust'. The lamentation in Troy was 'most like what would have happened if all lowering / Ilion had been burned from top to bottom in fire' (tr. Lattimore). Only through the intervention of Apollo was Hector's body not irredeemably mutilated and destroyed. *Iliad* 24.18–23 recounts how the dead man was to be thrown down and left 'to lie sprawled on his face in the dust. But Apollo / had pity on him, although he

---

[44] There is detailed discussion of these resonances in Vandiver 2010: 299. Vandiver makes the point that the elision of 'spirits' and 'breath' in Homer and its transposition in Rosenberg nuances the relationship between the earthly world and the Underworld at the point of death.

was only a dead man, and guarded his body from all ugliness'. In an extended sequence (lines 1–38), Rosenberg's poem denies the possibility of divine intervention but adds additional elements. The bodies in the opening lines are of men who are dead—the wheels 'pained them not.../ Their shut mouths made no moan'. However, in the closing lines it is an open question whether it is the wheels that crush the last hope and the last breath out of the wounded man—'We heard his very last sound, / And our wheels grazed his dead face'. The desecration portrayed in Homer imports into Rosenberg's poem the associations with the decaying remains of a hero. However, complete parallelism with this association is then subverted by Rosenberg's denial that the soldiers had ichor in their veins. This adaptation is reinforced by the echoes of Psalm 103 and by the 'pounding' and 'trampling' associated in Hebrew poetry with killing (pp. 75–8). Rosenberg's reference to the pyre (line 32) is counter-intuitive. It both evokes the role of the funeral pyre in Homer and represses its associations. The pyre in Rosenberg's poem shrieks, evoking the sounds of burning wood but also suggesting that it is the living who are burned, not dead heroes who are being honoured with funeral rites. In contrast to the *Iliad* there is no divine intervention to preserve the bodies, no funeral rites and games, and the dead will be lost without trace, crunched and hammered into the ground. In terms of Rosenberg's poetics, this is a good example of how he appears to transfer a motif but then subverts it (enacting his belief in the 'perversity' of the poet).

The recurrent image of the wheels in lines 63–79 has further resonances with earlier and contemporary literature in English. There are affinities with Wilfred Gibson's 'Wheels' composed in the aftermath of a pre-war accident and published in August 1914. That poem includes the lines 'Amid the scurry of wheels that cashed and whirred / About his senseless head' (*New Numbers*, vol. 1, no. 3, discussed in Noakes 2008: 389). There is also an allusion to William Blake's *The Marriage of Heaven and Hell*, line 2 'Drive your cart and your plough over the bones of the dead' (see Noakes 2008: 390). Owen's 'Strange Meeting' has 'when much blood had clogged their chariot wheels' (see the discussion of that poem pp. 155–62 below). While Owen and Rosenberg would not have known of one another's images, it is possible that both were alluding to Achilles' chariot wheels and subsequent readers might well triangulate their readings.[45]

---

[45] 'Wheels' can be regarded as a hanging motif, carrying multiple resonances from ancient and modern literature, captured and recontextualized by both Rosenberg and Owen.

The wheels motif also resonates with Rosenberg's *The Amulet* lines 22–37, which allude to a cart stuck in the mud and pulled out by mules (text in Noakes 2008: 175–6 with discussion 398). In *The Amulet* lines 35–7 we find: 'Saul fiercely dug from under. He tugged the wheels, / The mules foamed, straining, straining, / Suddenly they went.' The preceding lines had imaged how 'the slime clung / And licked and clawed and chewed the clogged dragging wheels'. These intratextualities between poems and plays emphasize how Rosenberg's war experience activates and illuminates the association between Greek and Hebrew referents. Comparisons between the plays and 'Dead Man's Dump' show the shift of emphasis from the debilitating mud of the plays to the intractable hardness of the earth, matching the aural texture of the poem. Comparison between the experimental plays and the pared-down poem also shows how the formal and aesthetic discipline of the poem focused and deepened Rosenberg's insights.

A distinctive feature of Rosenberg's poem is that the associative aspects of reception—verbal and visual—can be read forwards and backwards. A comparison poem that in terms of reception theory carries both association and affinity, probably reflecting the influence of Rosenberg and also shedding further light on 'Dead Man's Dump', including its reticence, is Michael Longley's 'Ballyboley', subtitled 'after A. T. Q. Stewart: a found poem' (Longley 2020: 12). Longley's poem is described in a note to the published collection as 'versifying' a passage from A. T. Q. Stewart's book *The Summer Soldiers: A History of the 1798 Rebellion in Antrim and Down* (first published 1995 with 1996 edition published by Blackstaff).[46] Longley's twelve-line poem describes how Samuel Skelton, the agent of Lord Massarine, watched from his window the Yeomanry burying parties for those killed in the rebellion. Cartloads of bodies were 'shot in' to mass graves. An officer asked where 'these rascals' came from. A blood-stained man in one of the carts feebly answered that he came from Ballyboley. The poem ends 'He was buried along with the rest'.

Associated works

The range of associations in and from Rosenberg's poetic work is especially wide and can be categorized under three main types: (i) poems by Rosenberg

---

[46] A. T. Q. Stewart (1929–2010) published a number of works on the history of Northern Ireland. He was from a Presbyterian family, educated at the Royal Belfast Academical Institution (as was Longley) and at Queen's University Belfast, where he became a lecturer.

that do not embed classical material but are closely related to or presage poems that do this to further refine the same or similar themes, for example 'On Receiving News of the War: Cape Town' (1914, published 1922; text in Noakes 2008: 71); 'The Dead Heroes' (written and published 1914; text in Noakes 2008: 73–4); 'Spring 1916' (composed and published 1916; text in Noakes 2008: 104). (ii) poems by Rosenberg containing brief classical allusions that are not worked up as a central part of the poem; (iii) other authors (predecessors, contemporaries, and later reception). Selected poems from categories (ii) and (iii) are included below.[47]

Associated poems are important for analysis of Rosenberg's work because they help chart phases in development of the inter-relationships between his poetics, use of classical material, his attitudes towards the war. Examples include mythological allusions, deployment of cultural emblems derived from history and myth, and 'glancing' encounters that Rosenberg went on to embed and refine in other poems.

'Returning we hear the larks' was written in 1917, in France, and published in 1922 (text in Noakes 2008: 113). It is considered to be one of Rosenberg's major poems. The text will be included in the full scholarly edition, Hardwick, Harrison, and Vandiver 2024, with detailed commentary considering how and to what extent the poem extends the reach of classical reception, and its implications for the stretched taxonomy discussed in this volume.

'On Receiving News of the War: Cape Town'

The poem was composed in South Africa in 1914 and was published in 1922 (text in Noakes 2008: 71). Its poetics provide a preview of motifs and strategies that Rosenberg was to develop in later phases of his work. In particular, line 17 ('ancient crimson curse') alludes here to the shedding of God's blood and also introduces the allusion to William Blake's 1794 poem 'The Sick Rose' that he embedded in the 1916 poem '[A Worm fed on the heart of Corinth]' as part of the association between the Trojan War and World War I (see pp. 77–80). Another significant feature is Rosenberg's use of images from the natural world to suggest the disruption represented by the war (line 1: 'Yet ice and frost and snow // From earth to sky / This summer land doth know. / No man knows why'). The reference to the 'malign kiss' from the past that is moulding lives and the mourning of God for dead children also trace motifs that became prominent in the poetry

---

[47] All the relevant texts will be included and discussed in the full scholarly edition, Hardwick, Harrison, and Vandiver 2024 with its digital functionality.

composed by Rosenberg in the light of his war experience and energised by his use of resonances with classical material. The poem is a good example of the 'poetry of unease' that is an important counterweight in the early poetry of the war to the less critical celebrations of heroism and sacrifice (see Introduction pp. 14–16).

'The Dead Heroes'

This poem was composed in the autumn of 1914 in South Africa and published in December of that year (text in Noakes 2008: 73–4). It is a transitional poem, both in its poetic allusions and in the development of Rosenberg's attitude to the war. The 'mailed seraphim', 'blazing spears', and repetitions of 'England' resonate with William Blake's poems 'Jerusalem' and other parts of 'Milton' (written and etched 1804–8, preface, lines 9–11). The apparent glorification of death in terms of heroism and religious sanction ('claim God's kiss') indicate that at this point Rosenberg was still flirting in style and motif with the mediaeval/chivalric formulations of patriotism that were common in much poetry composed in the early stages of the war. Rosenberg's letters provide evidence of the attitude that he subsequently developed towards this kind of poetry, for example in his disparaging comments about Brooke's 'begloried sonnets'; 'they remind me too much of flag days'; 'gaudy and reminiscent' (Noakes 2008: 304, 309, 310). However, a scattering of appreciative comments about Brooke also appears in the letters (Noakes 2008: 273: '[Brooke] was beginning to do great things'). In a letter to Marsh, October 1916, he described Brooke's poems 'Clouds' as 'as near to sublimity as any modern poem' (Noakes 2008: 319). Brooke's sonnet 'Clouds' was published in *The Pacific*, 1913. It is a meditation on what happens after death, suggesting in the sestet that the dead occupy a middle sphere, from which they can watch the oceans and 'men coming and going on earth'.

Other classical interactions

'Dusk and the Mirror' (thought to have been composed 1915, published 1937; text in Noakes 2008: 100–1). Line 39 alludes to 'Narcissian augurs browse'. Narcissus was a figure in Greek mythology who fell in love with his own image reflected in water but every time he tried to touch it the eddies took it away. The locus classicus for Narcissus is Ovid *Metamorphoses* 3.342ff., but it is not known whether Rosenberg was familiar with this. Rosenberg's allusion is to foreboding, to fear arising from the 'cool apparition'. Seamus Heaney's poem 'Personal Helicon—for Michael Longley' (in Heaney 1966: 44) refers to himself as a child looking Narcissus-like at the well water in his father's farm and then later, as a poet, 'I rhyme / To see myself, to set the darkness echoing'.

'The Immortals' (date of composition unknown, published 1922; text in Noakes 2008: 109–10). An example of 'mock-heroic'—'I killed them but they would not die', with the subject matter related to 'Louse Hunting' (composed between 1916 and 1917 in France, published 1922; text in Noakes 2008: 110). The theme of lice (as a main feature of military life and as a source of comedy) draws on Rosenberg's interest in authors as varied as Aeschylus, John Donne, and Robert Burns. In a letter to Bottomley, postmarked 23 July 1916 (Noakes 2008: 305), that discussed 'In the Trenches' and Rosenberg's intention to write a series of 'dramatic war poems', Rosenberg commented that he had 'plenty of amusing and serious material' and that 'last night we had a funny hunt for fleas' in which the soldiers 'all stripped by candlelight and the funniest drollest and dirtiest songs and conversations ever imagined. Burns' "Jolly Beggars" is nothing to it'.[48] Burns' comic poem 'To A Louse' (probably 1785) images the louse as a challenge to the finger-nails that seek to destroy it and as a means of seeing ourselves as others see us. In a letter dated 19 March 1917 (Noakes 2008: 386), Bottomley refers to a sketch of the flea hunt sent to him by Rosenberg as 'like a Witches' Sabbath of long slim bodies as if Botticelli had gone mad and designed a naked ballet for the Russian dancers. And it would be as much your own as the other, for it is all summarised in your letter of last summer'. The exchange points to the intersection between mock-heroic and the grotesque in Rosenberg's imagination.

'Marching – as seen from the left file', composed mid-late December 1915 at Bury St Edmunds and published 1916 in *Poetry: A Magazine of Verse*, vol. 9, no. 3, December, 128; text in Noakes 2008: 102–3. The poem is in two parts, differentiated by the instruction [BREAK]. The first part marks the rhythm of the marching of automated feet. The second part reflects metaphorically on the implications, alluding in line 10 to the ancient god of war 'Not broke is the forge of Mars' and continues 'But a subtler brain beats iron / To shoe the hoofs of death . . . Blind fingers loose an iron cloud / To rain immortal darkness / On strong eyes' (cf. the allusion to the forge of Hephaestus/Vulcan in *Iliad* 18 and *Aeneid* 8).

---

[48] Burn's 'The Jolly Beggars – a Cantata' is thought to have been inspired by an evening in Poosie Nansie's tavern, Mauchline, in September–October 1785. The characters are vagabond soldiers, 'sons of Mars' (text in Mackay 1993: 182–91).

'Girl to Soldier on Leave', composed in France, September or October 1917, published 1922; text in Noakes 2008: 119–20. The poem includes references to the Titans (line 1), early Greek gods who were dethroned after a massive struggle for supremacy with Zeus (also alluded to by Owen in 'Strange Meeting', 'The End', and 'An Imperial Elegy', all discussed below). Line 6 refers to Prometheus, one of the Titans, who stole fire to benefit mankind and was punished by Zeus by being chained to Mount Caucasus with an eagle eating his liver each day—it was replenished over-night to allow the torture to continue. Rosenberg admired Prometheus and referred to him as 'my splendid rebel' (line 5). A reference in line 15 to 'the sleep of Circe's swine' alludes to the goddess Circe who, in Homer's *Odyssey* 10, bewitched Odysseus' men on the return from Troy and turned them into swine.

'Soldier Twentieth Century', thought to have been composed in the autumn of 1917, published 1922 (text in Noakes 2008: 120–1). This poem reworks the allusions in 'Girl to Soldier on Leave' in a more condensed and focused way, reflecting on how cruelty underlies the triumphs of the immortal gods, predecessors of the historical tyrants Napoleon and Caesar. Lines 11–12, 'They have stolen your sun's power / With their feet on your shoulders worn' implicitly elide the soldier with the fire-thief Prometheus. The reference to Circe's swine (line 15) suggests that the soldier has been, like Odysseus' men, drugged into lack of awareness of what is really happening.

'Daughters of War', begun October 1916 and completed after June 1917 in France, published 1922 (text in Noakes 2008: 116–19). Line 27 refers to the 'Amazonian wind of them / over our corroding faces / That must be broken—broken for evermore'. The Amazons were warrior women in Greek legend who figure in the poems of the Trojan Cycle (Achilles was supposed to have killed the Amazon queen Penthesilea). Any sons born to the Amazons were sent away or killed as theirs was an all-female society. The poem is obscure in places and did not meet with the approval of his advisors. Rosenberg was disappointed that the poem was not included in Marsh's volume *Georgian Poetry 1916–17* and commented when sending a typescript of 'Returning we hear the larks' to Rodker that he thought 'Daughters of War' was his best poem (Noakes 2008: 390–1).

Rosenberg's relationship with other authors—intertexts and later receptions
This section notes briefly three earlier poets whose work was particularly important to Rosenberg and who can be directly linked to poems composed

by Rosenberg during the war. Rosenberg's comments on these poets indicate the development of a sophisticated poetic sensibility. They also show which poets were crucially important to him under battlefront conditions. Also listed are contemporary poems that are important for comparison with Rosenberg's treatment of key aspects of his war experience. Finally, selected examples of work by later poets are included that either directly allude to or add to understanding of Rosenberg's work. Those poems are especially important for associative models of reading.

Predecessors
John Donne (1573–1631). Donne's poem 'The Flea' was written to his (perhaps notional) mistress. Two aspects are crucial for Rosenberg. The first is that the flea is a link between people ('It suck'd me first and now sucks thee'). Rosenberg elaborates an additional dimension to this in his address to the rat in 'Break of Day in the Trenches'—'Now you have touched this English hand / You will do the same to a German' (see commentary ad loc.) The second significant aspect is that the encounter with the flea results in blood-stained nails that scratch the irritation, an image that Rosenberg deployed in 'The Immortals' and 'Louse Hunting'. There is ample evidence in Rosenberg's letters and prose that he admired Donne and considered him one of the most important poets writing in English. He was introduced to Donne's work from 1900 onwards by Winifreda Seaton and found Donne 'so choke sic full of profound and meaningful ideas' (undated letter to Seaton; Noakes 2008: 230).

Donne, an ordained clergyman, was one of the most erudite Metaphysical poets. His work was characterized by sophisticated word play (including sexual innuendo) and inversions of context and expectation. Rosenberg was intrigued by what he called Donne's 'sort of mental gymnastics' (letter to Seaton written between October 1913 and January 1914; Noakes 2008: 253). Despite some early uncertainty, Donne's importance to Rosenberg grew—Miss Seaton wrote to Lawrence Binyon that Rosenberg 'grew to care for Donne almost as much as I do' (18 November 1919; Noakes 2008: 229). In a letter to Miss Wright (October or November 1912; Noakes 2008: 248), Rosenberg refers to Stanley Spencer's painting of the Nativity that won a special prize. This depicted John Donne arriving in Heaven (the painting was set in Cookham and depicted the unfolding of divine events in contemporary life). After he enlisted, the importance of Donne to Rosenberg increased and he carried an edition with him in his pocket (together with Browne's *Religio Medici,* mentioned in a letter to Sydney Schiff, pre-12

November 1915; Noakes 2008: 280). In war conditions, his pocket was the only safe place to prevent loss or theft. Rosenberg wrote to Edward Marsh from the Military Hospital Depot at Bury St Edmunds that 'I have only taken Donne with me and don't feel for poetry much in this wretched place. There is not a book or paper here' (Noakes 2008: 282).

William Blake (1757–1827, poet and artist). Rosenberg's prose writing and letters indicate the extent of Blake's influence on him. Rosenberg was given a copy of Blake's poems by Alice Wright, his teacher at Birkbeck College (Noakes 2008: 414). His discussion of Blake forms part of his critical evaluation of the literary and visual arts. Rosenberg ranks Blake alongside Keats and Donne for their fulfilment of his *desiderata* in a poet—'vigorous intellect, a searching varies power that is itself and an independent nature' (prose essay 'Emerson', written ?1915; Noakes 2008: 211). In his essay 'Art' (summer–autumn 1914), Rosenberg criticized Blake's drawing technique but admired his art for 'that inspired quality, that unimpaired divinity that shines from all things mortal when looked [at] through the eye of imagination' (Noakes 2008: 219). There are allusions to Blake's poetry in 'The Dead Heroes' (1914; see commentary above p. 101), and in the thickly layered reference to 'sleeping green', line 12 of 'Break of Day in the Trenches' (see commentary ad loc.). In 'Dead Man's Dump', Rosenberg alluded to Blake's words in 'The Marriage of Heaven and Hell', 'Drive your cart and your plough over the bones of the dead' (see commentary ad loc.). '[A Worm fed on the heart of Corinth]' directly echoes the image of sexual exploitation and disease in Blake's poem 'The Sick Rose' (*Songs of Innocence*, 1789), and reworks it in the context of the rise and fall of the cities of myth and history in the ancient and contemporary Near East (see comm. ad loc.).

Walt Whitman (1819–92), for whom texts and commentaries are freely available in the Whitman Archive (www.whitmanarchive.org). Whitman's poetic treatment of the American Civil War is comparable with the stages of response to conflict evident in WWI poetry (excitement laced with doubt, direct observation, deep compassionate involvement—in Whitman's case, with the care of casualties). Rosenberg admired Whitman and contrasted him favourably with Brooke—'Whitman in "Beat drums beat" has said the noblest thing on war' (letter to Mrs Cohen, ?summer 1916; Noakes 2008: 304). When Rosenberg was in France, Whitman's poetry was sent out to him by friends and he commented 'The Homer for this war has yet to be found— Whitman got very near to the mark 50 years ago with "Drum Taps"' (letter to Edward Marsh, ?December 1916; Noakes 2008: 325). 'Drum Taps' was written in 1865, in the context of the American Civil War. Several poems in the sequence of forty-three poems seems Homeric in its focus on stock episodes and scenes of armies on the march and at rest, especially 'By the Bivouac's Fitful Flame'. Whitman also provides a preview of some of the tropes deployed by WWI poets, for example in the lines 'yours is the face of Christ himself', in response to a body in 'A sight in camp in the day-break grey and dim'. The poem was worked up from an entry in Whitman's journal. Although not a combatant, Whitman visited the battlefields in search of his brother and subsequently worked as an assistant in field hospitals. His poetry of witness grew from his first sight of a cartload of amputated limbs—'human fragments, cut, bloody, black and blue, swelled and sickening'.[49] Rosenberg's admiration of Whitman is echoed in his use in 'Daughters of War' (October 1916–June 1917) of Whitmanesque free verse and a visionary persona to communicate a hideous afterlife in which soldiers' bodies are violated (text in Noakes 2008: 116–19, with facsimile of extract from a fair copy presented to Bottomley in 1917: 117).

Contemporaries

In Rosenberg studies, the most important contemporary comparative material is broadly of two kinds: (i) poems by contemporary authors that highlight motifs or situations that are prominent in Rosenberg's war poetry; and (ii) poems that add a 'thick' dimension to analysis of Rosenberg's poetics, in respect both of technique and of his sometimes problematic relationship to movements in poetic imagination, ancient and modern.

The first category provides poems for comparative analysis. These are poems focused on the outbreak of war and the changes and portents it ushered in, for example May Wedderburn Cannan's (1893–1973) poem 'August 1914' (written in March 1915 just before she crossed into France to work in a soldiers' canteen; text in Kendall 2013: 179). Alice Meynell's 'Summer in England 1914' (published in her volume *Poems*, 1921; text in Giddings 1988: 15) threads in the hanging motifs of flora to frame a poetical exploration of foreboding and unease '…while this rose made round her cup / The armies died convulsed'. The closing image—'a thousand shattered men, / One wet corruption, heaped the plain' anticipates Ivor Gurney's 'To his love'—'that red wet / Thing I must somehow forget' (January 1918; text in Kendall 2013: 122). Vera Brittain's 'Perhaps—(*To R.A.L. Died of Wounds in France, December 23rd 1915*)', opens 'Perhaps the sun will shine again'

---

[49] For the text see Grier 1984: 2.504 and Stovall 1963–4: 1.32. See further, the discussion in Folsom and Price 2005: ch. 5, 'Blood-stained memoranda'.

(text in Reilly 1997: 14–15).[50] The disparity between the 'golden summer' of 1914 and the outbreak of war became a literary trope but the most significant poems give this a distinctive twist. Edward Thomas' (1878–1917) 'The Sun used to Shine' (composed 22 May 1916; text in E. Longley 2008: 122) is structured in a layered timeframe in which the poet moves between history and literary musing, brought together in the 'microcosm of landscape' (E. Longley 2008: 299) and framed by rumours of war, its approach, and an elegiac sense of what is to be. Thomas' poems provide an important counterpoint to Rosenberg's treatment of the temporalities and spatialities of the experiences of war and environment.

Mary Borden (1886–1968) was American by birth. After the birth of her third child she worked extensively as a Red Cross nurse in France from January 1915 and set up a field hospital in 1916 (as she also did in the Second World War).[51] Much of her WWI poetry was written under bombardment. In 'The Song of the Mud' (part of her sequence *At the Somme*, which dates from between October 1916 and March 1917; text in Kendall 2013: 78–80), she portrayed how the mud, which is a recurrent referent in Rosenberg's poetry and letters, became a major visible, audible, and material force in treading down and despoiling the living and the dead.[52] 'The Song of the Mud' opens with a vista that is almost tactile:

> This is the song of the mud,
> The pale yellow glistening mud that covers the naked hills like
>   satin,
> The grey gleaming silvery mud that is spread like enamel over the
>   valleys,
> The frothing, squirting, spurting liquid mud that gurgles along
>   the road beds,
> The thick elastic mud that is kneaded and pounded and squeezed
>   under the hooves of the horses...

---

[50] The poem was written when Brittain (1896–1970) was working at the 1st London General Hospital in February 1916. She also served as a VAD in France. Her memoir *Testament of Youth* was published in 1933.

[51] Borden's life, war memoirs, and art relating to her experiences in France has been researched by the nursing historian Christine E. Hallett, who commented 'now her only problem was how to explain the unspeakable to people at home' (Hallett 2021: 62).

[52] The first poem of the three in the sequence was 'Where is Jehovah?' It ends 'a desert, a promised land, a nation in agony waiting—/ Jehovah's not here—/ There's only a man standing,—quite still.' Borden was married to a Scottish missionary, Douglas Turner, who enlisted at the start of the war.

The poem ends in almost incantatory style:

> Mud, the fantastic disguise of the War Zone;
> Mud, the extinguishing mantle of battles;
> Mud, the smooth fluid grave of our soldiers.[53]

The sequence that follows 'The Song of the Mud' in Borden's work is 'The Hill' (text in Kendall 2013: 80–1). This portrays the landscape surrounding the battle zone, including the beauty of the hills that are still carrying crops, the shadows of the valleys and the intimations of peace, the cattle and the Homeric associations of images such as 'Camp fires gleamed down there' (cf. the evening scene in *Iliad* 8, especially lines 553ff.).[54] Then the vista is momentarily disturbed by the image of the despair of a prisoner being driven through the detritus of the war landscape. The juxtaposition and contradictions in the French landscape explored by Borden provide a link to the second category of comparative contemporary poems. These are poems that illuminate ways in which (notably in 'August 1914' and in 'Returning we hear the larks') Rosenberg reimagines pastoral, not only subverting the Georgian movement that he was previously associated with but also, with others such as Edward Thomas, extending in almost Virgilian spirit the capacity of georgic and pastoral to recognise the force of nostalgia for lost opportunities and also to move beyond this, testifying to the remorseless and lasting impact of violence.

The most important of those *comparanda* are Edward Thomas' poems 'In Memoriam, Easter, 1915' (composed 6 April 1915; text in Kendall 2013: 57 and E. Longley 2008: 80) and 'As the Team's Head Brass', an exploration of effects of absence on the landscape of England (composed 27 May 1916, on a walk from Hare Hall Camp, before Thomas went to France; text in Kendall 2013: 61–2 and E. Longley 2008: 123–4). The four-line poem 'In Memoriam, Easter, 1915' images the thickness of flowers left in a wood that will never be gathered; the word 'left' suggests they are left as memorials; the selection of the word 'gathered' rather than 'picked' intensifies the ambivalence. Edna

---

[53] The motif of mud is as important as that of the poppy in the poetry of the war. William Orpen's poem 'The Church, Zillebeke' (October 1918) uses mud as the literal and metaphorical signifier of the destruction that permeates the landscape (text in Dawe 2008: 46).

[54] The Homeric scene has provided a *topos* for other classical reception poems connected with war, e.g. Michael Longley's 'Campfires' (first published 1995; text from Longley 2006: 224), which begins 'All night crackling campfires boosted their morale / As they dozed in no man's land in the killing fields'.

Longley has commented that 'Thomas' woodland flowers are partly a wreath and partly a metaphor, they primarily mark a socio-ecological rupture: the loss of pre-war customs and futures' (E. Longley 2008: 225). In 'As the Team's Head Brass', the poet sits on a fallen tree and as the ploughman moves his team of horses up and down the field contemplates the effects of the intrusion of the war on the landscape of rural England and the way in which the land is worked, revealing agriculture and war as inter-related rather than separate (see further the discussion of the poem's rhythm and structure, the collapse of cyclical paradigms and comparison with Thomas Hardy in E. Longley 2008: 300–2). The ploughman tells Thomas that if his workmate had not been killed in France 'we should have moved this tree'. The poet reflects that he would not then have sat there—'Everything / Would have been different. For it would have been / Another world'.

Later receptions/associations and intertexts
Ezra Pound (1885–1972). In Pound's poem 'Hugh Selwyn Mauberley' (1920), sections IV and V are intertexts for WWI poetry. Pound uses classical referents throughout the poem to highlight *comparanda*. Section IV shows the influence of Aeschylus' *Agamemnon*, also found in Rosenberg. However, in writing post-war Pound's emphasis was on how soldiers 'came home to a lie / home to many deceits / home to old lies and new infamy'. Pound's allusion to Horace resonates with Owen's treatment of the *topos* in 'Dulce et Decorum Est' ('Died some, pro patria, non "dulce" non "et decor"…/ walked eye-deep in hell'; see further in the commentary on Owen's poem, pp. 126–34 below). Although Pound would not have read Owen's poem when he composed 'Hugh Selwyn Mauberley', subsequent readers would triangulate the ancient author and the two modern receptions. Section V of Pound's poem ('For an old bitch gone in the teeth, for a botched civilisation') similarly resonates for subsequent readers with the broken mouth image from Rosenberg's 'August 1914' (not published until 1937). Pound's post-war exploration of the abyss caused by the war is part of a broader poetic response to the war, most significantly evident in T. S. Eliot's poem 'The Waste Land' (1922). Pound's dismissive and anti-Semitic attitude to Rosenberg is discussed p. 70 above (see also Noakes 2008: 383). However, there are synergies between Rosenberg and Pound in their responses to images from ancient Greek poetry. Some of Rosenberg's poems embryonically play with the juxtaposition without explicit connection that was a characteristic of early Imagist poetry. Pound developed this technique to correlate images or lines

without subordinating one to the other. Liebregts compares this to the deployment of parataxis in early Greek poetry (Liebregts 2019: 30).

Keith Douglas (1920–44) provided a significant direct reference to Rosenberg in 'Desert Flowers' (text in Douglas 2011: 102; the poem was probably written in a military hospital in Palestine 1943). The first two lines explicitly acknowledge Rosenberg's poem 'Break of Day in the Trenches':

> Living in a wide landscape are the flowers—
> Rosenberg I only repeat what you were saying—
> the shell and the hawk every hour
> are slaying men and jerboas, slaying
> the mind: but the body can fill
> the hungry flowers and the dogs who cry words
> at nights, the most hostile things of all.
> But that is not new.

The poem is discussed by Brearton 2013, who points to the elegiac tribute to Rosenberg and the foreshadowing of Douglas' own death that together form Douglas' reflection on the 'tautology' involved in perceiving one war through the lens of another. This relationship is taken up in Michael Longley's poems that link the Trojan War and World War I.

Michael Longley (1939–). Longley's poem 'A Poppy' (first published in 2000; text in Longley 2006: 255) selects Homer's poppy simile as a trope for a trans-temporal alignment of war experience in the Trojan War and WWI. Longley self-reflexively alludes to the origin of the simile in Homer and to Virgil's response ('an image Virgil steals—*lasso papavera / Collo*— and so do I'). Longley's poem provides important comparative material to Rosenberg's treatment of the image of the poppy, although there is no overt reference to Rosenberg. The next poem in Longley's sequence is 'Poetry', which refers specifically to Edward Thomas and Edmund Blunden (Longley 2006: 255). This is followed by 'War Graves'. That poem describes the flowers planted on war graves of ordinary soldiers who are named but not known to him. In contrast to the native flowers on the graves, 'Around the shell holes not one poppy has appeared, / No symbolic flora' (Longley 2006: 256–7). Towards the end of the poem he refers to the poets Sorley, Thomas, and Owen, but again there is no mention of Rosenberg. Longley's deployment of the 'hanging motif' of the poppy echoes the same Homeric and historical associations found in Rosenberg but, in a further contrast with Rosenberg, Longley inserts himself into the poem (an extended metalepsis) not in terms of lived experience of the war but as a literary figure, placing himself on an equal footing with Virgil as a poet in relation to the founding poet, Homer.

Longley's poem 'A Pebble', published in his collection *The Stairwell* (Longley 2014: 38), does reference Rosenberg. Longley describes Rosenberg's nephew placing a pebble on his headstone ('a paperweight / Holding down the poems').[55] The poem directly references 'Dead Man's Dump' ('one of the greatest poems / In the world, I say') and alludes to the persistent image of Rosenberg's self-portrait ('His long sad Treblinka face'). Longley's poem 'Ballyboley' (Longley 2020: 12) also has strong affinities with 'Dead Man's Dump' (see discussion p. 99).

Long after Rosenberg's death, Nobel Laureate Seamus Heaney, a poet who was also writing at a time of violent conflict, commented on integrity in poetry: 'it is the poet's job to be sensitive to the tensions and strains which run through the life of the times. *What distinguishes the good poet is the ability to trace these tensions home through the fault lines of his or her own sensibility, and to be true to the workings of his or her own spirit while remaining alert to the working of the world.* That is what we might call artistic integrity, and is a sine qua non' (Heaney 2000: 5, emphasis added). Much earlier in his career, Heaney had alluded to Auden's comment that 'poetry makes nothing happen' ('In Memory of W.B. Yeats, Auden 2009: 89), responding to the idea that poetry is 'a way of happening' and that 'It can eventually make new feelings, or feelings about feelings happen' (Heaney 1972: n.p.). Both of Heaney's seem to provide a fitting epitaph for the Trench poems of Rosenberg.

---

[55] For observant Jews a stone placed on a tomb is a symbol of mourning and remembrance.

Wilfred Owen (1893–1918)

Elizabeth Vandiver

1. Poet—education, cultural context, output

Wilfred Edward Salter Owen (1893–1918) was largely self-educated in classics. Owen learned some Latin in school; it is unlikely that he ever studied any Greek. Throughout his life he was intensely interested in classical literature and fiercely determined to improve his knowledge of it, by reading translations and essays as well as by studying Latin. He considered his lack of formal education in the classical languages a fundamental gap in his training as a poet, and from his school years on he was concerned about how to remedy this. In an early poem, 'To Poesy' (1909 or 1910), Owen refers to 'the vasty seas / Of learning to be travelled o'er'. He singles out 'the Greeks of old' as those whose 'clear accents' he longs to hear, and specifies that 'In divers tongues my thoughts must flow out free' (ll. 53–4, 56, 63; Stallworthy 1983/2013: 1.4). But the great public (i.e. elite private) schools with their classical curriculum were out of financial reach for Owen's family; furthermore, his education had to prepare him to earn his living. Owen attended two fee-paying independent schools, the Birkenhead Institute (1900–7) and the Shrewsbury Technical School (1907–11). The Birkenhead Institute offered Latin but not Greek, while Shrewsbury Technical offered neither language.

Owen entered the Birkenhead Institute on 11 June 1900, at age 7, and left it in January 1907, two months before his fourteenth birthday, when the family moved to Shrewsbury. Owen studied Latin at Birkenhead but it is unclear how far he progressed in the language there. He appears to have shown some linguistic promise; in 1905 he won a prize (a copy of Macaulay's *Essays and Lays*) for 'excellence in languages' (Hibberd 2002: 37). Fourteen was the normal school-leaving age, but Owen's parents supported his wish to continue his education, although it had been a struggle for them to afford the Birkenhead fees (Owen 1963–5: 1, 96). Their finances limited the

Greek and Roman Antiquity in First World War Poetry: Making Connections. Lorna Hardwick, Stephen Harrison, and Elizabeth Vandiver, Oxford University Press. © Lorna Hardwick, Stephen Harrison, and Elizabeth Vandiver 2024. DOI: 10.1093/oso/9780198907879.003.0005

available possibilities, so Owen was enrolled as a probationer at the Shrewsbury Pupil-Teacher Centre on 19 March 1907, the day after his fourteenth birthday (Hibberd 2002: 37). This meant that he paid no fees and in fact he earned a small salary during 1909–11 (Hibberd 2002: 37, 52). In addition, enrolment as a Pupil-Teacher provided Owen with a possible career as a schoolteacher. But his attendance at Shrewsbury Technical put an end to his formal study of Latin, and in later years he struggled to gain competency in the language so that he could meet the requirements to undertake a university degree. During his last term as a Pupil-Teacher (April 1911) he gained distinction in English and French and could have gone on to training college, but he hoped to avoid teaching as a career. He longed fervently to go to university, specifically to Oxford, and in later years he continued to resent that he had not been able to study there. He realized early, however, that his financial situation required him to set his sights lower. Accordingly, he decided to take the Matriculation examination for a University of London external degree. The examination required passing papers in English and mathematics and three other subjects, which had to include either Latin or a science; Owen's choice of French, history, and botany suggests that he knew his Latin was very weak (Hibberd 2002: 54, 59). He took the Matriculation examination in September 1911 and passed. The next step was the second-year examination, Intermediate Arts, which required papers in Latin and Roman History.

As Hibberd says, 'The big obstacle was Latin' (2002: 65); the immediate problem was how Owen could support himself while also making time for the necessary study. In October he took a position as lay reader to the vicar of Dunsden, near Reading, where he studied for the Matriculation examinations, perhaps with the vicar's help for Latin and Roman history.[1] In a letter to his mother (12 June 1912) Owen mentions the possibility that the vicar will teach him Greek, and says that while he 'dreads' the process of learning it, 'I should love to read Greek, whose spirit giveth life to so much poetry' (Potter 2023: 57). However, he makes no further reference to this and although he occasionally included a transliterated Greek word in a letter

---

[1] On Owen's education, his struggles to learn Latin, and his hopes for a university education, see Vandiver 2010: 114–18. Owen's mother was intensely religious, and he was a pious child. The two shared daily Bible readings as he was growing up (Potter 2014: 26). She had hoped that he would be ordained and in 1910 he wrote to her that he was considering it but was unsure if he had a calling (Potter 2023: 13). When he arrived in Dunsden, Owen 'had never had any occasion to question his basic commitment to religion' (Hibberd 2002: 57), but doubts grew upon him during the time he spent there (see below). For his time at Dunsden, see Hibberd 2002: ch. 4.

and often referred to classical gods and goddesses by their Greek rather than their Roman names, there is no evidence that he ever studied Greek. This remained a matter of regret to him. In a letter of February 1918 to his mother, Owen mentions reading H. A. Vachell's novel about Harrow, *The Hill*, and calls it 'lovely and melancholy reading'; he comforts himself by recalling a family visit to Broxton Hill, 'whose bluebells it may be, more than Greek iambics, fitted me for my job' (Potter 2023: 358). The juxtaposition of the study of Greek verse with direct experience of nature as two possible paths to poethood is striking.

Owen's interest in the ancient world extended to material culture. He had a keen visual aesthetic sense and an interest in art, especially statues; his letters frequently mention visits to museums and galleries. He owned a small bronze statuette of Hermes, apparently a reproduction of a Gallo-Roman original from around the second century CE, which he probably bought in Bordeaux in 1915.[2] He frequently cycled from Shrewsbury to the Roman site of Uriconium or Viroconium (modern Wroxeter), where he dug in the fields and occasionally found 'shards and bones' (Hibberd 2002: 48).[3] He was also fascinated by the Roman artefacts from Uriconium in the Shrewsbury Museum. Owen's personal library[4] includes a copy of George Fox's *Guide to the Roman City of Uriconium* (1911), and he drew on this book for his 112-line 'Ode' on Uriconium, written in July 1913, which describes Roman artefacts in loving detail and enjoins the reader to 'lift the gloomy curtain of Time Past / And spy the secret things that Hades hath' (Stallworthy 1983/ 2013: 1.65).[5] Visits to his Gunston cousins in Reading in 1909 and 1910 included excursions to nearby Silchester, the site of the Roman town Calleva Atrebatum. A letter to his mother of 31 December 1909 gives an elated description of a visit to the Reading Museum, where the Assistant Curator showed him over the Silchester artefacts (Owen and Bell 1967: 57). He mentions Silchester in several other letters, and a guide to the Silchester collection in the Reading Museum survives in his library. The Owen Archive in the Bodleian Library contains some Roman coins, pottery fragments, and

---

[2] The statuette passed to Owen's cousin Lesley Gunston after Owen's death. Photographs of it appear in Hibberd 1986: pl. 6 and Potter 2014: 55.

[3] On the history of Uriconium and the excavations there, see White 2022, which discusses Owen's 'Ode' on pp. 56–9.

[4] Owen's library survives nearly intact in the Weston Library, University of Oxford; see below. Stallworthy 2013 includes a 1974 checklist of the library as Appendix B; this is almost complete, although a few additional items have been added to the collection.

[5] Owen's Uriconium Ode is discussed in Hardwick, Harrison, and Vandiver 2024 and in the digital version.

nails that Owen owned; these probably include the cache of artefacts from Silchester that the wealthy antiquarian, amateur geologist, and local historian Llewellyn Treacher (1859–1943) gave to Owen and Leslie Gunston in 1910.[6]

As part of his ongoing work towards a university degree, Owen decided to enrol in classes at University College, Reading, which prepared students for degrees awarded by the University of London. He registered for botany classes in April 1912; he had hoped to take classes in Latin and French as well, but could not manage the time while still working in the parish. His botany instructor introduced him to the Professor of English, Edith Morley, who encouraged him to try for a scholarship that would allow him to enrol in Reading's new residential college (Hibberd 2002: 65, 80, 94). He left his position as lay assistant in Dunsden in February 1913, apparently due to a crisis of faith,[7] and took the Reading scholarship examination in June 1913. He was unsuccessful; to his mother he wrote 'I feel sure that the Latin [?Boggle is to blame for] that and the fact that Miss Morley was not examining this year' (Hibberd 1982: 280).[8]

In September 1913 Owen took up a post as a teacher at the Berlitz School in Bordeaux. He had not yet relinquished his goal of attending university, but found that the long hours required by his teaching post left no time for private study. He stayed on in France for two years, although the war caused the Berlitz School to close by September 1914. In December 1914 Owen accepted a position as tutor for two young English boys stranded in France. He wrote to his mother in January 1915 that tutoring the boys in Latin would be useful for his examination preparation (Potter 2023: 162) and in March asked his sister to send him copies of Caesar's *De bello Gallico* and an elementary Latin reader *Gradatim* (Owen and Bell 1967: 326).[9] In addition, his letters mention working on Roman history with his pupils, and enjoying the process (Potter 2023: 155).

---

[6] Oxford, Bodleian Libraries, Owen Archive, JL 980, items 27–40. Owen describes this gift in a letter to his mother dated 18 August 1910 (Potter 2023: 12).

[7] Owen's letters to his mother and sister indicate increasing discord during his last few weeks at the Dunsden Vicarage, but Harold Owen censored the letters so heavily that it is impossible to tell precisely what happened. Potter says that 'what is described rather cryptically in his letters as a "furor" leads to his finally revealing the true state of his spiritual and religious feelings', at which point the vicar agreed that Owen should leave his post (Potter 2014: 44). For more on Owen's state of mind and growing religious doubts, see Hibberd 2002: 91–8.

[8] The text is uncertain; Dominic Hibberd restored it from a passage Harold Owen had inked out.

[9] Owen's postcard to his sister implies that he owns the books he is requesting, but neither *De bello Gallico* nor *Gradatim* survives in his library or on a checklist Harold Owen prepared in 1920 (Stallworthy 2013: 341).

By March 1915, however, Owen had lost enthusiasm for the idea of a university education, writing to his mother that 'I can find only two or three flimsy arguments for the B.A. Craze' and declaring his intention to be a poet, although to do so would require 'a period of study, then of intercourse with kindred spirits, then of isolation. My heart is ready, but my brain unprepared, and my hand untrained' (Potter 2023: 167). The question of whether or not to enlist was pressing on him as well. When the war broke out he had felt little inclination to join up, but as the months passed he became more uneasy with remaining a civilian. When he learned that the German shelling of Scarborough on 21 December 1914 had killed fifteen schoolboys, he told his mother 'I raved' (Potter 2023: 156). He continued to weigh his options through most of 1915. During a visit to London in May he could not have avoided the ubiquitous recruiting posters; at this time he saw a notice in his hotel that 'any "gentleman returning from abroad" could obtain a commission by joining the Artists' Rifles' (Hibberd 2002: 158). He returned to England in September and on 21 October enlisted in the Artists' Rifles. During the parts of his military training that took place in London, Owen sought out Harold Monro's (1879–1932) Poetry Bookshop, where he attended poetry readings and bought copies of Brooke's *1914 and other Poems*, Housman's *A Shropshire Lad*, and Monro's latest book, *Children of Love* (Hibberd 2002: 170).[10]

He was commissioned as a second lieutenant in the 5th Battalion, Manchester Regiment, in June 1916, was sent to the Western Front in January 1917, and was very soon in the thick of horrors, holding an advanced post in no man's land from 13–15 January. His experiences there would later form the subject of his poem 'The Sentry'. He soon returned to the line and he and his men spent 23–6 January on Redan Ridge, unsheltered on frozen ground (Hibberd 2002: 209–19). On 4 February he wrote to his mother that his platoon 'had to lie in the snow under the deadly wind. . . . The marvel is that we did not all die of cold. As a matter of fact, only one of my party actually froze to death' (Potter 2023: 246). This experience found poetic expression in 'Futility' and 'Exposure'. On 15 March he suffered a concussion after a fall and was sent to hospital, but he rejoined his battalion on 4 April. He was sent back into the line on 12 April, and 'it was during these nine days, 13–21 April 1917, that Wilfred's nerve finally gave way' (Hibberd 2002: 240). Details are uncertain, but it

---

[10] On the importance of the Poetry Bookshop, see Grant 1967.

appears that he was blown into the air and knocked unconscious by a shell that exploded near him, and when he regained consciousness had to shelter in a shell-hole for several days, surrounded by the dismembered remains of a fellow officer who had been killed on 2 April (Hibberd 2002: 239–41).

After these experiences, Owen was evacuated on 2 May to the Casualty Clearing Station, with shell shock. He was sent back to England and ordered to Craiglockhart War Hospital near Edinburgh. He arrived on 26 June, and began therapy with Dr A. E. Brock (1879–1947) the next day. A strong proponent of 'ergotherapy' based on Patrick Geddes' (1854–1932) theories, Brock immediately assigned Owen practical tasks such as metalwork.[11] Recognizing his patient's strengths, Brock also gave him the task of writing a poem on the myth of Heracles and Antaeus ('The Wrestlers', discussed below) and appointed him as editor of *The Hydra*, Craiglockhart's in-house journal. Owen brought out six issues, beginning with Number 7, for 13 July 1917; the last issue he edited was Number 12, for 29 September (Hibberd 1986: 206). He contributed several anonymous editorials and prose pieces to these issues, as well as printing (also anonymously) his own poems 'Song of Songs' in Number 10, 1 September 1917, and 'The Next War' in Number 12, 29 September 1917 (Hibberd 1986: 206n29; 2002: 260).

In Owen's view, the most important occurrence at Craiglockhart was his meeting Siegfried Sassoon (1886–1967) there. Shortly after Sassoon's arrival in August 1917, Owen (who greatly admired Sassoon's collection of poems *The Old Huntsman*) summoned up his courage and introduced himself. The friendship between the two men sparked Owen's poetic *annus mirabilis* (see Hibberd 1992). Through Sassoon, Owen also met Robert Graves (1895–1985); the two corresponded and Graves offered Owen suggestions on his work. When Owen was discharged from Craiglockhart in October 1917 and had three weeks' leave, Sassoon urged him to contact Robert Ross (1869–1918) in London. Ross encouraged Owen and introduced him to Arnold Bennett (1867–1931) and H.G. Wells (1866–1946), amongst others. At Robert Graves' wedding, Owen met Edward Marsh (1872–1953) and C. K. Scott Moncrieff (1889–1930) who would become a close friend and would include Owen as one of three dedicatees for his 1919 translation of the *Song of Roland* (Hibberd 1992: 58–60, 83–5, 117–19).[12] Scott Moncrieff also

---

[11] On Brock's theory of 'ergotherapy' and his debt to the ideas of Geddes, see Hibberd 1977 and Hibberd 2002: 253–7.

[12] On Scott Moncrieff's original dedication to the *Song of Roland*, headed 'To Mr. W. O.' and beginning 'To you, my master in assonance, I dedicate my part in this assonant poem', see France 2012: 367–8, 370. As printed, the dedication includes a sonnet addressed to Owen and

introduced Owen to Philip Bainbrigge (1890–1918), a Shrewsbury classics master now in the Army; Owen and Bainbrigge 'seem to have been intimate' and to have shared a 'rapport' (Ingleheart 2018: 36–7).

After leaving Craiglockhart, Owen spent ten months in England. In late November 1917 he was judged fit for four months of 'light duty of a clerical nature' (Hibberd 2002: 279) and was posted to Scarborough, where he stayed until 12 March 1918; he was then posted to the Northern Command Depot in Ripon and remained there until he was 'graded fit' for general service on 4 June (Hibberd 2002: 279, 319). In Scarborough Owen had a private room in an attic, with a turret overlooking the sea. In Ripon he shared a hut with thirteen other officers, but soon rented a room in a cottage on Borrage Lane, where he was able to retreat for several hours on most evenings. It was in these two places, Scarborough and Ripon, that he wrote and revised several of his most important poems (Hibberd 1992: 69–70, 106–7). He was posted back to Scarborough on 5 June and from that point forward his 'life was the comfortless one of a serving soldier' (Hibberd 2002: 320).

Owen was sent back to France on 31 August 1918. On 29 September–3 October he took part in the successful assault on the Beaurevoir-Fonsomme line, and was awarded the Military Cross for his actions in an attack on the night of 1/2 October. According to the official citation, Owen 'personally manipulated a captured enemy M[achine] G[un] from an isolated position and inflicted considerable losses on the enemy' (Hibberd 2002: 376).[13] He was killed in action on the morning of 4 November 1918, trying to lead his men across the Sambre and Oise canal. His parents received the telegram announcing his death as the church bells were ringing to celebrate the Armistice on 11 November (Stallworthy 1983/2013: 1.xix; Cuthbertson 2014: 287–90, 293–4).

Owen had continued his disciplined self-education through reading, even when on leave from the Front (Vandiver 2010: 118–19). He bought a copy of

poems to Philip Bainbrigge and Ian Mackenzie, both of whom also died in the last months of the war (France 2012: 368). Scott Moncrieff is best known for his English translation of Proust, *Remembrance of Things Past* (1922–30).

[13] The official War Office document survives in a scrapbook kept by Owen's father (Hibberd 2002: 376) and was printed in the London *Gazette* of 30 July 1919 (Potter 2023: 398n168). Owen and Bell print a different version of the citation, replacing the sentence about inflicting losses on the enemy with 'He personally captured an enemy Machine Gun in an isolated position and took a number of prisoners' (1967: 580). Hibberd comments that this is 'presumably a family forgery; capturing prisoners would have seemed a more appropriate activity for a war poet than inflicting "considerable losses" with a machine gun' (Hibberd 1992: 174; see also Hibberd 2002: 376–7).

Andrew Lang's (1844–1912) translation of Theocritus, Bion, and Moschus in Scarborough in December 1917 and included it on a handwritten 'reading list' he kept for that month (Hibberd 1992: 71). The book survives in Owen's library, which also includes a copy of Plutarch's *Life of Julius Caesar* in North's translation. His extant library by no means represents all of his reading, however. His letters record that he read many books now missing from the library and he shows familiarity, at least by reputation, with several works that there is no record he ever owned (see Vandiver 2010: 120–1, 129). For example, he ends an editorial for *The Hydra* with allusions to Homer and Hesiod, though neither is in his library: 'The great poets are above the pains of careful endings. Thus, Homer ends with lines that might as well be in the middle of a passage; Hesiod, one knows not how; and *The Hydra*, the new voice from Craiglockhart, does not end at all, but is still going on' ([Owen] 1917). Clearly, he had at the very least read enough about Homer and Hesiod to be able to characterize the ending of their works accurately. No copy of Homer or Vergil survives amongst his books, but so devout a disciple of Keats would almost certainly have read Chapman's Homer, and his possession of Cary's Dante suggests that his investigation of poetic tradition would have led him to read the *Aeneid*, probably in translation— a surmise supported by apparent allusions to the *Aeneid* in several of his poems. Although his library contains no volumes of Horace or Ovid, allusions to both poets are quite frequent in his work and strongly suggest that he had read some Horace, at least in translation and possibly in Latin.

The question of how much Owen's awareness of classics was mediated through English writers is complex and cannot be definitively answered. His direct knowledge of Ovid is particularly difficult to determine, although there is a strong current of Ovidian imagery running through several of his poems (discussed individually below). His library includes two children's books, *The Greenwood Tree* and *Contes fabuleux de la Grèce antique* (Adams [1910], a translation of an English original), which both contain many retellings of stories from Ovid's *Metamorphoses*, interspersed with modern adaptations and additions. *The Greenwood Tree* cites Charles Kingsley's (1819–75) *The Heroes* as a source of additional information about Jason (70n[3]), and a copy of *The Heroes* is in Owen's library. *The Greenwood Tree* also refers its readers to Andrew Lang's translation of Bion's 'Lament for Adonis' (40n[3]), which Owen was reading in late 1917 in the translation he bought in Scarborough. Whether he sought out other ancient texts whose contents he had first encountered in these children's books cannot be known, but it seems likely. He also engaged with classics mediated through the poems of Keats, Shelley, and Tennyson. Classics became one of the foremost sources of allusions, motifs, and associations in his poetry, matched only by the Bible, with which his religious upbringing had made him thoroughly familiar.

Owen's status as one of the foremost poets of the First World War is due almost entirely to the work of his editors after his death, since only five of his poems ('Song of Songs', 'The Next War', 'Miners', 'Hospital Barge', and 'Futility') were published during his lifetime (Hibberd 2002: 367). Owen's friendship with Osbert Sitwell (1892–1969) had led him to submit several poems to the Modernist journal *Wheels*, which Osbert and his sister Edith Sitwell (1887–1964) edited, but these arrived too late to be included in the 1918 issue.[14] Edith Sitwell dedicated the 1919 issue of *Wheels* to Owen's memory and printed seven of his poems: 'The Show', 'Strange Meeting', 'A Terre', 'The Sentry', 'Disabled', 'The Dead-Beat', and 'The Chances', none of which had been published previously (Sitwell 1919: 52–64). The first edition of his poems, edited by Edith Sitwell with a preface by Sassoon and containing twenty-three poems, appeared in December 1920. It was followed in 1931 by Edmund Blunden's (1896–1974) edition, which added some thirty-five additional poems and fragments. In 1963 C. Day Lewis (1904–72) published his edition, *The Collected Poems of Wilfred Owen*, including nineteen more poems, and Dominic Hibberd's (1941–2012) *Wilfred Owen: War Poems and Others* followed in 1973. These editions varied in many details of readings and in the assumed chronology of the poems. Jon Stallworthy's (1935–2014) magisterial two-volume *Wilfred Owen: The Complete Poems and Fragments* (1983, rev. edn. 2013) established the chronology and texts of all the extant poems and fragments. It immediately became, and remains, the standard edition for Owen scholarship. Stallworthy's fascinating account of his own and earlier editors' work, 'Owen and his editors', appears both in Stallworthy 2008 and as Appendix D in the 2013 revised *Complete Poems and Fragments* (hereafter CPF).

In 1962 Benjamin Britten (1913–76) incorporated several of Owen's poems into the text of his 'War Requiem', commissioned for the consecration of Coventry Cathedral, and this began a groundswell of interest in Owen (Hibberd 2002: 370; Stallworthy 2008: 84–6). Owen's most famous poems, especially 'Anthem for Doomed Youth', 'Dulce et Decorum Est', and 'Strange Meeting', now appear in almost every anthology of First World War poetry.

---

[14] On *Wheels*, see http://modjourn.org/journal/wheels/.

Owen's position as probably the best known of the First World War poets is due in part to the apparent anti-war stance of his most famous poems, which matched so well the anti-war feeling (motivated by the American involvement in Vietnam) of the 1960s and 1970s. His reworking of Horace's tag *dulce et decorum est pro patria mori* has changed the way modern students read Horace, but Owen's hegemony over presentations of war goes beyond reshaping modern readers' understanding of Horace to reshaping their understanding of ancient war literature in general. Modern students (at least in the US) unquestioningly assume that any literature *about* war must be literature *against* war. This powerful assumption that war poetry can only mean anti-war poetry owes a very great deal to the war poets in general and to Wilfred Owen in particular; poets who did not denounce war tend to be discounted.[15] Owen's attitude towards war is actually far more nuanced than is often realized, but his presentation of ancient militarism as an 'Old Lie' in 'Dulce et Decorum Est' has carried the field, and teachers of classics now have to persuade their students to believe that there were in fact times and contexts in which such exhortations to die for one's country were not meant ironically. Owen famously said that 'the true Poets must be truthful' (Stallworthy 1983/2013: 2.535); for many readers, 'Dulce et Decorum Est' in particular and Owen's work in general have recast basic assumptions about what can be 'true' concerning war and the experience of death in battle.

On the formal level, Owen's most important achievement was his development of the form of rhyme variously called pararhyme, half-rhyme, slant rhyme, consonantal rhyme, and other terms; he himself referred to it in a December 1917 letter to Siegfried Sassoon as 'my vowel-rime stunt' (Potter 2023: 341).[16] In its strictest form, pararhyme consists of word pairs where the initial and final consonants are the same but the vowel varies: escaped/scooped, laughed/left, killed/cold.

In a letter to Leslie Gunston about his use of pararhyme, Owen wrote that 'I suppose I am doing in poetry what the advanced composers are doing in music. I am not satisfied with either' (Potter 2023: 354). His comparison of pararhyme to the work of 'advanced composers' is his clearest comment on

---

[15] See above on the tendency to view Brooke's war poetry as 'politically naive', for instance.

[16] The fullest treatment of Owen's development of pararhyme and its possible sources is Bäckman 1979: 168–91, who gives a full typology for different forms of partial rhyme on pp. 171–2. See also Welland 1978: 104–24 (ch. 6, 'Half-Rhyme') and Hibberd 2002: 257–8.

his purpose in developing that form of rhyme. Unfortunately he does not specify which composers he has in mind, but it seems most likely that he intended to compare his use of pararhyme to the contemporaneous development of atonality in music by composers such as Alban Berg (1885–1935) and Arnold Schoenberg (1874–1951). Other poets before Owen had used approximate or half-rhyme, but he was the first to develop it fully into strict pararhyme. Later poets including Auden, Heaney, and Walcott have followed his example.

2. Paramaterial—manuscripts, *The Hydra*, letters

Since only five of Owen's poems—and those not his most famous—were printed during his lifetime, the difficult task of establishing a 'standard' text for his work depends on his unfinished and often unclear manuscripts. Owen wrote to his mother in late May 1918 that he was planning to have his poems 'typed at once', and to send the typescript to Heinemann (Potter 2023: 372). But if this typescript was made, it has disappeared. Many of Owen's surviving manuscripts are rough working drafts in a bewildering state of ongoing revision, with text scribbled in the margins and between lines, and variants written, crossed out, and rewritten, and in many cases there are several manuscripts in differing stages of revision for one poem. For such poems, which (if any) of several cancelled readings Owen would ultimately have used cannot be known. These difficulties involve some of his most significant poems. Owen's manuscripts are therefore far more important for evaluating his poetic achievement than is the case with most poets, since we cannot assume that Owen had finally rejected readings that have been cancelled on one manuscript but still appear on others. Fortunately for scholars and readers, images of most of the manuscripts of Owen's poems are available on the First World War Poetry Digital Archive (FWWPDA). The manuscripts themselves are housed primarily in two sites: the British Library and the Bodleian Library, Oxford. Three are at Columbia University, a few remain in private hands, and some are lost and known only from photocopies or transcripts.

The six issues of *The Hydra* that Owen edited contain several editorials and articles by him. Transcriptions of all extant copies of *The Hydra* are available through the Edinburgh Napier University Library. In addition, digital images of many issues are available at FWWPDA, including five of the six that Owen edited (the 15 September 1917 issue is not included).[17]

Owen's *Collected Letters* (Owen and Bell 1967) are an invaluable source for context and chronology of his poems, which has now been supplemented by the new edition of *Selected Letters* (Potter 2023). Unfortunately, Harold Owen censored his brother's letters heavily, blacking some passages out with heavy ink and cutting others away with scissors, and much important information is lost. Nevertheless, the remaining material gives rich background on Owen's thought processes, interests, state of mind, and experiences. There are several instances when it is possible to compare Owen's description of a war experience in a letter with his treatment of the same experience in a poem.

Owen's letters are mainly held by the Harry Ransom Center, University of Texas, Austin. Some letters (including several to Sassoon) are at Columbia University. The Harry Ransom Center and Columbia University also hold correspondence relating to the publication of Owen's work, by Sassoon, Blunden, Owen's mother Susan, and his brother Harold.

Owen's personal library has largely survived, although as discussed above some books that he is known to have owned are no longer present. In 1975, Phyllis Owen, Harold Owen's widow, donated Wilfred's personal library along with many of his manuscripts, his school notebooks, and various family photographs and memorabilia to the English Faculty Library, Oxford (Hibberd 2002: 370). The archive also includes correspondence of Owen's family members with his editors and biographers and the working files of Dominic Hibberd and Jon Stallworthy. This archive was moved from the English Faculty Library to the Weston Special Collections Library (part of the Bodleian Library) in 2016.

3. Poems

These are presented in the versions printed by Stallworthy in CPF. Stallworthy's number for each poem or fragment is provided, as is the volume and page number.[18]

---

[17] The Napier transcripts are at https://www.napier.ac.uk/about-us/our-location/our-campuses/special-collections/war-poets-collection/the-hydra.

[18] The Owen Archive was recatalogued after the move to the Weston Library, but since Stallworthy's edition uses the abbreviation OEF (for Oxford English Faculty) for items in the Owen Archive, I follow that usage when discussing specific manuscripts.

The full printed edition (Hardwick, Harrison, and Vandiver 2024) and the digital version of that commentary will include discussion of every poem that references classics in any way, from Owen's earliest juvenilia onward. For the present volume, space requires limiting the discussion to his war poems, taking 'war poem' to mean any poem written from August 1914 onward that in some way refers to or concerns the war. Poems written during this period that have no discernible connection with the war are not included.

The war poems are grouped into three categories, to foreground the most significant forms of classical reception that Owen employs.[19] The first category covers poems that allude to Horace. The section begins with the most obvious of these, 'Dulce et Decorum Est', probably Owen's most famous poem and one of the best-known English poems of the twentieth century. Following the discussion of 'Dulce et Decorum Est', the section comments on 'Arms and the Boy', 'Schoolmistress', 'With an Identity Disc', '1914', 'The End', and 'Insensibility'. The second category covers poems that allude, directly or indirectly, to the classical *katabasis* (Underworld journey) or to the Underworld itself. Once again, the section begins with one of Owen's best-known poems, 'Strange Meeting', and goes on to discuss 'Spring Offensive', 'Exposure', 'Apologia pro Poemate Meo', 'A New Heaven', and 'An Imperial Elegy'. Finally, the third category contains two unfinished poems, 'The Wrestlers' and the very fragmentary 'Perseus', which are Owen's only direct retellings of classical myths.

The poems in these three categories are discussed in detail. The chapter's final section, 'Other classical interactions', gives brief discussions of a selection of Owen's poems that contain glancing or peripheral connections with classics.[20]

3.1 Horatian intertexts

Owen's extant library contains no copy of Horace. Our assessment of whether Owen was familiar with Horace's work must therefore rely on indirect evidence and inference from Owen's own writings. The balance of

[19] This arrangement highlights the necessity of different forms of taxonomy for discussing different poets; for Isaac Rosenberg, for instance, phases of development are more important than groupings based on particular classical texts, such as the ones used here for Owen.

[20] On glancing references, see Introduction, p. 11.

probability indicates Owen had read at least some of Horace's poems, at the very least in translation.[21] Owen included an untranslated quotation from Horace—*aequam memento rebus in arduis / Servare mentem* (*Odes* 2.3.1–2, 'remember to keep a tranquil mind in difficult situations')—in a letter to his sister dated 23 June 1912 (Potter 2023: 60). At this time Owen was studying Latin for his university entrance examinations, while serving as a lay assistant at Dunsden. He could, of course, have found this very well-known Latin tag in a book of common quotations, but in any case it is the earliest indication that he is familiar with at least one example of Horace's Latin, wherever he found it.[22]

Far more significant is the appearance of Horatian quotations, allusions, and echoes in at least seven of Owen's poems. The most famous is the title and the concluding line and a half of Owen's 'Dulce et Decorum Est', which quotes Horace *Odes* 3.2.13. Strikingly, 'Arms and the Boy' begins with words that clearly echo the opening lines of that same ode. These two poems were written within about six months of one another; it seems likely that Owen had read *Odes* 3.2 and was responding to it in both poems. In addition, 'With an Identity Disc' engages directly and substantively with *Odes* 3.30, and '1914', 'The End', 'Insensibility', and—less directly—'Schoolmistress' all include Horatian connections. These Horatian intertexts will be discussed in detail in the commentary on the individual poems.

'Dulce et Decorum Est' (1917; rev. 1918)
(a) **Text of poem** [CPF 144, 1.140–1]

> Bent double, like old beggars under sacks,
> Knock-kneed, coughing like hags, we cursed through sludge,
> Till on the haunting flares we turned our backs
> And towards our distant rest began to[23] trudge.
> Men marched asleep. Many had lost their boots   5
> But limped on, blood-shod. All went lame; all blind;

---

[21] Working on this commentary has changed my position on this point; I had previously argued that Owen had probably not read Horace (Vandiver 2010: 129–30; Vandiver 2018).

[22] School editions of Horace (such as Pitt's, Gow's, and Page's) were readily available, as were translations. Horace was included in Bohn's Classical Library, for instance.

[23] Norgate points out that the fair copy clearly reads 'began the trudge', not 'began to trudge' (2020: 10–11). Stallworthy transcribes the manuscript correctly (CPF 2.292), but prints the earlier reading 'to trudge' in his text (CPF 1.140). The difference is a small one, but not insignificant; as Norgate discusses, 'began the trudge' implies a habitual action, 'one the soldiers have made before and become accustomed to—and so are that bit less alert' (11).

Drunk with fatigue; deaf even to the hoots
Of tired, outstripped Five-Nines that dropped behind.

Gas! GAS! Quick, boys! — An ecstasy of fumbling,
Fitting the clumsy helmets just in time;   10
But someone still was yelling out and stumbling,
And flound'ring like a man in fire or lime...
Dim, through the misty panes and thick green light,
As under a green sea, I saw him drowning.

In all my dreams, before my helpless sight,   15
He plunges at me, guttering, choking, drowning.

If in some smothering dreams you too could pace
Behind the wagon that we flung him in,
And watch the white eyes writhing in his face,
His hanging face, like a devil's sick of sin;   20
If you could hear, at every jolt, the blood
Come gargling from the froth-corrupted lungs,
Obscene as cancer, bitter as the cud
Of vile, incurable sores on innocent tongues, —
My friend, you would not tell with such high zest   25
To children ardent for some desperate glory,
The old Lie: Dulce et decorum est
Pro patria mori.

(b) Poem—date, form, and content

The poem was drafted at Craiglockhart in early October 1917 and revised
between January and March 1918. The earliest manuscript is dated 8 October
1917 and Owen apparently enclosed a copy of some version of the poem in
a letter to his mother on the 16th (CPF 1.140). There are four manuscript
drafts (available on FWWPDA). The earliest has the subtitle '(To Jessie Pope,
etc.)'; Pope (1868–1941) was a popular writer of jingoistic verse. On the
second version this is crossed out and replaced by 'To a certain Poetess'
(CPF 2.294, 296). The third draft is also headed 'To a certain Poetess'; only
on the final draft does the title stand by itself and the 'you' of the final stanza
become not one particular individual but, implicitly, any and every reader.[24]

---

[24] Norgate argues that the target of the final version may be the journalist Horatio Bottomley
(1860–1933) instead of or as well as Jessie Pope (2021: 7–14).

Hibberd argues that the poem's structure reveals a 'tight formal discipline'. It begins with what appears to be a Shakespearean sonnet, a form that features three rhymed quatrains followed by a rhymed couplet, with the rhyme scheme ABABCDCD EFEFGG. The sestet of Owen's 'sonnet' proceeds normally through its first four lines (9–12), leading to the expectation that lines 13–14 will be a rhymed couplet. Instead, line 14 disrupts the rhyme, and underlines this disruption by the feminine ending of 'drowning';[25] in place of a final couplet, 'there is instead the first half of a quatrain, so that the sonnet does not end but instead makes the reader pause in anticipation' (Hibberd 1986: 114). Lines 15–16, the second half of the quatrain in Hibberd's terms, then form a pivot around which the whole poem turns: from the past-tense description of the front-line gas attack in the first fourteen lines, to the horrifying dream-haunted present tense of 'In all my dreams...he plunges at me', to the conditional future that structures the final twelve lines of the poem: 'If you...could pace/watch/hear...[then] you would not tell'. As Hibberd notes, the second section of fourteen lines, beginning with line 15, 'bears no resemblance to a sonnet and is held together only by its rhymes'.[26] The central section, lines 13–16, also moves the poem from the first person plural where the experience of intolerable weariness is shared by the group ('we'), through the first-person singular introduced in line 14, with its focus on the single individual speaker's reaction ('I saw him drowning') to the accusatory second-person singular[27] of the final twelve lines. This metalepsis turns the poem into a direct confrontation between the speaker and the reader, who is both pulled into the horrific experience and simultaneously accused of being detached from it.

The poem features very regular iambic pentameter, with skilfully handled substitutions of choriambs (a trochee followed by an iamb) for two iambs at the beginnings of lines ('drúnk with fatígue') and occasionally in mid-line as well ('coúghing like hágs'). The use of monosyllables in line 25 is noteworthy and effective. In the standard version printed by Day Lewis and Stallworthy, the regularity of the metre throughout throws emphasis on the last line, the only short line in the poem as they print it. However, Sitwell and Blunden

---

[25] On feminine endings, see discussion of Brooke's 'The Old Vicarage, Grantchester', above.

[26] Martin's statement that the poem is 'two sonnets, bent and doubled in the middle at lines 13 and 14', is unfounded, since the pivotal lines 15–16 would in that case have to begin the 'second sonnet', which both syntax and rhyme scheme make clear they do not (Martin 2012: 175).

[27] The address 'my friend' makes it clear that 'you' is singular, not plural; the speaker is addressing a single auditor, or perhaps it would be better to say is addressing each reader individually.

print line 8 as 'of gas-shells dropping softly behind', a nine-syllable line which cannot be scanned as iambic pentameter. Editors thus confront a decision; does the metrical regularity of the rest of the poem argue for 'restoring' a metrical version of line 8? The possibilities are either the reconstructed, partially cancelled 'Of tired, outstripped Five-Nines that dropped behind' or an earlier cancelled version: 'Of disappointed shells that dropped behind' (CPF 2.294, 296).

Norgate argues that line 8 should be taken as a half-line, 'Of gas-shells dropping softly', that breaks off in mid-thought. He points out that Five-Nines were in fact German explosives, *not* gas shells, and that the manuscripts that include the words 'tired, out-stripped Five-Nines' also include four cancelled lines describing gas shells falling in *front* of the soldiers. If those lines about gas are removed, then the revision of 'Five-Nines' into 'gas shells' introduces gas into the poem, but that gas should be in front of, not behind, the soldiers (2020: 16–21). The difficulty here, of course, is that Norgate's suggested reading disrupts the rhyme-scheme of the poem, which is otherwise completely regular. It seems clear that Owen had not decided on a final revision of line 8, and thus we are left with the choice of maintaining the sonnet-form rhymes, either by keeping the unmetrical version of Sitwell and Blunden or by restoring a cancelled version with Day Lewis and Stallworthy, or of accepting Norgate's proposed half-line and so losing the apparent sonnet. Examination of the manuscripts does seem to indicate that the 'sonnet' is probably a mirage caused by Owen's cancellation of the four lines about gas shells. This cancellation leaves what appears to be a sestet of a sonnet in lines 9–14, but in the earlier manuscripts containing those cancelled lines, the poem falls either into rhymed quatrains or into stanzas of eight lines each. The six-line apparent sestet, *pace* Hibberd, may be only an artefact of Owen's decision to excise four lines.

(c) Reception commentary

'Dulce et Decorum Est' is without question the most famous example of classical reception in First World War poetry. In this instance, Owen's reception is framed as a rejection. He cites the Horatian tag only to denounce it as an outmoded lie, and in so doing denounces likewise the whole traditional view of warfare and what death in war 'means'. Owen's linguistic code-switching in the poem, using Latin as a title and as the final lines of the poem, forms an indictment of the traditional view by underlining its distance from the trenches; Latin here functions as a kind of hyper-literary vehicle, exactly the sort of thing that Owen would denounce in his draft 'Preface' by saying 'Above all I am not concerned with Poetry' (CPF Appendix A, 2.535).

It is worth considering what resonances readers in Owen's day would have heard in the Latin phrase *dulce et decorum est pro patria mori* and, as a corollary, what the precise target of his denunciation is.[28] Is he renouncing classics as such, or is his bitter anger directed less at the Latin original and more at the use of the tag in contemporary society? The only comment about this Latin phrase that we have from Owen himself is in a letter of mid-October 1917 to his mother, in which he enclosed a copy of his poem. He writes 'The famous Latin tag means of course It is sweet and meet <u>to die</u> for <u>one's country. Sweet</u>! And <u>decorous</u>!' (Potter 2023: 322; 'sweet' and 'decorous' are both underscored with a double line). Most unfortunately, this letter is one that Harold Owen chose to 'edit' by scissoring a passage out. The passage that attracted Harold's censoring scissors was probably on the front side of the page, where Owen was discussing family friends, and the removal of whatever more he may have written about 'the famous Latin tag' on the back of the page was simply collateral damage.[29]

If we had only the brief comment that remains in Owen's letter to judge by, it would be impossible to say if he even knew that the 'famous tag' was Horace's. But as we shall see below, 'Arms and the Boy' also references *Odes* 3.2. Assuming that Owen did know this ode, then the Horatian context becomes important for our interpretation of 'Dulce et Decorum Est':

> dulce et decorum est pro patria mori:
> mors et fugacem persequitur virum,
> nec parcit imbellis iuventae
> poplitibus timidove tergo. (Horace *Odes* 3.2.13–14)

(It is sweet and fitting to die for one's fatherland: death pursues the fleeing man as well, nor spares the hamstrings of the unwarlike youth or his timid back.)

Hipp contends that the quotation from Horace 'suggests that part of Owen's need to write the poem came from the fear that, having broken down in battle, he was one of these "faint-hearted youths"' (Hipp 2002: 37–8). This implies that Owen read Horace's ode as straightforwardly militaristic, although Horace's rather cynical statement that cowards who flee also die

---

[28] On the target of Owen's accusation, see Hobbs 2018.

[29] Jane Potter, personal communication to Elizabeth Vandiver, 21 April 2021.

problematizes the most simplistic reading of the ode, and some of Horace's other odes provide further nuance. Horace himself, if we can trust *Odes* 2.7.9–14, threw his shield away in battle and ran (see Winkler 2000: 211–12). But Owen probably also knew the tag from more modern sources, in contexts that allowed for no nuance at all and may have been more likely than Horace's ode to rouse the anger that is so evident in the speaker of the poem.

Dulce et decorum est pro patria mori was a popular tag for gravestones and monuments by the nineteenth century. It was used on Boer War memorials, in 1913 it was engraved on the chapel wall at Sandhurst, and it appears with no hint of irony on individual gravestones at Gallipoli and on British war memorials in the 1920s. When Owen enlisted, he may well have heard a rousing speech by Lieutenant-Colonel W. Shirley, which used the phrase (Kerr 1993: 174), and he may have seen it used as the title of a poem in an issue of *Boy's Own Paper* in 1916 (Cuthbertson 2014: 163). Galloway Kyle's anthologies *Soldier Poets: Songs of the Fighting Men* (1916) and *More Songs by the Fighting Men* (1917) each contained a poem titled 'Dulce et Decorum est Pro Patria Mori', and the second of these volumes survives in Owen's library (Norgate 1989: 521). Along with these literary sources, Owen could also have seen the tag in one particular setting that would have been particularly memorable to him. In late October 1915, Owen spent two weeks in London, during which he enlisted in the Artists' Rifles. Owen's letters mention two visits to the Headquarters of the Artists' Rifles on Duke's Road, on 15 September 1915 and 21 October. St Pancras New Church stands just opposite the Headquarters, and although Owen's letters do not mention the church, he must have noticed it. Someone standing in the doorway of the Headquarters and looking across the road sees one of the church's two famous Caryatid Porches. This is an architectural feature that could well have drawn Owen's attention to the building, given his strong interest in classical statuary. If his interest was piqued and he went into the church, he would have seen in the vestibule a memorial to Alfred Frederick Cleave, who died in the Boer War in August 1900. The first two lines of the memorial plaque read: 'THE CITY OF LONDON IMPERIAL VOLUNTEERS / DULCE ET DECORUM EST PRO PATRIA MORI', followed by personal information about Cleave, including that he was 22 years old when he died, the age at which Owen enlisted.[30] There is no direct evidence that Owen saw this memorial, but it is an intriguing possibility.

[30] IWM, War Memorials Register; © WMR-47616; https://www.iwm.org.uk/memorials/item/memorial/47616.

In any case, all these possible sources remind us how fully the tag *dulce et decorum est* was embedded in contemporary British culture, as a standard form of praising and commemorating death in battle. For readers who have come to the tag only through Owen, his poem's emotional power and rhetorical force make it extremely difficult to step back and interrogate the poem's reading of the Latin line. Owen's interpretation has driven competing readings from the field so thoroughly that the modern reader scarcely considers the possibility of disagreeing with him. Thus, readers who know the Latin phrase only through Owen may miss the shock value that the poem had at the time, when it was forcefully repudiating a standard commonplace and one that carried with it the cultural and moral authority conveyed by classics' prestigious position in the public schools (see discussion of Brooke's and Sorley's education in this volume).

Owen clearly assumes that the 'you' of the poem, who tells 'the Old Lie', does not have first-person knowledge of warfare. This would simply be untrue of Horace, who was himself a veteran, but Owen is speaking directly to civilians who use the tag to urge children towards 'some desperate glory'. It is these civilians whom Owen wants to force to confront the horror of death in modern warfare. His presentation is so powerful that most readers take it to mean that absolutely nothing could be worth this kind of suffering. The implicit claim—couched in Owen's searing language—that no end could possibly justify these means is the message that has resonated most clearly throughout the late twentieth and early twenty-first century's reading of his poem. And yet for anyone except the absolutely committed pacifist, such a position is not, in point of fact, self-evident in any and all circumstances. It is also worth remembering that Owen's own position on war was not simple. As has often been noted, far from being wholly pacifist or even 'anti-war', he was quite willing to return to the Front after his time at Craiglockhart, and his Military Cross was awarded in part because he 'inflicted considerable losses' on the Germans with a captured machine gun (Hibberd 2002: 376). Owen, who memorably described himself to his mother in May 1917 as a 'conscientious objector with a very seared conscience' (Potter 2023: 280) was certainly not a fully committed pacifist with regard to the actual war being fought, whatever he may have hoped for a future when war would be obsolete.

'Dulce et Decorum Est' is in many ways an outlier amongst Owen's poems on the war, as he chooses to focus unflinchingly on the actual physical cost of combat. Owen insists that his reader face what *pro patria mori* actually entails in this war, in unsparing and gruesome detail. If the war is to be considered worth this suffering, any such evaluation must take full account of the cost, not euphemise it into invisibility by calling it 'sweet' and 'decorous'. In contrast, 'Apologia pro Poemate Meo', 'Exposure', and 'Spring Offensive' all to some degree argue for the bond between soldiers as being, indeed, something 'sweet' and 'meet', and Owen uses those precise words to describe death in battle in the fragmentary 'The Women and the Slain', on which he was working as late as 1917. Famous though it is, 'Dulce et Decorum Est' may represent a passing mood of Owen's rather than a fixed stance towards the war.

(d) Associated works

In Owen's own poems, the closest connection is with the fragmentary poem 'The Women and the Slain', which quotes an English paraphrase of *dulce et decorum est pro patria mori* with apparent approval (see discussion below in Section 4, 'Other classical interactions'). 'Arms and the Boy' also draws on Horace Ode 3.2, as its first four lines directly echo the beginning of that ode. The poem 'Schoolmistress' also evokes a Horace—although primarily the character Horatius from Livy and the *Lays of Ancient Rome*, rather than the poet—and has some thematic parallels to 'Dulce et Decorum Est'. These poems are discussed below in this section.

Owen was not alone in focusing bitterly on Horace's tag. Ezra Pound too turned to Horace *Odes* 3.2 for his denunciation of the war in 'Hugh Selwyn Mauberley': 'Died some, pro patria, / non "dulce" non "et decor"' sounds the same embittered note as the ending of Owen's poem, expanded to include bitterness at how the survivors 'came…home to old lies and new infamy'. Pound could not have been alluding to Owen, since 'Hugh Selwyn Mauberley' was published in June 1920 and Owen's poem appeared first in Sitwell 1920, published in late November of that year (Vandiver 2019: 196n86; Palaima 2021: 245–6). The two writers' use of the same Horatian tag is a coincidence, but hardly a surprising one, however striking it may be that both gloss that tag as the 'old lie[s]'. *Dulce et decorum est pro patria mori* provided an obvious synecdoche for the type of traditional war-writing that seemed to endorse war too easily and glibly.

Carol Ann Duffy's 2009 'Last Post', which takes lines 15–16 of Owen's poem as its epigraph, epitomizes the extent to which Owen's refiguring of the tag has itself become canonical. The end of her first stanza echoes Pound as well as Owen, and assumes without any question that death in the battles of World War I was pointless as well as brutal, as she writes 'Dulce— No—Decorum—No—Pro patria mori' (Duffy 2013: 112). Duffy (1955–)

allows no room for writers who experienced battle in the Great War, knew what it meant, and yet considered that it was, nevertheless, worthwhile—Rex Freston, Will Streets, Julian Grenfell, Noel Hodgson, and many others are elided out of the picture as though their reactions to the war were self-evidently mistaken.

The overall assumptions engendered by Owen's reworking of Horace's words have had striking effects even on some translators and scholars of Horace, so that *Odes* 3.2 itself becomes a poem associated with Owen. For instance, in his commentary on his own translation of Horace, Slavitt says:

> This ode is well known because of the Wilfred Owen poem.... The temptation is to read the entire ode in the light of the Owen and figure that Horace doesn't mean a word of it. My guess, though, would be that he does. (2014: 96)

Slavitt assumes that modern readers know Owen's work before they know Horace's ode, which in most cases is now undoubtedly true. But he further assumes that Owen's reading is not only so powerful, but also so self-evidently accurate, that it almost irresistibly imposes its own interpretation of Horace's words back onto Horace himself.

There is an irony here, since Owen was not arguing for any kind of satirical or destabilizing meaning in the original tag itself. Calling the words 'the old Lie' makes sense only if he wants his readers to recognize the tag as something that has been accepted as true in a straightforward and unironic sense, which Owen now refutes by marshalling the evidence of what death in modern battle is actually like. Yet so powerful has Owen's indictment been that it is now almost impossible for scholars of Horace, let alone a modern reader unfamiliar with Horace, to read the line in its original context *without* backreading Owen's fierce protest into it.

'Arms and the Boy' (1918)
(a) **Text of poem** [CPF 151, 1.154]

> Let the boy try along this bayonet-blade
> How cold steel is, and keen with hunger of blood;
> Blue with all malice, like a madman's flash;
> And thinly drawn with famishing for flesh.
>
> Lend him to stroke these blind, blunt bullet-leads,   5
> Which long to nuzzle in the hearts of lads,

> Or give him cartridges whose fine zinc teeth
> Are sharp with sharpness of grief and death.
>
> For his teeth seem for laughing round an apple.
> There lurk no claws behind his fingers supple;   10
> And God will grow no talons at his heels,
> Nor antlers through the thickness of his curls.

(b) Poem—date, form, and content

The fair copy of this poem is dated 3 May 1918, when Owen was in Ripon (CPF 1.154). One draft appears on the verso of Owen's famous 'Preface'. The poem consists of three four-line stanzas; this is itself reminiscent of Horace, since although he used a variety of metres most of his Odes are in four-line stanzas. Each of Owen's stanzas contains two pararhymed couplets, a pattern that Owen used throughout a poem in only two other instances, 'Wild with All Regrets' and 'Strange Meeting'. The first stanza features strict pararhyme, where the consonants remain exactly the same and the vowel shifts (blade/blood, flash/flesh). The second couplet of the second stanza departs from strict consonant correspondence with 'teeth/death', and the third stanza's rhymes are even freer (apple/supple, heels/curls). The metre is iambic pentameter, with feminine endings in lines 9 and 10. The first two lines each have an extra syllable but not a feminine ending, and line 8 is a syllable short.

Owen listed this poem in his draft Table of Contents under the heading 'Protest — the unnaturalness of weapons' (CPF 1.154; Hibberd 1986: 148), and the contrast between the soldiers' manufactured weapons and the boy's complete lack of natural weapons (talons, antlers) forms the culmination of the poem. Hibberd notes that Owen refers in a letter to children playing soldiers outside his Borrage Lane cottage and surmises that the irony of this may have suggested the poem to Owen (1986: 143).

(c) Reception commentary

The title reworks the opening words of the *Aeneid*. This could indicate direct familiarity with Vergil (as assumed by O'Keefe 1972: 73 and Cuthbertson 2014: 123), but caution is needed here; Owen was certainly aware of the well-known tag 'arms and the man', which Shaw used as the title for an 1894 anti-war play and Sassoon for the title of a poem in 1916.[31] The title alone, therefore, cannot be taken to prove Owen's familiarity with Vergil's Latin.

---

[31] Owen mentions Shaw in his letters, so presumably he would have been aware of Shaw's play *Arms and the Man*. Sassoon's 'Arms and the Man' appeared in his collection *The Old Huntsman*. Owen introduced himself to Sassoon at Craiglockhart by asking him to autograph copies of this book.

The most striking classical intertext for the poem is in fact not Vergil but Horace. The first stanza of Owen's poem refers directly to the opening stanza of *Odes* 3.2, the same Ode from which *dulce et decorum est pro patria mori* comes:

> Angustam amice pauperiem pati
> robustus acri militia puer
>   condiscat et Parthos ferocis
>   vexet eques metuendus hasta...

> Let the boy learn to endure constraining hardship
> As a friend, strengthened by energetic military service,
> And to harry the ferocious Parthians
> As a cavalryman to be feared for his spear...

Horace's poem treats the boy's education in arms as an important part of his maturation; Owen stresses the ironic contrast between the supposed glory accruing to grown men through arms and the innocence of boys who are not yet skilled in using those arms. But the parallels in wording strongly suggest that Horace's ode lies behind Owen's poem. Both poems feature a third-person jussive subjunctive as the main verb of their opening sentence, and 'boy' as its subject: 'Let the boy try' / *puer condiscat* ('Let the boy learn'). Both emphasize the necessity of the boy's gaining mastery over a weapon meant for stabbing, Owen's bayonet and Horace's spear (*hasta*). And in both, the conditions of war are at least lightly personified. Horace says that hardship should be greeted 'as a friend' (*amice*), and Owen treats the bayonet, as well as the bullets and cartridges of the second stanza, as hungering for blood—a metaphor that also recalls Homer's presentations of weapons as hungry for human flesh (e.g. *Il.* 20.75 and 168).

In its final stanza, Owen's poem turns from descriptions of weaponry to the natural world and from Horace to Ovid. The first line of the stanza evokes idyllic images of a child laughing as he eats an apple.[32] But this apparently positive image is immediately problematized as the stanza moves on to evoke Ovid's *Metamorphoses*, raising but rejecting the idea that the innocent boy could be transformed into a clawed animal, a bird of prey, or a beast with antlers. Owen owned the mythological handbook *The Greenwood Tree* (see above), which included prose versions of Ovid's accounts of

---

[32] The 'hanging motif' of the apple evokes both the apple's role as a love token in classical poetry and the biblical fruit that led to Adam and Eve's fall, traditionally identified as an apple.

various humans' transformations into bears (Callisto and Arcas) and birds (Procne, Philomela, Tereus, Nisus, Perdix), and *Contes fabuleux* (Adams [1910]) which included the story of the hunter Actaeon in its section on Diana; because Actaeon inadvertently saw Diana naked, she transformed him into a stag and he was torn apart by his own hounds. The implicit contrast between what the Ovidian gods could do to rescue humans from disaster (as in Arcas' case) and what the Christian God (signalled by the upper-case G) will *not* do for the modern boy underlines the sense of foreboding in this poem of unease (see Introduction, pp. 14–16). Furthermore, the choice of Ovidian human-to-animal metamorphoses as a point of reference adds to the poem's ominous tone; such metamorphoses, in Ovid, are frequently divine punishments, not forms of deliverance, and often end unhappily for the one transformed. Of such unhappy examples, Actaeon is perhaps the most memorable, so that the poem's last line bears a doubly ominous weight: God will not transform the boy, as Diana transformed Actaeon, but the boy's fate at the hands of modern weaponry will be as savage as Actaeon's was amongst his hounds.

(d) Associated works

This poem's clear reference to Horace *Odes* 3.2 links it to 'Dulce et Decorum Est', since that Latin phrase occurs in the same ode. 'Dulce et Decorum Est' was written at Craiglockhart, so probably predates 'Arms and the Boy' by several months. As noted above, it seems likely that Owen was reading Horace, perhaps in translation, at some point during those months. Ovidian references are very common in Owen's work and are discussed below.

'Schoolmistress' (1918)

(a) Text of poem [CPF 143, 1.139]

Having, with bold Horatius, stamped her feet
And waved a final swashing arabesque
O'er the brave days of old, she ceased to bleat,
Slapped her Macaulay back upon the desk,
Resumed her calm gaze and her lofty seat.   5

There, while she heard the classic lines repeat,
Once more the teacher's face clenched stern;
For through the window, looking on the street,
Three soldiers hailed her. She made no return.
One was called 'Orace whom she would not greet.   10

(b) Poem—date, form, and content

Stallworthy dates the poem to early 1918 (January to March). It is thus later than the first drafts of 'Dulce et Decorum Est', which date to late 1917, and was written at about the same time that Owen was revising that poem.

The form is two five-line stanzas in iambic pentameter, linked to one another by the rhyme scheme ABABA ACACA. Line 7 is a foot short, having only eight syllables; the rough draft has the metrical 'then suddenly again her face clenched stern' (CPF 2.291). There is a strong preference for trochaic inversion in the first foot, so that the first four syllables form a choriamb (e.g. 'háving with bóld', l. 1).

This deceptively simple-looking poem features several themes that are important in Owen's work: an unpleasant strand of misogyny; the complete separation of the imaginative worlds of soldiers and civilians; the educational system's investment in indoctrinating children into traditional views of the glory of warfare; and, most importantly for our purposes, the distance between the classical world of such glory (here already mediated through Macaulay's nineteenth-century reception of Livy) and the lived experience of the modern soldier.

(c) Reception commentary

The main referent here is 'Horatius at the Bridge' in Macaulay's *Lays of Ancient Rome*. Owen's schoolbooks preserve a notebook used for essays on English literature, written by him in 1907.[33] One of these essays is a detailed prose recounting of the 'Horatius' episode, incorporating some lines of quoted verse. As already noted, Owen had won a copy of Macaulay's *Lays* as a prize in 1905. In 'Schoolmistress', Owen assumes that his reader is also deeply familiar with Macaulay, so that he can allude to Macaulay's Horatius poem quite elliptically, with only one direct quotation, 'The brave days of old', from the end of the Horatius lay. Horatius himself is called 'brave' rather than 'bold' in Macaulay: 'Then out spake brave Horatius, the Captain of the gate'.[34] But Owen's choice of 'bold' as an epithet for Horatius resonates with the teacher's scorn for the three soldiers in the second stanza, since 'bold' can refer to inappropriate and presumptuous actions, such as

---

[33] Owen Archive, MS 12282/31.

[34] The Romans as a group are called 'bold' when Astur confronts them: 'He smiled on those bold Romans, / A smile serene and high', https://victorianweb.org/authors/macaulay/lays/3.html, accessed 21 December 2022.

'cheeky' greetings from lower-class men to higher-class women.[35] The fact that this 'bold' modern soldier, for whom the teacher feels such contempt, is named 'Horace' underlines the contrast between what the teacher claims to admire and her reaction to actual soldiers, in an unexpected and satirical final 'turn' that is reminiscent of Sassoon's characteristic style.

Owen's poem contains a link to Macaulay's in the number of soldiers. Horatius Cocles, in Livy and Macaulay, was the primary focus of the story and the primary volunteer to hold the bridge, but he was joined by two companions, Spurius Lartius and Titus Herminius (Livy 2.10). In 'Schoolmistress', too, the modern soldier named 'Horace' has two companions. Three soldiers hail the teacher, but only one is identified by name, which foregrounds him as the main character and the point of the poem. An earlier draft of the poem made the connection with Macaulay more explicit. That draft includes the line 'How brave Horatius kept the bridge to Rome', and says, of the soldier, 'His name was 'Orace, and his surname Cockles'. This draft also gives the names of his companions as 'Bill and 'Ern' (CPF 2.290–1).

(d) Associated works

While the obvious connection of the name 'Horace' here is to Macaulay's 'Horatius', there is also a resonance with the poet whose name is normally Anglicized as 'Horace'. However, even without the connection of the name 'Horace', the intratextual elements in 'Schoolmistress' and 'Dulce et Decorum Est' are strongly marked.[36] Both poems indict a civilian observer for trying to instil ardour 'for some desperate glory' into children, and the drafts of 'Dulce et Decorum Est' addressed 'To Jessie Pope, etc.' and 'To a certain poetess' indicate that at one point in Owen's thinking about 'Dulce et Decorum Est', the civilian whom the poem addresses, like the Schoolmistress, was female. Both poems deny ('Dulce et Decorum Est' directly, 'Schoolmistress' implicitly) that the experience of the modern soldier can in any way achieve the sort of glory that Macaulay's poem celebrates.

'Schoolmistress' is one of only three works in which Owen engages directly with an ancient myth or legend. The other two are 'The Wrestlers'

---

[35] The *OED* lists under sense 4 of 'bold, adj.': 'In bad sense: Audacious, presumptuous, too forward; the opposite of 'modest'. *OED Online*, Oxford University Press, December 2022, www.oed.com/view/Entry/21056, accessed 21 December 2022.

[36] On intratextuality, see Introduction, p. 10.

and 'Perseus' (discussed below). 'The Wrestlers' is a straightforward retelling of the myth of Heracles and Antaeus. 'Perseus' is so fragmentary that it is unclear what form that poem would eventually have taken.

'With an Identity Disc' (1917)
(a) Text of poem [CPF 91, 1.96]

> If ever I had dreamed of my dead name
> High in the heart of London, unsurpassed
> By Time for ever, and the Fugitive, Fame,
> There taking a long sanctuary at last,
>
> I better that; and recollect with shame   5
> How once I longed to hide it from life's heats
> Under those holy cypresses, the same
> That keep in shade the quiet place of Keats.
>
> Now, rather, thank I God there is no risk
> Of gravers scoring it with florid screed,   10
> But let my death be memoried on this disc.
> Wear it, sweet friend. Inscribe no date nor deed.
> But let thy heart-beat kiss it night and day,
> Until the name grow vague and wear away.

(b) Poem—date, form, and content
This poem was written in March 1917 and revised later at Craiglockhart. It is a Shakespearean sonnet, consisting of three quatrains followed by a couplet, with the rhyme scheme ABAB CDCD EFEF GG.[37] (On the sonnet form and Greek epigram, see above on Brooke, 'The Soldier'.) Owen included a draft of the poem in a letter to his brother Colin, written 24 March 1917, in which he says he began the sonnet the day before. Owen was at the Casualty Clearing Station at the time, with concussion; the letter discusses his hopes for a quiet life after the war, and says that he has decided he will keep pigs (Potter 2023: 264). In line with this mood of longing for a rural life, the sonnet rejects the idea of lasting fame or public memorials for a poet. It focuses instead on the dead soldier's identity disc, to be worn by the speaker's friend until the disc becomes illegible.

---

[37] Owen transcribed Shakespeare's 'To me, fair friend, you never can be old' on the verso of one of the manuscripts of 'With an Identity Disc' (Welland 1978: 45).

(c) Reception commentary

This sonnet offers the strongest evidence that Owen was familiar with at least some of Horace's *Odes*, since it is structured to parallel Horace's sixteen-line *Odes* 3.30 thematically, as well as featuring clear verbal echoes of Horace (and to a lesser degree Ovid). The poem is framed in terms that recall, only to reject, Horace's proud claim 'I have completed a monument more lasting than bronze' (*exegi monumentum aere perennius*, *Odes* 3.30), and its further elaboration by Ovid ('my name will be indelible forever', *nomenque erit indelebile nostrum, Metamorphoses* 15.876).

 Odes 3.30 reads:

Exegi monumentum aere perennius
regalique situ pyramidum altius,
quod non imber edax, non Aquilo impotens
possit diruere aut innumerabilis
annorum series et fuga temporum.   5
non omnis moriar, multaque pars mei
vitabit Libitinam: usque ego postera
crescam laude recens, dum Capitolium
scandet cum tacita virgine pontifex.
dicar, qua violens obstrepit Aufidus   10
et qua pauper aquae Daunus agrestium
regnavit populorum, ex humili potens
princeps Aeolium carmen ad Italos
deduxisse modos. sume superbiam
quaesitam meritis et mihi Delphica   15
lauro cinge volens, Melpomene, comam.

I have finished a monument more lasting than bronze, more lofty than the regal structure of the pyramids, one which neither corroding rain nor the ungovernable North Wind can ever destroy, nor the countless series of the years, nor the flight of time.

 I shall not wholly die, and a large part of me will elude the Goddess of Death. I shall continue to grow, fresh with the praise of posterity, as long as the priest climbs the Capitol with the silent virgin [a Vestal]. I shall be spoken of where the violent Aufidus thunders and where Daunus, short of water, ruled over a country people, as one who, rising from a lowly state to a position of power, was the first to bring Aeolian verse to the tunes of Italy.

> Take the pride, Melpomene, that you have so well earned, and, if you
> would be so kind, surround my hair with Delphic bay. (Rudd 2004: 216–17)

Both poems move from a description of the poet's fame reflected in his
capital city to a description of poetic fame outside of that city. Both end with
a direct address to an interlocutor whose existence is only revealed by this
address and in both instances, the poet tells the addressee how to treat the
poet himself or his reputation and memory. The structural parallel underlines the poems' differences; as Horace's poem builds to ever-greater triumphant claiming of public fame, Owen's moves towards ever-greater
privacy and, eventually, the complete erasure of the poet's name.

The setting for the poet's fame, in the heart of his capital city, in each case
centres on a religious site of great cultural importance: the Temple of Jupiter
Capitolinus on Rome's Capitoline Hill, and Poets' Corner in Westminster
Abbey. In both poems, the reference to the particular site is very elliptical;
Horace simply mentions a priest and a (Vestal) virgin climbing the
Capitoline, and Owen alludes only to a poet's name 'in the heart of
London' where Fame finds a 'sanctuary'. But in each instance, the reference
to the specific site is unmistakeable. If there were any doubt in Owen's case,
the manuscripts demonstrate that he was unquestionably thinking of Poets'
Corner (where he is in fact now memorialized), since early drafts of the
sonnet show the wording 'kept by Westminster in sanctuary' and 'a sanctuary in Westminster at last' (available on FWWPDA).

Horace confidently states that the rustic inhabitants of his native area,
Apulia, will be proud of him and in effect claims that his glory will spread
from Rome to his place of birth. Owen's inversion of this idea is complicated. Rather than imagining that his success in London will reflect glory on
his hometown, the speaker imagines himself 'hiding' his poetic success at the
grave of another English poet, who died far from London and whose grave
carries no name (Keats' grave famously was inscribed 'Here lies one whose
name was writ in water')—and, to add another twist, who is buried in the
Protestant Cemetery in Rome, the city where Horace claims his public
triumph. Owen's exact meaning is less clear in Stallworthy's text than in
the version printed by Blunden, Day Lewis, and Hibberd, where lines
5–7 read:

> Or if I onetime hoped to hide its shame,
> —Shame of success, and sorrow of defeats,—
> Under those holy cypresses... (Hibberd 1973: 67)

In both versions, the speaker seems to be imagining the remoteness and perhaps the anonymity of Keats' grave as a refuge to protect him from either success or defeat, until he 'betters that' by restricting any memory of him at all to the identity disc, which will be seen only by his friend.

Horace and Owen both end their poems with an address to someone whose presence has not previously been indicated. For Horace, this is the Muse Melpomene, and his request of her is that she will further his fame, and take pride in it, by crowning him with bay and thus making him quite literally a poet laureate. For Owen, the person addressed is an anonymous 'sweet friend', whose age and even gender are unspecified. Owen's request is the opposite of Horace's. Far from asking his interlocutor to further his fame, Owen asks his friend to wear his identity disc until the inscription is entirely effaced. The disc serves as an ironic parallel to, and refutation of, the laurel wreath. Both are items to be worn on the person, but the wreath openly declares the fame of the poet it crowns while the disc, in Owen's poem, will be worn privately by someone else, and the purpose of its being so worn is to erase the poet's name. Not merely an intensely private act of memorial, this is a private act of forgetting, which repudiates any idea of a poet's reputation surviving him. This is directly at odds with Owen's often-expressed hopes for lasting fame, so that this poem is a notable outlier amongst his writings.

Along with the overall structural parallels, Owen alludes to Horace in specific details and wording, especially in the first three lines. Owen's 'high in the heart of London' reflects the Capitoline Hill's location, a site that was literally 'high' in the heart of Rome as well as being central to religious practice and social interactions. In the third line, the wording 'unsurpassed / by Time for ever, and the Fugitive, Fame' specifically recalls Horace's *fuga temporum* (the flight of time), reversing the terms and using the English derivative 'fugitive' to echo the Latin *fuga*.

The poem also engages with Ovid's epilogue to *Metamorphoses* (itself an intertext with Horace), with its triumphant final statement 'and throughout all ages, I shall live through Fame' (*perque omnia saecula fama / . . . vivam*, *Met.* 15.878–9). The final line, urging that the friend wear the identity disc 'Until the name grow vague and wear away' directly opposes Ovid's 'indelible name' (*nomen . . . indelebile*, 15.876).

(d) Associated works

Apart from its connection to other Horatian poems and to the recurrent references to Ovid in Owen's work, 'With an Identity Disc' is associated with other poems that address the topic of remembrance after death. Owen revisits the topic of how the dead may be remembered in 'Miners', 'Strange Meeting', and 'Anthem for Doomed Youth'.

'1914' (1914, rev. 1917 or 1918)
(a) **Text of poem** [CPF 113, 1.116]

War broke: and now the Winter of the world
With perishing great darkness closes in.
The foul tornado, centred at Berlin,
Is over all the width of Europe whirled,
Rending the sails of progress. Rent or furled   5
Are all Art's ensigns. Verse wails. Now begin
Famines of thought and feeling. Love's wine's thin.
The grain of human Autumn rots, down-hurled.

For after Spring had bloomed in early Greece,
And Summer blazed her glory out with Rome,   10
An Autumn softly fell, a harvest home,
A slow grand age, and rich with all increase.
But now, for us, wild Winter, and the need
Of sowings for new Spring, and blood for seed.

(b) Poem—date, form, and content

This Petrarchan sonnet[38] was drafted in late 1914, when Owen was living in France. Owen revised the sonnet in late 1917 or early 1918 (CFP 1.116). The rhyme scheme is ABBAABBA in the octave, followed by CDDCEE in the sestet. The sonnet was Owen's preferred form for much of the poetry he wrote between 1914 and early 1917 (Hibberd 1986: 41).[39] Several of the poems he showed to Siegfried Sassoon at their first meeting were sonnets, but Owen reported to his mother that 'certain old sonnets of mine did not please S. at all' (Owen and Bell 1967: 487; letter dated 22 August 1917). There is no way to know if '1914' was amongst these.

Stallworthy notes the 'apparent echo of Rupert Brooke's "red / Sweet wine of youth"' in line 7, but considers it 'probably fortuitous', since Brooke's sonnet 'The Dead' was first published in December 1914 (CPF 1.116).

---

[38] See above, on Brooke's 'The Soldier'.

[39] Many of the war poets favoured the sonnet; Kendall 2013 includes sonnets by Wilfred Gibson, Siegfried Sassoon, Rupert Brooke, Ivor Gurney, Charles Sorley, and Edmund Blunden, as well as Owen's 'Anthem for Doomed Youth'.

However, in the rough draft Owen's phrase 'Love's wine's thin' appears as 'Blood runs thin' (CPF 2.270), suggesting that Brooke's famous sonnet may have influenced Owen's later revision of the line and produced this glancing contact. A copy of Brooke's *1914 and other Poems*, in its thirteenth impression, survives in Owen's library, with a magazine photograph of Brooke's grave on Skyros filed in the book (Stallworthy 2013: 140n). Although there is no possibility of influence between Rosenberg and Owen, this poem of unease is reminiscent of Rosenberg's 'On Receiving News of the War: Cape Town' (see discussion in chapter on Rosenberg) in its harnessing of the imagery of the seasons to express the poet's anxiety as he contemplates the implications of the war while living in a foreign country.

(c) Reception commentary

The entire sonnet takes the cultures of ancient Greece and Rome as unquestioned touchstones for other, later cultures. Owen may have Edgar Allen Poe's famous tag 'the glory that was Greece and the grandeur that was Rome' ('To Helen') in mind, and could also have been aware of two recent books by J. C. Stobart which took those phrases as their titles (Stobart 1911 and 1912). Owen's use of 'glory' and 'grand' in his poem perhaps supports this connection. The association of Greece with 'Spring' and Rome with 'Summer' suggests that later cultures (here, most obviously, British culture) represent deterioration and inevitable decline. The 'rich harvest home' of European culture can only lead to barren winter.

Lines 5–6 recall Horace's depiction of the State as a tempest-tossed ship with rent sails: *O navis, referent in mare te novi / fluctus.... Non tibi sunt integra lintea* ('O ship, new waves will carry you back into the sea.... Your sails are not whole'; *Odes* 1.14.1–2, 9). The final line of the octave (l. 8) glances at a common trope that treats war as a reaper harvesting human lives (see discussion of Rosenberg's 'August 1914' above). This draws on a famous simile in the *Iliad*, where Greek and Trojan warriors' slaughter of one another is compared to harvesters reaping grain (11.67–71). Here the trope is modified so that the grain that is reaped rots uselessly, as part of the 'famines of thought and feeling'; the 'grain' of the old civilization can no longer be used, making the term 'increase' in the sestet bitterly ironic. The trope returns in the final line of the sestet with the words 'blood for seed,' but there it is presented as part of a new sowing, a return of Spring.

This metaphor of the seasons motivates the sestet in particular. The presentation of present European culture as 'Autumn...rich with all increase'[40] looks back to the recent time when it was possible to believe in 'the sails of progress', but treats that era as irrevocably disappeared into 'wild Winter'. The final couplet turns to another common trope, the idea that shedding young men's blood will somehow nourish or enrich the earth, or (as here) the culture; see, for instance, Vergil's description of the gods choosing to fatten fields with Roman blood (*Georg.* 1.491–2, discussed above on Brooke's 'The Soldier'). Owen may also be referring to J. G. Frazer's extremely influential theories; although no copy of Frazer's *Golden Bough* (1st edn. 1890) survives in Owen's library, Hibberd thinks that Owen 'may have been aware' of the work, a 'study of pagan vegetation rites in which kings or gods … were sacrificed in winter to guarantee a fertile spring' (1986: 59).

(d) Associated works

The final couplet touches on ideas that Owen would treat much more memorably in 'Exposure', and in drafts of the unfinished poem 'The Women and the Slain' (both discussed below).

'The End' (?1917–18)

(a) **Text of poem** [CPF 154, 1.159]

> After the blast of lightning from the east,
>   The flourish of loud clouds, the Chariot Throne;
> After the drums of time have rolled and ceased,
>   And by the bronze west long retreat is blown,
> Shall Life renew these bodies? Of a truth,   5
>   All death will he annul, all tears assuage?
> Or fill these void veins again with youth,
>   And wash, with an immortal water, age?
>
> When I do ask white Age, he saith not so:
>   'My head hangs weighed with snow.'   10
> And when I hearken to the Earth, she saith:
>   'My fiery heart shrinks, aching. It is death.
> Mine ancient scars shall not be glorified,
>   Nor my titanic tears, the seas, be dried.'

---

[40] *Chambers' Etymological Dictionary*, which survives in Owen's library, derives the word Autumn from *augeo, augere*, to increase, so Owen is engaging in a kind of bilingual pun here. There is also an echo here of Shakespeare's Sonnet 97: 'the teeming autumn, big with all increase'; Hibberd 1973: 113; Bäckman 1979: 20.

(b) Poem—date, form, and content

Stallworthy thinks this poem was 'begun probably in late 1916' and was then 'continued either at Craiglockhart in October-November 1917, or at Scarborough between November 1917 and January 1918' (CPF 1.159). Hibberd thinks that it is 'probably late 1916'; his dating supports his opinion that this poem 'may be read as a comment on war, but one could hardly call it a war poem' (1986: 62, 65). If we accept Stallworthy's assumption that Owen worked on this poem while at Craiglockhart or shortly thereafter, its connection with the war seems clear, and the poem can be read as a type of poetry of survival where the anxiety about physical survival is extended to encompass rejection of the idea of spiritual survival.

'The End' is a sonnet with an ABBACDDC EEFFGG rhyme scheme and one line of iambic trimeter rather than pentameter (line 10).[41] This was one of at least ten sonnets on set themes that Owen wrote as part of an agreement with his cousin Leslie Gunston and their friend Olwen Joergens; each of the three poets would write a sonnet on the same theme, they would exchange copies, and critique one another's work. Owen's contributions were written between September 1916 and August 1917 (Hibberd 1986: 62).

Owen's mother chose to quote line 5 and half of line 6 on his tombstone in France, but changed the second question into a positive answer by omitting the question mark:

> "SHALL LIFE RENEW
>   THESE BODIES?
>   OF A TRUTH
> ALL DEATH WILL HE ANNUL" WO (Hibberd 1992: 193; Potter 2014: fig. 53)

(c) Reception commentary

The poem is a prime example of 'thick' reception in Owen, with its blending of biblical and classical material. The octave begins with strong Christian associations in the biblical resonances of the first four lines; the Chariot-Throne recalls the first chapter of Ezekiel, and the overall setting is clearly

---

[41] Welland notes that the manuscripts show the reading 'everlasting snow', but that Owen has struck out the adjective in the latest fair copy. Since Owen apparently intended to think of another adjective rather than to shorten the line, he suggests that 'there is perhaps a case for retaining Owen's rejected word with an explanatory note' (1978: 126).

the Apocalypse. The opening lines also recall Horace, specifically *Odes* 1.34.5–8, which describes the unexpected and terrifying appearance of a divine chariot accompanied by thunder: *namque Diespiter / igni corusco nubila dividens / plerumque, per purum tonantis / egit equos volucremque currum* ('For Jupiter, who normally splits the clouds with his flashing fire, drove his thundering horses and flying chariot across a clear sky'; Rudd 2004: 84–5). There may also be a glancing reference, in 'white Age' whose 'head hangs weighed with snow', to *Odes* 1.9, an extremely well-known and much imitated poem. That ode begins 'Do you see how Soracte stands white with deep snow' (*Vides ut alta stet nive candidum / Soracte*, ll. 1–2) and later reveals that the description of the mountain is a metaphor for old age ('do not spurn sweet love...while peevish whiteness is absent from your green age'; *nec dulcis amores / sperne... donec virenti canities abest / morosa*, ll. 15–17).

The Christian tone diminishes as the force who might possibly 'renew these bodies' is named not as God, but rather as 'Life', a personification which signals a shift from Christian to pagan imagery. The final line of the octave underlines this turn to the classical, where the image of reversing or preventing age and death by washing with an immortal water recalls both Eos' failure to give Tithonus immortality (*Homeric Hymn to Aphrodite* 218–38) and, more directly, the post-Homeric story of Thetis' washing of Achilles in the water of Styx to make him invulnerable.[42] In the sestet, the personified Earth and Age both recall the Titans of Hesiod's *Theogony*.

One of the early manuscripts shows the tentative lines 'The light so smote the forehead of the earth / She lay in daze as dead' (CPF 2.325). This suggests a trace of the Phaethon story in Ovid, where Phaethon drove the sun-chariot so far off course that Earth herself was scorched (*Met.* 2.272ff.).

For most readers, these submerged references to Greek myth would be 'low-intensity' gestures towards shared cultural allusions. Owen's devoutly Christian mother, however, refocused the lines she quoted on his tombstone by changing Owen's second question to a statement, so that 'Life' becomes a 'high-intensity' reference to the Christian resurrection.[43] She uses Owen's own words to reclaim him for the unquestioning evangelical Christianity of his childhood (see discussion above), although this requires ignoring the clear negative answer given by the poem itself (l. 9).

---

[42] The earliest mention of this story is from the first century CE, in Statius' *Achilleid* 1.133–4; see Gantz 1993: 231.

[43] On 'low-' and 'high-intensity' religious belief, see Introduction, pp. 19–20.

(d) Associated works

The echo of Horace ties this poem to the other Horatian-influenced works discussed in this section. The reference to the Earth's 'titanic tears' links the poem to 'Strange Meeting' with its 'titanic wars' and to the fragment 'Imperial Elegy', which imagines the Western Front as a 'titan's grave'. The poem's question about whether there is any afterlife in prospect is closely related to the similar rhetorical questions of 'Asleep' and especially 'Futility'.

'Insensibility' (late 1917/early 1918; revised April 1918)
(a) **Text of poem** [CPF 147, 1.145–6]

1

Happy are men who yet before they are killed
Can let their veins run cold.
Whom no compassion fleers
Or makes their feet
Sore on the alleys cobbled with their brothers.   5
The front line withers.
But they are troops who fade, not flowers,
For poets' tearful fooling:
Men, gaps for filling:
Losses, who might have fought   10
Longer; but no one bothers.

2

And some cease feeling
Even themselves or for themselves.
Dullness best solves
The tease and doubt of shelling,   15
And Chance's strange arithmetic
Comes simpler than the reckoning of their shilling.
They keep no check on armies' decimation.

3

Happy are these who lose imagination:
They have enough to carry with ammunition.   20
Their spirit drags no pack.
Their old wounds, save with cold, can not more ache.
Having seen all things red,
Their eyes are rid

Of the hurt of the colour of blood for ever.   25
And terror's first constriction over,
Their hearts remain small-drawn.
Their senses in some scorching cautery of battle
Now long since ironed,
Can laugh among the dying, unconcerned.   30

     4

Happy the soldier home, with not a notion
How somewhere, every dawn, some men attack,
And many sighs are drained.
Happy the lad whose mind was never trained:
His days are worth forgetting more than not.   35
He sings along the march
Which we march taciturn, because of dusk,
The long, forlorn, relentless trend
From larger day to huger night.

     5

We wise, who with a thought besmirch   40
Blood over all our soul,
How should we see our task
But through his blunt and lashless eyes?
Alive, he is not vital overmuch;
Dying, not mortal overmuch;   45
Nor sad, nor proud,
Nor curious at all.
He cannot tell
Old men's placidity from his.

     6

But cursed are dullards whom no cannon stuns,   50
That they should be as stones.
Wretched are they, and mean
With paucity that never was simplicity.
By choice they made themselves immune
To pity and whatever moans in man   55
Before the last sea and the hapless stars;
Whatever mourns when many leave these shores;
Whatever shares
The eternal reciprocity of tears.

(b) Poem—date, form, and content
The first drafts were written either at Craiglockhart in late 1917 or at
Scarborough between November 1917 and January 1918, and the poem
was perhaps revised in April 1918, at Ripon (CPF 1.147).

The poem is an ode in six numbered stanzas of varying lengths.
Individual lines range from four to thirteen syllables, predominantly
iambic with frequent trochees and choriambs. The poem's flexible line
length, intricate rhyme scheme, and variable stanzas recall odes such as
Wordsworth's 'Intimations of Immortality'.[44] Its flexible metrical structure,
handled with great skill, also clearly shows the influence of Owen's reading
of free verse poems in *Wheels* 1917.[45] The poem is structured as a kind of
priamel, with the repetition of 'Happy are men...Happy are these...'
yielding in the end to 'But cursed are dullards'. The rhyme scheme is very
complex, employing extensive pararhyme at line-ends and internally, one
true rhyme in lines 34–5, and occasional words that are not quite pararhyme
but approach it. In the first stanza, for instance, the pararhyme is patterned
A A B C D __ B E E C D:

killed	A
cold	A
fleers	B
feet	C
brothers	D
withers	
flowers	B
fooling	E
filling	E
fought	C
bothers	D

The stanza's pivotal line, 'The front line withers', is emphasized both by its
position (five lines before it, five after it) and by the fact that it alone does not
end with a pararhyme to anything else in the stanza, though it echoes the

<hr>

[44] I owe this comparison to the anonymous OUP reader.
[45] A copy of the 1917 *Wheels*, which Owen bought when Edith Sitwell invited him
to submit poems for the 1918 issue, survives in his library. The 1917 issue includes frequent
examples of free verse; Hibberd calls it 'Wilfred's introduction to Modernist poetry'
(2002: 323).

pararhyme of 'brothers/bothers'. This kind of intricate patterning continues throughout the poem, differing from stanza to stanza and enhanced by frequent alliteration and assonance throughout.[46]

(c) Reception commentary

The poem's classical resonances begin with the first line, which sets up the poem's repeated use of the words 'Happy (are men who)…'. This formulation recalls the Greek *makarismos*, the pronouncement 'Happy / Blessed are those…', that appears, for instance, in the chorus of Euripides' *Bacchae* lines 72ff. and the *Homeric Hymn to Demeter* line 480, more generally in formulations such as Odysseus' words to Nausicaa about how 'happy' her parents are (*Od.* 6.154), and of course most famously in the Beatitudes of the Gospels (Matt. 5:3–12; Luke 6:20–2).[47] The more immediate source is Horace's *beatus ille* ('happy the man', *Epodes* 2.1), which begins, in Abraham Cowley's (1618–67) translation, 'Happy the Man whom bounteous Gods allow / With his own Hand Paternal Grounds to plough!' (published 1668). Another striking resonance is with Vergil's *Georgics* 2.490–2: 'Happy is the man who has been able to understand the causes of things, and has placed beneath his feet all fear and inexorable fate' (*Felix, qui potuit rerum cognoscere causas, / atque metus omnis et inexorabile fatum / subiecit pedibus*). Owen's 'happy' men, like Vergil's *felix*, have overcome the fear of death, although their situations are entirely different.

The poem's main engagements with classics come in the first and last stanzas. Lines 6–9, 'The front line withers / But they are troops who fade, not flowers / For poets' tearful fooling, / Men, gaps for filling' inverts and rejects the trope of the dying warrior resembling a flower that figures in *Iliad* 8.306–8, where a dying man's head is compared to a drooping poppy. This trope has a complex literary history in itself, having been refigured by Sappho, Catullus, and Vergil, and reaches its culmination in Isaac Rosenberg's 'Break of Day in the Trenches' (see discussion above). Here, Owen interweaves the drooping flower image with another common trope, of troops as mown grass or, in Homeric terms, a 'generation of leaves' (*Il.* 6.146–50). Owen's 'troops who fade, not flowers' also reflects the biblical imagery so prevalent throughout his work, referencing 1 Peter 24 ('the grass withereth, and the flower thereof falleth away') and Isaiah 40:6–7 ('all flesh is

---

[46] On the 'intricate pattern' of rhyme in 'Insensibility', see Welland 1978: 120–3.
[47] R. C. T. Parker, 'makarismos', in *OCD*.

grass, and all the goodliness thereof is as the flower of the field: The grass withereth, the flower fadeth'). Owen's gloss of such images as 'poets' tearful fooling' returns the image to the secular realm. Where the simile of reaping is normally used to underline the transitory nature of human life or the numbers of battle dead, Owen resists and refuses the comfort of the standard simile by reminding his readers that these are *not* flowers or reaped grain, but 'Men, gaps for filling'. His reference to 'poets' tearful fooling' here resonates with his famous statement in his unfinished draft 'Preface' that 'Above all, I am not concerned with Poetry' (CPF 2.535).

In the last stanza 'Whatever mourns when many leave these shores' (l. 56) is a ghosting of Vergil's *tendebantque manus ripae ulterioris amore* ('they stretched out their arms in longing for the farther shore', *Aen.* 6.314), which describes the souls Aeneas sees in the Underworld waiting to be transported across the Styx. Charon, the ferryman of Styx, thrusts most of them back; the Sibyl tells Aeneas that the rejected souls are those whose bodies are unburied. The striking image at the beginning of 'Insensibility' of soldiers' 'feet / Sore on the alleys cobbled with their brothers'' strengthens this resonance with Vergil's unburied dead. A rejected manuscript version of line 56, 'when mortals leave these shores' (CPF 2.303), provides a clearer trace of Vergil's unburied dead and their longing.

This Vergilian trace may come through an intermediate source, J. A. K. Thomson's 'Mother and Daughter', in the collection *The Greek Tradition*. In this imaginative prose retelling of the Persephone myth, Persephone describes what she saw in Hades by directly translating Vergil: 'The shapes were holding out their hands in a passion of longing for the farther shore'. She goes on to explain that 'these were the unhappy dead who had not found burial on earth' (Thomson 1915: 103–4). We know that Owen was reading Thomson's book at the time he was working on 'Insensibility', since he mentions it in a letter to his cousin of 8 January 1918, although he garbles the author's name: 'I've been reading…a glorious book of critical essays by A. K. Thompson, called *The Greek Tradition*' (Potter 2023: 350).

Lines 58–9, 'Whatever shares / The eternal reciprocity of tears' reflect crucial scenes from both the *Iliad* and the *Aeneid*. In *Iliad* 24, the resolution depends on the 'reciprocity of tears' between Achilles and Priam, as each man mourns for his own dead. Vergil remodels this scene of reciprocal mourning into Aeneas' own tears; as Aeneas looks at images of Troy, he imagines the tears of others for Troy's suffering: *sunt lacrimae rerum et mentem mortalia tangunt* (1.462)—one of Vergil's most untranslatable lines. Williams renders it as 'here too there are tears for human happenings and mortal sufferings touch the heart' (1972: 196). Context is important here; the shipwrecked Aeneas is gazing at a mural in Carthage that depicts scenes from the Trojan War, and finds in the sympathetic portrayal of Priam, in particular, reason to think that these strangers feel compassion for the suffering of others. The *lacrimae rerum* ('tears of things') are less a comment on the underlying sorrows of existence, as the phrase is often taken, than they are a comment on the ability of human beings to feel for one another. In Owen's poem, this is reshaped into 'the eternal reciprocity of tears'; and again, a draft makes the connection with both Homer and Vergil clearer, since Owen tried the phrase 'the eternal reciprocity of mortal tears' (CPF 2.306).

(d) Associated works

The Horatian echo in the repeated 'Happy are those...' connects this poem with the others discussed above, where Owen appears to draw directly on Horace. Cowley was not the only English poet to use 'Happy the man who' in translating Horace. At age 12, Alexander Pope (1688–1744) wrote the 'Ode on Solitude' (1700), which begins 'Happy the man whose wish and care / A few paternal acres bound', and in 1685 Dryden (1631–1700) had used the same phrase to translate lines from *Odes* 3.29. The Latin word Horace uses there is *laetus*, not *beatus*, but Dryden's English echoes Cowley's in using the same phrase, 'Happy the man who'. Along with these two possible sources for a mediated reception of Horace, Owen was very likely familiar with Charles Wesley's (1707–88) well-known hymn that begins 'Happy the man who finds the grace'.

Apart from the Horatian connections, the direct reference to crossing the Styx in 'A New Heaven' (discussed above) parallels the subtler references in the final stanza here. In both poems the dead on the shores of Styx are evoked as counterparts of the dead of the Great War.

In a fragmentary poem 'Spring not, spring not in my wild eyes, O Tears', written probably between October 1911 and May 1912, Owen wrote that long ago 'Far in the dim antiquity / ... tears were honoured things' (CPF 2.393).

'Insensibility' makes a fitting transition to the next section in our discussion, since its final stanza touches on the afterlife and the Underworld.

3.2 Underworld journeys and visions

The classical *katabasis* was a narrative describing a journey to, and return from, the Underworld by a living human being. These Underworld journeys undertaken by mythic figures such as Heracles, Odysseus, and Aeneas clearly had a powerful appeal to Owen and form one of the most important strands of intratextuality in his work. He returns to the *katabasis* theme repeatedly in his works, with references that range from glancing to sustained. Even his 1913 poem 'Uriconium: An Ode' had invited the reader to look at things hidden in Hades (see Hibberd 2002: 106), and his war poetry includes several reworkings of the *katabasis* theme, the most sustained of which is of course 'Strange Meeting'. The classical Underworld had an obvious resonance with the semi-subterranean conditions of trench warfare and Owen was far from the only poet to explore those connections (see e.g. above on Charles Sorley's evocation of Homer's Underworld). This section will look at Owen's varied uses of the *katabasis* and at poems that allude to the classical Underworld in general.

'Strange Meeting'
(a) Text of poem [CPF 148, 1.148–9]

> It seemed that out of battle I escaped
> Down some profound dull tunnel, long since scooped
> Through granites which titanic wars had groined.
>
> Yet also there encumbered sleepers groaned,
> Too fast in thought or death to be bestirred.   5
> Then, as I probed them, one sprang up, and stared
> With piteous recognition in fixed eyes,
> Lifting distressful hands, as if to bless.
> And by his smile, I knew that sullen hall, —
> By his dead smile I knew we stood in Hell.   10
>
> With a thousand pains that vision's face was grained;
> Yet no blood reached there from the upper ground,
> And no guns thumped, or down the flues made moan.
> 'Strange friend,' I said, 'here is no cause to mourn.'
> 'None,' said that other, 'save the undone years,   15
> The hopelessness. Whatever hope is yours,
> Was my life also; I went hunting wild
> After the wildest beauty in the world,
> Which lies not calm in eyes, or braided hair,
> But mocks the steady running of the hour,   20
> And if it grieves, grieves richlier than here.

> For by my glee might many men have laughed,
> And of my weeping something had been left,
> Which must die now. I mean the truth untold,
> The pity of war, the pity war distilled.   25
> Now men will go content with what we spoiled,
> Or, discontent, boil bloody, and be spilled.
> They will be swift with swiftness of the tigress.
> None will break ranks, though nations trek from progress.
> Courage was mine, and I had mystery,   30
> Wisdom was mine, and I had mastery:
> To miss the march of this retreating world
> Into vain citadels that are not walled.
> Then, when much blood had clogged their chariot-wheels,
> I would go up and wash them from sweet wells,   35
> Even with truths that lie too deep for taint.
> I would have poured my spirit without stint
> But not through wounds; not on the cess of war.
> Foreheads of men have bled where no wounds were.
>
> 'I am the enemy you killed, my friend.   40
> I knew you in this dark: for so you frowned
> Yesterday through me as you jabbed and killed.
> I parried; but my hands were loath and cold.
> Let us sleep now....'

(b) Poem—date, form, and content

'Strange Meeting' is one of Owen's best-known poems, and one of the most famous poems of the First World War. Stallworthy dates its composition to the period January–March 1918 and comments that the manuscripts 'suggest that WO may not have regarded the poem as complete' (CPF 1.149). Hibberd notes that the latest fair copy of the poem (available at FWWPDA) has line 39 'circled in pencil and arrowed to the foot of the page, as though Owen intended this to be the start of a continuation to the poem; the present last line is a hasty addition and was perhaps originally intended to be only temporary' (1973: 45). Stallworthy notes that 'The pencil of the last line has been overwritten in a later ink' (CPF 2.307), which may indicate that Owen had decided to keep those words, although this does not solve the question of what he would have done with the circled line 39. The possibility remains that, effective though it is, the half-line 'Let us sleep now' and its closing ellipsis would not have been Owen's final ending for the poem.

'Strange Meeting' is in very regular iambic pentameter with frequent use of choriambs, especially in the first two feet, occasional substitutions of anapaests for iambs (ll. 11, 25), and feminine endings (ll. 28, 29). The poem showcases Owen's pioneering use of 'pararhyme' (escaped/scooped; groined/groaned; bestirred/stared; etc.). The poem is in couplets with one triplet at lines 19–21 (hair/hour/here).

The poem consists of a brief introduction by a first-person narrator, lines 1–13, which gives the setting: an underground tunnel, filled with 'encumbered sleepers', that the narrator recognizes as 'Hell'. In line 14, the narrator addresses one of the sleepers, whose response comprises the rest of the poem, lines 15–44.

'Strange Meeting' is a richly allusive poem, including echoes of, amongst other works, the Bible, Shelley, Keats, Cary's 1814 verse translation of Dante's *Divine Comedy*, Harold Monro, and Siegfried Sassoon (Bäckman 1979: 105–10). Its classical allusions include direct and indirect references to Homer and Vergil in particular, along with the overall setting of the classical Underworld. The poem takes the classical *katabasis* as its model, and its main speaker—the 'I' of the poem—enacts a descent to the Underworld that connects him to Odysseus, Aeneas, and later Dante as narrators of their own Underworld journeys. Simultaneously, the poem's opening words ('It seemed') place it firmly in the tradition of dream-apparitions by ghosts, such as Aeneas' dream of Hector (*Aeneid* 2.270ff.) and Achilles' dream of Patroclus (*Iliad* 23.69ff.). As it stands, the abrupt end with the unresolved half-line leaves unclear how the speaker returns from the Underworld, or how he awakes from his dream, but the poem itself acts as evidence that he did; its past-tense setting ('it seemed' ... 'I knew we stood in Hell' ... 'I said') indicates that the speaker is reporting back to the living in the aftermath of his Underworld journey, as Odysseus reported to the Phaeacians in his Underworld narrative of *Odyssey* 11, as Plato's Er does also in *Republic* 10.614–21, and crucially (given Owen's known reading of Cary's translation) as Dante does in the *Divine Comedy*. *Pace* many critics who think that both speakers in the poem are dead (see e.g. Minogue and Palmer 2018: 45), the poem's logic requires that the speaker of the frame narrative be alive, a visitor to the Underworld. The opening statement 'It *seemed* that out of battle I escaped' argues against reading the poem as referring to that speaker's own death; cf., for instance, the statement in 'Mental Cases' that 'Surely we have perished / Sleeping, and walk hell' (CPF 1.169, ll. 8–9), where the speaker does assume that he and his companion are dead. Furthermore, the 'Strange Friend' uses the present tense to describe the narrator's hopes but the past tense to describe his own: 'Whatever hope *is* yours, / *Was* my life also' (16–17). This contrast in tenses clearly indicates that the main narrator can still feel hope, i.e. is still alive, while the dead Friend cannot. There may also be a glancing connection to the messengers in 'Job' who repeat 'I only am escaped alone to tell thee'; Job 1:15–19.[48]

(c) Reception commentary

'Strange Meeting' signals its status as both dream and *katabasis* in its opening three-line sentence. The first two words, 'It seemed,' reference the standard Latin introduction of a ghost's appearance to a living person, whether in a dream or not, with *visus* [*est*], as in the appearances to Vergil's Aeneas of the shades of his former commander Hector (*Aen.* 2.271 *visus*, a dream) and his dead wife Creusa (*Aen.* 2.773 *visa*, a waking vision) at the sack of Troy.[49] The poem's interaction with ghost and dream narratives of ancient epic continues in the speaker's description of the 'Strange Friend': 'By his dead smile I knew we stood in Hell'. The Strange Friend/ghost's face reflects the circumstances of his death, just as Hector's ghost appears with many traces of his end in Aeneas' dream.

At the same time that it is a dream-narrative, 'Strange Meeting' also reflects the ancient literary *katabasis*. The speaker's escape from battle into a 'profound dull tunnel' takes him, literally, underground; the phrase 'titanic wars' gives the first indication that this tunnel leads to the classical Underworld. The next two lines emphasize the classical setting, as the groaning 'encumbered sleepers'[50] recall the Titans imprisoned in Tartarus by Zeus after the very first 'titanic war', the Titanomachy, in which the Titans attempted to overthrow Zeus' supreme power.[51] The Titans' presence in the Underworld is mentioned in *Aeneid* 6.580–4, where the Sibyl

---

[48] Noted by Stallworthy 2008: 22.

[49] Hibberd recognizes that 'it seemed' signals 'a dream poem' but does not note the classical connection, saying only that Owen is 'drawing on the Romantic tradition of visionary poetry' (1986: 173).

[50] Interestingly, in a 1916 letter to his mother Owen used the term 'encumbered' to describe an actual experience of being trapped underground in the dark during a threatened Zeppelin attack on London: 'When I was going up the subway at Liverpool St. from the Underground to the Gt. Eastern Platform, I noticed the passages unduly encumbered, and found the outlet just closed, and Liverpool St. in complete darkness. We were corked down in those subways for close on 3 hours.... There was just room to move from one Exit to another seeking an escape' (Potter 2023: 203).

[51] *Mythologie Gréco-Latine*, which Owen owned, includes a long though idiosyncratic description of the Titanomachy, Vol. 1, 5–10. For the fragments of the ancient *Titanomachy*, see West 2003: 222–33.

identifies them for Aeneas, and is echoed in *Inferno* 31.44–5, where Dante calls them 'horrible giants' whom Jupiter still threatens with thunder. Yeats pointed to the adjective 'titanic' as an example of why he disliked Owen's writing, apparently considering it overblown and artificial (1940: 113); but the manuscripts of 'Strange Meeting' show that Owen chose the word 'titanic' carefully. In the earliest draft, he first wrote 'the nether fires' and then revised this to 'the nether flames' (CPF 2.308). In the corrected fair copy, he changed 'nether flames' to 'plutonic flames', moving the setting from the Christian to the classical Underworld, and then further revised 'plutonic flames' to 'titanic wars' (CPF 2.306), cementing the classical setting of the poem and changing the emphasis from the suffering of those in the Underworld to the role of war in establishing that Underworld's existence (Vandiver 1999: 447–50; Vandiver 2010: 303–4). The opening of 'Strange Meeting' encompasses specifically Vergilian motifs as well; the 'profound dull tunnel' is reminiscent of the long cavern of the Sibyl (*Aeneid* 6.237, 262), through which Aeneas makes his descent. The 'encumbered sleepers' recall Charon's words at 6.390: *umbrarum hic locus est, somni noctisque soporae*: 'this is the place of shades, of sleep and slumberful night'.

The most fully developed *katabasis*-episodes in classical literature are in the *Odyssey* (Book 11) and the *Aeneid* (Book 6), and these episodes are the ones most likely to be familiar to Owen and other autodidacts. 'Strange Meeting' clearly signals its connection to both these narratives. Odysseus appears to stand at the border of the Underworld rather than descending into it, though the episode several times implies that he has entered (a famous problem), but Aeneas does enter the Underworld bodily and speaks there with the ghosts of former comrades. Odysseus begins by pouring the blood of sacrificial animals into a pit (or trench?) so that the souls of the dead can approach, drink the blood, and regain their powers of speech. He holds off the souls he does not want to approach with a weapon of war, his sword (*Od.* 11.48–50). Aeneas too performs complicated sacrificial rites before entering the Underworld. For the 'I' of 'Strange Meeting', no such preparations are required: 'no blood reached there from the upper ground / And no guns thumped, or down the flues made moan' (ll. 11–12). Both the sacrificial blood and the weapon of war are absent, and yet the 'vision' who confronts the narrator—the 'Strange Friend'—is nevertheless able to speak.

The conversation between the two, the presumably still-living speaker of the frame narrative and the dead Strange Friend, closely parallels Odysseus' conversation with Achilles in *Odyssey* 11.467–540. Odysseus urges Achilles not to grieve, even in death (l. 486), and Achilles responds by forcefully stressing the superiority of life over death:

> O glorious Odysseus, do not console me for death. I would rather be alive upon the earth as a hired man of someone else, even a landless man with little to live on, than to rule over all the perished dead. (488–91)

The narrator of 'Strange Meeting' echoes Odysseus in his words 'Strange friend…here is no cause to mourn', as the Strange Friend's reply echoes Achilles: 'None…save the undone years / The hopelessness' (ll. 14–15).

Odysseus and Aeneas both converse with the spirits of dead comrades in the Underworld, and in both epics the dead are eager to recall events from the Trojan War as they interact with their living visitors. In Owen's poem, as the Strange Friend's speech progresses, he recalls that war as well, by incorporating allusions to the *Iliad* into his soliloquy. Describing what he would have done had he lived longer, the speaker says that 'when much blood had clogged their chariot-wheels, / I would go up and wash them from sweet wells' (34–5). This couplet juxtaposes two Iliadic images. The first, the blood-clogged chariot-wheels, recalls Achilles' chariot at the end of Book 20, where blood splashes the wheel-rims, the rails, and the horses' feet (20.499–502).[52] The second, the sweet washing-wells, no less vividly recalls one of the *Iliad*'s most memorable images of peace, the vignette of the two springs of water where the Trojan women used to wash their clothes in the days before the Achaeans came (22.147–56). Homer mentions these wells when Hector runs by them with Achilles in hot pursuit, evoking the image of Troy-at-peace at the moment when the city's downfall becomes inevitable. Owen reflects and recalls this juxtaposition of the worst of war with the best of peace by calling up the image of the blood-spattered Achilles in his war-chariot and immediately turning to the image of washing from sweet wells. The feminine realm of washing, here claimed by the Strange Friend, stands in opposition to the traditional masculine configuration of glory in battle (Vandiver 2010: 132–5, 308–9).

Owen's most complex Homeric allusion in 'Strange Meeting' lies in the terminology he uses to describe the second speaker and the climactic line of that speaker's speech: 'Strange friend' and 'I am the enemy you killed, my friend' recall two crucial scenes in the *Iliad*, where warriors on the battlefield

---

[52] For Rosenberg's strikingly similar use of the image of wheels in 'Dead Man's Dump', see discussion above.

greet one another with terms meaning 'friend'. In the first, from *Iliad* 6, the Greek Diomedes and the Trojan Glaucus address one another in battle, realize that they are *xeinoi*, hereditary guest-friends, from the generation of their grandfathers, and agree not to attack one another. Each accepts the other as, quite precisely, a 'strange friend'. But in *Iliad* 21, the outcome is quite different. When the young Trojan prince Lycaon (whom Achilles had previously captured and sold into slavery) begs Achilles for his life, Achilles greets him as 'friend', but slays him nonetheless.[53] The Strange Friend's declaration 'I am the enemy you killed, my friend' gives an unexpected turn to a conversation that seemed to parallel the interaction between Diomedes and Glaucus by revealing that the poem's narrator had, instead, played the role of Achilles and killed his interlocutor. In Greek, the words that Diomedes and Achilles use are not the same; Diomedes calls Glaucus his *xeinos*, a word that depending on context means friend, stranger, guest, host, or foreigner, while Achilles addresses Lycaon with the much more emotionally immediate term *philos*. But Owen would have read Homer in English; if, as seems likely, he read Chapman's translation, he would not have known that Chapman uses 'friend' to translate a different Greek word in each passage. Thomson's *The Greek Tradition* includes a discussion of the Achilles-Lycaon passage, which says that *philos* means, in that passage, 'something a little less than "beloved", but certainly, in the context, a great deal more than "friend"' (Thomson 1915: 146). As noted above, Owen was reading Thomson in January 1918; it seems very likely that he had Thomson's discussion in mind when he used the term 'friend' in lines 14 and 40 of 'Strange Meeting' (Vandiver 2010: 305–8).

The poem's final words, 'Let us sleep now', recall and rework Palinurus' words to Aeneas at 6.371, where he says he would like to 'rest in peaceful abodes' (*sedibus ut saltem placidis in morte quiescam*). Aeneas can grant his dead comrade's wish, once he leaves the Underworld, by burying Palinurus' body; the 'I' of 'Strange Meeting' presumably can provide no such resolution for his interlocutor. If Owen did in fact intend the poem to end with the half-line followed by an ellipsis, this final line highlights the poem's double nature as dream-vision and *katabasis*. The Strange Friend asks to be left in

---

[53] This scene is also crucial for Sorley's 'When you see millions of the mouthless dead', discussed above. Owen had probably read Sorley's poem. He wrote the note 'Marlboro' & Other Poems/Chas Sorely' on the back of the manuscript of 'Has your soul sipped' (CPF 1.91), and Sassoon and Graves are both likely to have recommended Sorley's work to him. Hibberd lists *Marlborough and Other Poems* (Sorley 1916a) as a book that Owen probably owned, although no copy survives in his library (1986: 233).

the realm of dream, while the speaker (presumably) wakes and reports back to the living on what he saw in his dream-*katabasis*. There is one final glancing parallel with the end of *Aeneid* 6, where Aeneas leaves the Underworld through the ivory gate (thus implying that his *katabasis*, too, was in some sense a dream).

'Let us sleep now' is most often taken as an invitation from the Strange Friend to the poem's speaker to join him in sleep. But the construction 'Let us sleep' is ambiguous and does not necessarily represent an invitation; it can just as easily be read as a rebuff or as a 'plea to be left in peace' (Graham 1984: 45). If 'let' here is an imperative meaning 'allow', then 'Let us sleep now' is a request from the Strange Friend that the narrator allow the 'encumbered sleepers' to sleep, presumably by departing, rather than a hortatory subjunctive—'let's sleep'—implicitly including the narrator amongst the dead. This is obviously an important interpretive point, but unfortunately Owen's usage elsewhere is not definitive for deciding the issue. In 'A New Heaven', Owen uses the contracted form 'Let's die home, ferry across the Channel!' for the hortatory subjunctive including the speaker and the person he is speaking to (CPF 1.82). In the fragmentary 'The Women and the Slain', where the women beg the dead to return to them, the slain respond 'We cannot come' and, in a cancelled line, say 'Keep silent. Let us sleep' (CPF 2.502); there, 'let us sleep' is very clearly an imperative meaning 'allow us to sleep'. It is striking that the clear subjunctive of 'A New Heaven' is in the form 'Let's', while the uncontracted 'Let us sleep' in 'The Women and the Slain' can only mean 'Allow us to sleep', excluding the addressees from the group indicated by 'us' as the dead men refuse to interact with the living women. However, in the fragment 'Earth's wheels', which contains several lines later used in 'Strange Meeting' (see below), the form 'let us' is used several times as a clear subjunctive; one draft begins 'Earth's wheels run oiled with blood. Forget we that. / Let us turn back to beauty and to thought', where 'Let us turn' clearly parallels the more archaic construction 'Forget we'. But the setting of 'Earth's wheels' is very different from the setting of 'Strange Meeting'; it is a direct plea from one comrade to another, suggesting a withdrawal from war and violence, and there is no possible ambiguity in its use of 'we'. In sum, 'Let us sleep now' in 'Strange Meeting' remains ambiguous, and how one reads the line probably depends on whether one thinks the main speaker is alive or dead.

(d) Associated works

Owen revisited the *katabasis* theme in the other poems discussed below in this section. In addition, several poems and fragments touch on the *katabasis* or the classical Underworld in passing, including 'The Unreturning', 'Mental Cases', 'The Sentry', and the fragments 'Purgatorial Passions' and 'It was an evening'.

The link to the classical myth of the Titanomachy is strengthened by Owen's use of the same adjective in 'The End' (see discussion above), where the personified Earth refers to 'my titanic tears, the seas'. The fragmentary 'An Imperial Elegy' pictures the Western Front as 'a titan's grave' (discussed below). Isaac Rosenberg also connected the Titans with the war in 'Girl to Soldier on Leave' (see discussion above).

The fragment 'Earth's wheels' (CPF 2.514–17) appears to have been written as a plea to Siegfried Sassoon not to return to the Front, at a time when Owen was considering applying for home service. The section that, in 'Strange Meeting', became wistful contrary-to-fact statements by the Strange Friend of what he would have done appears in this earlier version as hopeful predictions of the future. The Underworld setting came later.

'Spring Offensive' (1918)
(a) Text of poem [CPF 177, 1.192–3]

Halted against the shade of a last hill
They fed, and eased of pack-loads, were at ease;
And leaning on the nearest chest or knees
Carelessly slept.
                But many there stood still
To face the stark blank sky beyond the ridge,   5
Knowing their feet had come to the end of the world.
Marvelling they stood, and watched the long grass swirled
By the May breeze, murmurous with wasp and midge;
And though the summer oozed into their veins
Like an injected drug for their bodies' pains,   10
Sharp on their souls hung the imminent ridge of grass,
Fearfully flashed the sky's mysterious glass.

Hour after hour they ponder the warm field
And the far valley behind, where buttercups
Had blessed with gold their slow boots coming up;   15
When even the little brambles would not yield
But clutched and clung to them like sorrowing arms.
They breathe like trees unstirred.

Till like a cold gust thrills the little word
At which each body and its soul begird   20
And tighten them for battle. No alarms
Of bugles, no high flags, no clamorous haste, —
Only a lift and flare of eyes that faced
The sun, like a friend with whom their love is done.
O larger shone that smile against the sun, —   25
Mightier than his whose bounty these have spurned.

So, soon they topped the hill, and raced together
Over an open stretch of herb and heather
Exposed. And instantly the whole sky burned
With fury against them; earth set sudden cups   30
In thousands for their blood; and the green slope
Chasmed and deepened sheer to infinite space.

Of them who running on that last high place
Breasted the surf of bullets, or went up
On the hot blast and fury of hell's upsurge,   35
Or plunged and fell away past this world's verge,
Some say God caught them even before they fell.

But what say such as from existence' brink
Ventured but drave too swift to sink,
The few who rushed in the body to enter hell,   40
And there out-fiending all its fiends and flames
With superhuman inhumanities,
Long-famous glories, immemorial shames —
And crawling slowly back, have by degrees
Regained cool peaceful air in wonder —   45
Why speak not they of comrades that went under?

(b) Poem—date, form, and content

'Spring Offensive' was probably begun in July 1918, and was revised in France in mid- to late-September 1918. Owen sent a fair copy of the first seventeen lines to Sassoon on 22 September 1918, with a note asking 'Is this worth going on with? I don't want to write anything to which a soldier would say No Compris!' (CPF 1.193). 'Spring Offensive' may well be the last poem Owen ever worked on,[54] and the manuscripts 'show that it was never

---

[54] 'Smile, Smile, Smile' also dates from September 1918.

finally revised' (CPF 1.193). It is one of Owen's most important works. In his unfinished 'Preface', Owen had written that 'This book is not about heroes. English Poetry is not yet fit to speak of them' (CPF 2.535), but Hibberd comments that with 'Spring Offensive' Owen 'began to fashion a kind of poetry that would be fit to speak of heroes while denying heroic qualities to war itself'. He calls the poem 'both a prologue to new writing and an epilogue to all he had written before' (1986: 184).[55] The poem is a profound example of the poetry of survival and its enmeshment with the poetry of unease (see Introduction, pp. 14–16). It uses a covert form of third-person metalepsis, where the poem's narrator clearly comments on the action and even the emotions of the soldiers but does not use the first person anywhere in the poem.

The forty-six-line poem is written in iambic pentameter, with four instances of feminine endings (ll. 27–8 and the final couplet, ll. 45–6). There are frequent examples of choriambs at the beginnings of lines (e.g. 'Hálted agaínst', l. 1; 'Véntured but dráve', l. 39), and occasional long lines where dactyls or anapaests substitute for iambs (e.g. l. 6, 'to the énd of the wórld'). There is one short line of six syllables: 'They breathe like trees unstirred' (l. 18) and one short line of eight syllables, 'Ventured but drave too swift to sink' (l. 39).

The poem's rhyme scheme is dominated by quatrains that are broken and somewhat disguised by stanza divisions. The most common pattern is ABBA (ll. 1–4, 5–8, 13–16, 26–9, 37–40), with one five-line variant in the pattern ABBBA (lines 17–21) and another where the unrhymed word 'slope' intrudes in the pattern A[X]BBA (ll. 30–4). There are also two quatrains of the AABB pattern (ll. 9–12, 22–5), and two rhymed couplets (ll. 35–6, 45–6). The use of stanzas, however, directs the reader's attention away from the rhyme scheme, so that the overall impression is one of complexity similar to the rhyme scheme of 'Insensibility'. For instance, the fourth stanza, read as a stanza, begins with a rhymed couplet (ll. 27–8) but then continues with four unrhymed lines (29–32); the reader accustomed to reading stanzas as self-contained units may not immediately notice the rhymes in the lines immediately preceding and following that stanza: 'spurned / together / heather / burned' (ll. 26–9) followed by 'cups / slope / space / place / up' (ll. 30–4).

The repetition of short 'u' in the rhymes is particularly noticeable; over one-third of the lines end in this or neighbouring sounds, often lengthened

---

[55] See Hibberd's whole discussion of 'Spring Offensive' 1986: 183–92, and Vandiver 2010: 309–14.

by a following 'r' (world/swirled; cups/up (twice); stirred/word/begird; done/sun; spurned/burned; surge/verge; wonder/under).[56] The one repeated rhyme, 'cups/up', forms an important pivot from the presentation of the personified Nature as beneficent though sorrowing ('buttercups', l. 14) to Nature that is actively hostile ('earth set sudden cups', l. 30), an effect that is heightened by the assonance and rhythmic similarity of 'buttercup' and 'sudden cups'. The one unrhymed end-syllable in the poem, 'slope' (itself almost a pararhyme for 'cups/up') in l. 31, highlights the moment at which the soldiers' world changes from a calm and pastoral landscape to a vertiginous and deadly precipice ('the green slope / Chasmed and deepened sheer to infinite space', ll. 31–2).

There is one heavily corrected draft manuscript of the poem and one fair copy of the first seventeen lines. The draft shows heavy revision of the first five stanzas and it is not always obvious which reading should be preferred. The final stanza, however, survives in remarkably clear form, with only two minor corrections: 'Who rushed' is crossed out and replaced by 'The few who rushed', and in the penultimate line 'their' is cancelled and replaced by 'cool &' (CPF 2.379; and on FWWPDA). This stanza is written in pencil; Hibberd surmises that it may have been written in October 1918, in which case it 'refer[s] to immediate experience' (1992: 161, 209n3).

'Spring Offensive' depicts a group of soldiers immediately before they launch an attack, and then describes the attack itself. The first two stanzas of the poem portray in minute particularity the surroundings in which the soldiers rest before battle, drawing sustained attention to the physical details of the natural world—the grass, the bees, the insects, the flowers. The warmth and even the sounds of the morning[57] are powerfully invoked. In the third stanza, the command that the soldiers advance acts 'like a cold gust' to break the somnolent and tranquil warmth of summer, and as they 'race' forward the very character of the land itself changes from a meadow to an 'open stretch of herb and heather'. At this point, the character of Nature itself changes as well, from a loving, though sorrowful, presence that tried to delay the soldiers' progress towards the Front to an implacable enemy. The sky 'burn[s] with fury' against the soldiers, the earth 'set[s] sudden cups...for their blood', and the ground itself tilts and casts the soldiers into 'infinite space'.

---

[56] Hibberd says that Owen 'is particularly fond of the short *u*...in his descriptions of war' (1973: 34).

[57] Hibberd identifies 'Spring Offensive' as a 'dawn piece' (1986: 186).

The opening stanza foregrounds key nature motifs from Romantic poetry, but the reader cannot be lulled into false security; there are repeated and unsettling hints that this apparently beneficent Nature will turn against these soldiers.[58] The stanza contains a disturbing thread of imagery of sharpness and shatterability, from the jarring likening of summer to a hypodermic needle through the description of the 'ridge of grass' as 'sharp' and the reference to the 'sky's mysterious glass', which flashes 'fearfully'. This imagery compels the reader to confront what will in fact happen to these soldiers: their world will indeed shatter around them, and its fragments will pierce and kill most of them.

(c) Reception commentary

The poem's main engagement with classics comes in the final stanza, which presents the soldiers' attack as a *katabasis*. There are, however, several points of contact with classical material in the earlier stanzas as well. In the third stanza, where Nature is benevolent and concerned for the soldiers, the 'little brambles' that 'clutched and clung to them like sorrowing arms' (16–17) reflect Ovidian stories of humans and nymphs who are transformed into trees or plants, but still retain their self-awareness and their emotions. The mythological handbook *The Greenwood Tree* which Owen owned (see above) retold Ovid's story of Dryope, who broke branches off a lotus and learned from the drops of blood that fell from the blossoms that the plant was in fact the nymph Lotis. Dryope was then transformed into a tree herself (23; cf. Ovid *Met.* 9.331–93). From *The Greenwood Tree* alone, Owen would also have known the stories of Phaethon's sisters turning into poplars (19), Daphne's transformation into a bay tree (20–1), Cyparissus' transformation into a cypress (24), and the transformations of Narcissus, Hyacinthus, Clytie, and the blood of Adonis into flowers (36–41). The anthropomorphic presentation of the brambles as compassionate beings that try to hold the soldiers back glances at such sorrowing humans, metamorphosized into plants. Line 18 inverts the allusion by presenting the soldiers themselves as undergoing metamorphosis, so that they 'breathe like trees unstirred'. Here, one thinks of Ovidian stories where transformation into a tree is a protection from violence—Daphne is the most obvious example—and of Homeric similes that liken warriors to trees. But Owen's soldiers are not, in fact, protected through transformation; they are not changed into trees, but are

---

[58] On the poem's relationship to the Romantic view of nature and some echoes of Keats and Shelley, see Hibberd 1986: 187–8.

only able, in their last minute of quiet rest, to 'breathe *like* trees unstirred'. The importance of this image is underscored by the shortness of the line, only six syllables long, four of them monosyllables with long vowels.[59]

Line 18 provides the pivot to the soldiers' preparation for battle, the moment at which they have to turn away from their rest in the warm and beneficent summer meadow and prepare for the attack. The change is signalled by another reference to nature, as the 'little word' of command comes 'like a cold gust'. The 'unstirred trees' to which the soldiers were compared are now hit by a cold wind; and outside the structure of similes, the soldiers 'begird / And tighten... for battle'. Since these soldiers are not being observed by any admiring onlookers, there are no 'bugles... [or] high flags'; instead, the moment at which they prepare for their deaths is presented in terms that again lightly anthropomorphise a natural object, this time the sun:

> Only a lift and flare of eyes that faced
> The sun, like a friend with whom their love is done. (23–4)

The presentation of young men's (willingly accepted) deaths as separation from the sun recalls Euripides' Iphigenia and Sophocles' Antigone, who both lament that their deaths mean they will no longer see the sun; for both tragic characters, their bidding farewell to the sun signals their recognition that death is imminent (Eur. *Iph. Aul.* 1218–19, 1509; Soph. *Ant.* 807–9, 879–80). The friend-like sun of 'Spring Offensive' is also linked intratextually to 'the kind old sun' of 'Futility', which is unable to awaken the dead soldier (see discussion below). In 'Spring Offensive', the soldiers already know that the sun can do nothing for them; he is a 'friend with whom their love is done'.[60] Their recognition of this prompts an exclamation in the narrator's voice:

> O larger shone that smile against the sun, —
> Mightier than his whose bounty these have spurned. (25–6)

---

[59] It is possible, however, that Owen did not intend to leave this line short. The manuscript shows that he crossed out 'All they [*sic*] strange day' at the beginning of the line, which would have made the line metrically complete (CPF 2.377). He rejected that phrase, but he may have intended to compose an alternative for it.

[60] Cf. Welland: 'As in "Futility" the sun is a life force, a creative principle from which the soldier is cut off, but this time it is by an act of deliberate rejection.... The sense of alienation in "Spring Offensive" is the more terrible because it is the result of active choice, not passive suffering' (1978: 83).

'His' in line 26 is ambiguous, with its antecedent unclear; the easiest reading takes it as referring to the sun, but it is also possible that it refers to God. In either case, the lines underscore that the soldiers' leave-taking encompasses the entire natural world, represented in the preceding lines by the sun, and that they are voluntarily renouncing the 'bounty' of the summer meadow, the flowers, trees, and sunshine that they now leave behind. (There is perhaps, here, a glancing trace of Brooke's sonnet 'III. The Dead', with its words 'These laid the world away'.)

Unlike the bystander addressed in 'Dulce et Decorum Est', these soldiers have already looked at what death in this war means, and voluntarily accept it for themselves. This presentation of the soldiers' voluntary sacrifice, undertaken in full recognition that it means their own deaths, explains the beginning of the next line: '*So*, soon they topped the hill' (l. 27). It also offers a motivation for the sudden hostility of Nature against the soldiers; they have chosen to turn their backs, literally, on life's 'bounty'. Lines 29–32 are simultaneously a continuation of the anthropomorphic treatment of Nature, now hostile, and a profoundly evocative description of the realities of battle on the Western Front, where bursting shells would make the sky 'burn... with fury' and would also 'set sudden cups' (i.e. shell holes) in the earth.

The soldiers themselves play the role of Homeric warriors, fighting against natural forces as Achilles does against the river Scamander and infused in the two final stanzas with a 'Joy of Battle'[61] and a superhuman strength that reflect the Homeric hero's *aristeia* (a scene that foregrounds a warrior's inspired prowess in battle). In the version of the poem as printed, the references to an *aristeia* are most evident in the final stanza (see below), but the manuscript shows that Owen repeatedly revised key lines, including 23 and 27, and that at some stages of composition he considered stressing the soldiers' superhuman exhilaration in battle in these earlier lines as well. In the standard version, lines 23–4 read 'Only a lift and flare of eyes that faced / The sun'. For 'lift and flare', Owen tried and crossed out versions that would have included the words 'mighty', 'kindle', 'lift and sparkle', 'blaze', 'glory', and 'radiance'. Even more strikingly, for line 27, 'So, soon they topped the hill', Owen considered 'Glorious', 'Lightly', 'Proudly', 'Bright-faced', and 'Splendid' before writing in 'So, soon' (CPF 2.378). As Das says, the manuscript reveals that 'a poem rooted in unthinkable horror was

---

[61] The phrase is Julian Grenfell's, 'Into Battle' l. 37 (Kendall 2013: 111). See below on Owen's probable knowledge of Grenfell's poem.

conceived as a poem not about killing or being killed but about exhilaration' (2005: 163; see also Hibberd 1986: 188–9).

The exhilaration is precisely that of an *aristeia*, in which, as Owen puts it in 'Apologia pro Poemate Meo', 'power was on us as we slashed bones bare / Not to feel sickness or remorse of murder' (ll. 6–7). Even in the standard printed version, some trace of this exhilaration remains in the penultimate stanza, in the opening lines describing the soldiers 'running on that last high place' who 'Breasted the surf of bullets'. The image is of exultant or even joyous youth, and 'Breasted the surf of bullets' may be another glancing reference to Brooke, who memorably wrote (in the first of his war sonnets, 'Peace') about soldiers 'turn[ing] as swimmers into cleanness leaping'; a cancelled version of Owen's phrase reads 'Leapt to unseen bullets'. 'That last high place' (l. 33) links the soldiers' actions to ancient religious sacrifice; Hibberd connects the 'high place' with sacrifices mentioned in the Hebrew Bible, especially those to Moloch and Baal (e.g. Jeremiah 19:5; 1 Kings 11:7), and he notes that Owen had read *Salammbô*, Flaubert's novel about Carthage that includes scenes of human sacrifice, before he enlisted (1986: 190).[62]

The stanza quickly moves away from any hints of joyousness with the shift to the description of the soldiers who 'went up / On the hot blast and fury of hell's upsurge / Or plunged and fell away past this world's verge', but the opening image is of sacrifice willingly undertaken. Even in the vertiginous imagery of plunging and falling, some sense of exultation remains, as Owen memorably wrote to his youngest brother Colin:

> The sensations of going over the top are about as exhilarating as those dreams of falling over a precipice, when you see the rocks at the bottom surging up to you. I woke up without being squashed. Some didn't. There was an extraordinary exultation in the act of slowly walking forward, showing ourselves openly. (Potter 2023: 277; letter dated 14 May 1917)

The pivot to the very different tone of the final stanza comes with line 37: 'Some say God caught them even before they fell'. This line is reminiscent not only of Christian consolation but also of the scene in *Iliad* 16.666–83, where Sleep and Death carry Sarpedon's body from the battlefield at Zeus' command. But Owen immediately questions the possibility that any such

---

[62] This is not the only time Owen associates 'high places' and sacrificial altars; in an unnamed sonnet (revised in late 1917 or early 1918, but probably written earlier), he writes 'on the mountain, that high altar-tomb / The sun stood full of wine, blood-sanctified' (CPF 1.105).

consolation can be found through divine intervention, both in the next line (38), which asks 'what say' the survivors, and in the poem's final unanswered question, 'Why speak not they of comrades who went under?' (45). The manuscript shows that Owen had considered a version of line 37 that would read 'Of them *we* say God caught them as they fell'. As Hibberd notes, this reading echoes a statement about the dead in one of Owen's letters to his mother: 'in poetry we call them … glorious' (Potter 2023: 248). Hibberd rightly points out that Owen's 'underlining of "*we*" shows how the final version of the line should be read'; in the revision, 'the myth is brushed aside. … Pagan slaughter leaves no room for Christian consolation' (1986: 190).[63]

In the final stanza, Owen revisits the classical *katabasis*, as he did in 'Strange Meeting'. Once again, he depicts living men who enter hell and then return to the world. But these soldiers return, not with new knowledge such as Odysseus received from Teiresias nor with a new sense of purpose such as Aeneas presumably achieved, nor even with an increased understanding of reality such as Dante gained. Instead, they 'crawl slowly back' to 'regain cool peaceful air'—perhaps reflecting the Sibyl's words to Aeneas: 'the descent to Avernus is easy … but to recall your steps and to climb back to the upper air, that is the task, that is the labour' (*facilis descensus Averno; / … sed revocare gradum superasque evadere ad auras, / hoc opus, hic labor est, Aen.* 6.126–9)—and are utterly silent about what they saw and did in the Underworld. The poem's narrator can describe their actions as 'long-famous glories, immemorial shames', but the revenants themselves are silent. Their silence underlines their distance from the Homeric *katabasis*; in the *Odyssey*, Odysseus himself narrates the deaths of many of his men and recounts the story of his journey to the Underworld, as part of which he describes speaking to the souls of Elpenor, Agamemnon, Achilles, and Ajax. Thus, he speaks specifically about 'comrades who went under', and he does so in part to confer glory and fame on them as well as on himself. Imperishable glory (*kleos aphthiton*) was precisely what the Homeric warrior fought for, and what epic itself conferred on the warriors it described.

But Owen's descriptive language of his soldiers' *katabasis* decisively forecloses the possibility of Homeric *kleos*. The warriors of 'Spring Offensive' did not merely observe the conditions of hell or speak to its inhabitants; they 'outfiend[ed] all its fiends and flames / With superhuman

---

[63] Cf. Das' description of l. 37 as 'a final dismissal of religious consolation' (2005: 164).

inhumanities, / Long-famous glories, immemorial shames' (41–3). Line 41 draws on traditional elements of the Christian Hell (fiends and flames), but line 43 changes the focus to the classical. In the *Odyssey*, when Odysseus speaks to the souls of his dead comrades in the Underworld, he discusses 'long-famous glories' with Agamemnon and Achilles; with Ajax, who will not speak to him, he touches on the 'immemorial shame' of Ajax's suicide. In Owen's treatment, the soldiers who have been in hell with their comrades 'who went under' collapse these two categories into one; the 'long-famous glories' of Homeric and Vergilian warfare, the deeds on which epic itself conferred renown, are introduced as 'superhuman inhumanities' and further glossed as 'immemorial shames'. The entire content of the traditional mode of discussing battle is emptied out, so that the soldiers are left with no words in which to describe their experiences. The poem does not answer its own final question, but one answer to 'Why speak not they...?' is that, when glory can no longer be distinguished from shame and when the superhuman includes inhumanities, there is no longer any language in which the survivors *can* speak of their dead comrades.

If Hibberd is correct that the final stanza of 'Spring Offensive' was written in October 1918, then a letter Owen wrote his mother about the action for which he won his Military Cross is especially pertinent: 'I can find no word to qualify my experiences except the word SHEER.... It passed the limits of my Abhorrence. I lost all my earthly faculties and fought like an angel' (Potter 2023: 397). The juxtaposition of 'the limits of my Abhorrence' with 'fought like an angel' (clearly a Miltonic angel, utterly implacable and fearless) reflects the same idea as 'superhuman inhumanities'. Even more strikingly, the choice of 'SHEER' to describe the fighting recalls the poem's description of the attack: 'the green slope / Chasmed and deepened sheer to infinite space' (31–2).

The letter and the poem's final stanza both foreground the combined exultation and horror of the subjective experience of battle and the inadequacy of language to convey that experience. In its attempt to compensate for that inadequacy, the final stanza of 'Spring Offensive' stands as one of Owen's most significant engagements with classical epic. If this stanza was indeed written less than a month before Owen's death, then it is also the very last poetry Owen wrote.

(d) Associated works

'Spring Offensive' has intratextual points of contact with several of Owen's other poems. The *katabasis* element of the last stanza appears also in 'Strange

Meeting', 'Apologia pro Poemate Meo', and 'The Sentry'. The treatment of nature as a force that becomes hostile to the soldiers connects the poem to 'Exposure', and the presentation of the sun as a 'friend' ties it to 'Futility'.

The presentation of nature in 'Spring Offensive' is strongly reminiscent of Julian Grenfell's (1888–1915) 'Into Battle', a poem that Owen almost certainly knew.[64] Grenfell's poem, like Owen's, elides the human enemy out of the description almost entirely; he mentions only 'lead and steel', not the soldiers who wield them, just as Owen mentions only 'the surf of bullets'. Furthermore, Grenfell's poem presents the 'Joy of Battle' as a Homeric *aristeia*, as 'Spring Offensive' does in its final stanza. But the effect of the two poems could scarcely be more different. For Grenfell, Nature is wholly benevolent and helpful to the warrior (the sun, wind, and earth cheer him on, the 'bright company of heaven' fortifies him, the blackbird sings to him), while for Owen Nature is either sorrowing and helpless or actively hostile. Both poets personify Nature, and both elide the human enemy out of the soldier's experience; but Owen's vision is ultimately anti-consolatory and leaves no room for any uncomplicated 'glory' of the sort that Grenfell still espouses.

'Exposure' (1918)
(a) Text of poem [CPF 174, 1.185–6]

Our brains ache, in the merciless iced east winds that knive us ...
Wearied we keep awake because the night is silent ...
Low, drooping flares confuse our memory of the salient ...
Worried by silence, sentries whisper, curious, nervous,
    But nothing happens.   5

Watching, we hear the mad gusts tugging on the wire,
Like twitching agonies of men among its brambles.
Northward, incessantly, the flickering gunnery rumbles,
Far off, like a dull rumour of some other war.
    What are we doing here?   10

The poignant misery of dawn begins to grow ...
We only know war lasts, rain soaks, and clouds sag stormy.

---

[64] Grenfell, 'Into Battle' (Kendall 2013: 110–11). In an August 1915 letter to Leslie Gunston Owen mentions a supplement, *War Poems from the Times*, published by *The Times* on 9 August 1915. 'Into Battle' was included in this supplement, although Owen does not single it out for comment in his letter (Owen and Bell 1967: 355, with note). On 'Into Battle' and its Homeric connections, see Vandiver 2010: 184–97.

Dawn massing in the east her melancholy army
Attacks once more in ranks on shivering ranks of grey,
    But nothing happens.   15

Sudden successive flights of bullets streak the silence.
Less deathly than the air that shudders black with snow,
With sidelong flowing flakes that flock, pause, and renew;
We watch them wandering up and down the wind's nonchalance,
    But nothing happens.   20

Pale flakes with fingering stealth come feeling for our faces —
We cringe in holes, back on forgotten dreams, and stare, snow-
    dazed,
Deep into grassier ditches. So we drowse, sun-dozed,
Littered with blossoms trickling where the blackbird fusses,
    — Is it that we are dying?   25

Slowly our ghosts drag home: glimpsing the sunk fires, glozed
With crusted dark-red jewels; crickets jingle there;
For hours the innocent mice rejoice: the house is theirs;
Shutters and doors, all closed: on us the doors are closed, —
    We turn back to our dying.   30

Since we believe not otherwise can kind fires burn;
Nor ever suns smile true on child, or field, or fruit.
For God's invincible spring our love is made afraid;
Therefore, not loath, we lie out here; therefore were born,
    For love of God seems dying.   35

Tonight, this frost will fasten on this mud and us,
Shrivelling many hands, puckering foreheads crisp.
The burying-party, picks and shovels in shaking grasp,
Pause over half-known faces. All their eyes are ice,
    But nothing happens.   40

(b) Poem—date, form, and content

Stallworthy dates this poem primarily to 1918: 'Begun at Scarborough in
December 1917,...revised there in early 1918; and finished in France in
September 1918' (CPF 1.186). The dating is complicated by the fact that
Owen wrote 'Feb. 1916' at the foot of the latest draft.[65] This date cannot be

---

[65] Stallworthy identifies 'five pages of rough working..., a preliminary and heavily corrected
draft..., and a heavily corrected fair copy' (CPF 2.365; available on FWWPDA).

correct; Owen was first in the trenches in January 1917 and the poem's description of freezing cold matches very closely his experiences from late January and early February of that year, when as he wrote to his mother on 4 February 'the marvel is that we did not all die of cold' (Potter 2023: 246). Blunden (1931: 122) suggested that the manuscript date of Feb. 1916 was a slip for 'Feb. 1917', but as Stallworthy points out, it is unlikely that Owen could have produced 'so astonishing and mature a poem from his initial exposure to the reality of the trenches' (2013: 246). He suggests that the '6' of the manuscript's date 'could be an imperfect "8"', but in fact the '6' appears quite clearly written. Perhaps the best explanation is that Blunden was correct to read '1916' as a slip for '1917', but that Owen intended the date to refer to the time of the experience the poem describes, not to the time of writing it. The title of 'From My Diary, July 1914' shows a similar approach, since that poem was actually written in late 1917 and early 1918 (CPF 1.120).[66]

Even by the standards of Owen's manuscripts, the text of 'Exposure' is very uncertain; Stallworthy is being rather optimistic when he refers to the latest manuscripts as 'a heavily corrected fair copy' (CPF 2.365). The poem would better be described as still in working-draft form. It consists of eight stanzas, each with four long lines followed by a short fifth line, which functions as a kind of refrain. The long lines are pararhymed in an ABBA pattern, with the rhymes changing in each stanza. The pararhyme is handled extremely skilfully, another argument for a late date of composition. The metre is predominantly iambic, but the long lines are expanded beyond standard iambic pentameter. Most contain twelve syllables, with variants of eleven, thirteen, fourteen, and even fifteen syllables, and from five to eight stresses, with six stresses most common. As in many of Owen's poems, choriambs are very frequent at the line beginnings (e.g. 'Weáried, we keép'; 'Wátching, we heár'; 'Slówly our ghósts'; 'Shútters and doórs').

The poem describes the hallucinations experienced by soldiers slowly freezing to death. As they begin to succumb to hypothermia, they imagine themselves experiencing the warmth of sunlight amongst grasses and blossoms, and realize (l. 25) that they may be dying. They next imagine returning—or trying to return—to their homes as ghosts, only to find the 'shutters and doors, all closed', so that they are excluded from their hearthsides and accept their approaching deaths (l. 30, 'We turn back to our dying'). The final stanza moves the focalization from the soldiers dying of

---

[66] For a thorough discussion of the dating of 'Exposure', see Hibberd 1976.

cold to the aftermath of their deaths, when their comrades will bury the frozen bodies.

The echo in the opening line of the beginning of Keats' 'Ode to a Nightingale' ('My heart aches, and a drowsy numbness pains / My sense') has been widely noticed and discussed. For explorations of Owen's debt to, and repudiation of, Keats in this poem, see especially Graham 1984: 63–5 and Kerr 1993: 7–10.

(c) Reception commentary

The classical interactions of 'Exposure' begin in the third stanza. The soldiers' experience of daybreak as 'poignant misery' leads to an arresting personification of Dawn, who far from bringing colour and warmth to the world brings only greyness, cold, and violence. Lines 13–14 combine the reality of the war, where grey-uniformed German soldiers attack from the East, with an evocative description of a cold and cloudy winter daybreak.[67] Most significantly, the personification of Dawn links 'Exposure' to the Trojan War cycle, since the dawn goddess Eos' son Memnon took part in the Trojan War and was killed by Achilles. The mythological handbook *The Greenwood Tree* (see above) contains a description of Dawn sending a young man into a situation that will prove fatal for him: 'Aurora, the goddess of the Dawn, threw open the purple eastern gates, and showed [Phaethon] the chariot-way strewn with roses' (74). Owen has drained away the colour from the Homeric 'rosy-fingered Dawn' and has left the grey, colourless remnant as an image of the cost of war. Even more strikingly, Owen changes the normal presentation of the arrival of Dawn as a welcome and beneficent presence (a presentation he would have found in Adams [1910], for instance) into an arresting image of Dawn herself as a hostile force. No longer the Eos/Aurora of myth, a devoted mother of an individual son who mourned his death in battle so deeply that she granted him immortality, this Dawn sends 'ranks on ranks' of undifferentiated soldiers against the poem's narrators.

The sixth stanza also engages with Homeric tropes. The freezing soldiers imagine a failed return or *nostos*, a homecoming that does not succeed, as they cannot gain entrance to their houses but can only see (through a window or a crack?) the embers glowing on the hearths in empty rooms.[68]

---

[67] 'Owen subverts the *topos* of dawn into puncturing emptiness…as the personification blends weather and war' (Lanone 2013: 24). Cf. Welland 1978: 78.

[68] On the theme of *nostos* and the poetry of unease, see Introduction, p. 15.

There is a poignantly ironic resonance with the popular song by Ivor Novello, 'Keep the Home Fires Burning', with its line 'Though the lads are far away they dream of home' (see e.g. Kerr 1993: 12–13). Hibberd notes another intertextual connection, with Tennyson's 'Lotos-Eaters', who say 'surely now our household hearths are cold / ... And we should come like ghosts to trouble joy' (stanza 6, ll. 72–4; Hibberd 1986: 169). The lotos-eaters, of course, are Odysseus' companions, and the *nostos* that they disavow is the theme of the *Odyssey*. In one of the manuscripts, line 30 reads 'Return back to our dying', which strengthens the resonance with the theme of *nostos*, figured here as an impossibility. In an eerie and evocative reframing of the longing for homecoming, not only are the soldiers 'ghosts' who 'drag home', but there are no humans waiting in the house to greet them. The hearth, the symbolic centre of a home and the scene of Odysseus' and Penelope's reunion in the *Odyssey*, here holds a fire that has died down to embers and the only creatures who lay claim to it are the crickets and the 'innocent' mice.[69]

Owen's soldiers recognize that the impossibility of *nostos* is a sign of their deaths. The manuscript readings for the seventh and eighth stanzas are uncertain, but as Stallworthy's text stands, the soldiers accept that they must die because they hope that their deaths may somehow preserve not just civilization ('kind fires', l. 31), but the natural world as well (l. 32). Their faith that this will be so is uncertain; in one of the poem's more puzzling lines, they say 'For God's invincible spring our love is made afraid' (l.33). Owen had used 'the invincible spring' before, in 'The Wrestlers' (discussed below), which he began writing shortly after arriving at Craiglockhart in July 1917. There, Earth is said to give her son Antaeus 'the grip and stringency of winter / And all the ardour of the invincible spring'. In one of the preliminary drafts of 'Exposure', Owen crossed out 'God's' and wrote in 'earth's', a reading that would tie the poem more closely to Owen's treatment of the Antaeus myth in 'The Wrestlers' (CPF 2.370).

The variant 'earth's invincible spring' also sheds some light on a cancelled final stanza that Owen drafted in three versions. This ninth stanza, which apparently Owen envisaged following the stanza about the burial party, would have made 'Exposure' contain at least a glancing reference to a

---

[69] Kerr comments that Dickens' *The Cricket on the Hearth* was 'among Owen's favourite childhood reading' (1993: 11). It is worth noting that insects (including crickets) and mice are in fact household pests who are ruthlessly killed to make houses 'clean' and 'safe'; their undisturbed possession of the empty house is a sort of inverted metaphor for the soldiers, houseless and vulnerable, who are ruthlessly killed outdoors supposedly to guarantee civilization's purity and safety.

katabasis and perhaps to the abduction of Persephone by Hades. In what appears to be the fullest draft of this stanza, Owen wrote:

> shock
> 'And some wait only till ~~at last shell~~ gulfs
>   the burst earth   for us
>   And our door opens.'

and then modified this to:

> 'Yet we are waiting ~~but~~ till the burst earth gulfs for us
> And our door opens'. (CPF 2.367)

As Hibberd notes, at this stage 'the poem was to have ended with an expected event, the opening of the hell door in the bottom of a crater' (1986: 168). And of course the archetypal scene of the earth 'gaping open' to swallow a young person alive is the abduction of Persephone, a 'child' who was gathering flowers in a 'field' and whose abduction was witnessed by the sun (*Homeric Hymn to Demeter* 32–3). Her return each year enacted the return of the 'invincible spring'. *The Greenwood Tree* contains a retelling of 'The Story of Proserpine', which begins 'In the Sicilian vale of Enna there reigned perpetual spring' and stresses the child-like nature of Proserpine/Persephone. She is described as 'playing' with her companions, who themselves are depicted filling their baskets of flowers 'with child-like eagerness' (29). It is worth noting that in this version the earth opens when Pluto hurls his sceptre into the bottom of the river Cyane: 'the waters parted, the earth opened, and the chariot sank quickly down to Pluto's kingdom' (30). The detail of the earth gaping at the bottom of a water-filled concavity is not so far away from Hibberd's 'opening of the hell door in the bottom of a crater'.[70]

In Owen's later draft of 'Exposure', which has become the standard text and which omits this stanza, any implicit references to Persephone's abduction and return are submerged so that only the faintest traces of them remain. (For a discussion of a trace allusion to Persephone in Rosenberg's 'Break of Day in the Trenches', see discussion above.) In the standard text, the soldiers' fear for 'God's invincible spring' remains puzzling—if the

---

[70] As noted above, Owen would also know Persephone's story from Thomson 1915, which includes a chapter called 'Mother and Daughter' and which Owen was reading in January 1918.

spring is 'invincible', why do they fear for it?—and the connection between the soldiers' deaths and the safety of 'kind fires' and 'suns [that] smile true on child, or field, or fruit' remains unclear. The difficulties only increase with the stanza's final two lines, where the imagery shifts towards Christian tropes as the soldiers state directly that they were born to undertake this sacrifice and do so willingly, or at least 'not loath' (l. 34). The stanza's final short line, which is presented as an explanation, leaves the reader's questions unanswered. 'For love of God seems dying' is bewilderingly ambiguous. Does 'love of God' mean God's love for his creation, or his creatures' love for him (in grammatical terms, is it a subjective or an objective genitive)? And the use of the verb 'seems' complicates our understanding of the line even more; does it seem to the soldiers that the love of God is dying, or does it seem so to the civilians whom the soldiers hope to protect? Or does 'seems' here have the meaning 'takes on the aspect of', so that love of God appears under the guise of (human) dying? The manuscripts show that Owen struggled with this line, trying out versions including 'We know what we are doing', 'This we are doing', 'To do this dying', and 'For God's redeeming', amongst others (CPF 2.370). Since even the version Stallworthy uses as his copy text shows several revisions of this line, it seems likely that Owen would have revised it more fully and clarified its ambiguities. As it stands, the seventh stanza is perhaps the most difficult section of a very difficult poem, toggling uneasily between apparent 'high-intensity' Christian belief in the reality of redemptive sacrifice and a much lower-intensity use of terms such as 'love of God' alongside traces of classical myth.

In the eighth stanza, the poem's focus shifts from the viewpoint of the soldiers who are freezing to death to the viewpoint of those who will bury the frozen bodies. For a reader familiar with Sallust's *Bellum Catilinae*, lines 38–40 of Owen's poem resonate strikingly with the conclusion of that work, where Sallust foregrounds the futility of war. In a haunting scene, those searching the battlefield after the combat turn over the dead bodies and recognize friends, guests, kinsmen, and enemies intermingled:

Nevertheless, the army of the Roman people had gained no joyful or bloodless victory. For all the most resolute had either fallen in the battle or come away with severe wounds. Many, too, who had gone out from the camp to have a look or to pillage, on turning over the bodies of the enemy found now a friend, now a guest or kinsman; some also recognized their personal enemies. Thus the whole army was variously affected with exultation and mourning, lamentation and gladness. (Ramsey 2013: 147)

This resonance is even stronger in a cancelled manuscript version, where Owen had written 'We'll steal their boots' as part of the description of the frozen dead (CPF 2.370), paralleling Sallust's matter-of-fact statement about pillage.[71] In earlier MSS versions, Owen had written 'We' or 'We others' or 'We living' instead of 'The burial party' (CPF 2.366). There is no evidence to indicate that Owen had ever read Sallust, so this may well be an example of a 'reader-activated' connection, one brought to the text by readers who are also familiar with Sallust rather than one 'seeded' by Owen (see Introduction, pp. 9–10).

After the January action on which the poem is based, in actuality the dead remained unburied until the ground had partially thawed. On 4 February 1917, Owen wrote to his mother about 'the distortion of the dead, whose unburiable bodies sit outside the dug-outs all day, all night, the most execrable sights on earth. In poetry we call them the most glorious. But to sit with them all day, all night...and a week later to come back and find them still sitting there, in motionless groups, THAT is what saps the "soldierly spirit"' (Potter 2023: 248; ellipsis and emphasis original). The poem's evocation of a burial party working with frozen corpses on frozen ground thus evokes a form of horror that differs from the experience on which the poem is based.

(d) Associated works

Several of Owen's other poems (all discussed in this chapter) engage intratextually with elements in 'Exposure'. One version of 'A New Heaven', printed by C. Day Lewis, includes the line 'Let's die back to the hearths we died for', which parallels the 'ghosts drag[ging] home'. 'Futility' treats the sun as a kind and benevolent entity, whose touch might warm a dead boy back to life. The fragmentary 'The Women and the Slain' spells out the sentiment hinted at in the antepenultimate and penultimate stanzas of 'Exposure', that soldiers' deaths somehow guarantee the continuation not just of society but of the harvest. In 'Perseus', Owen appears to have considered juxtaposing references to Persephone and to a *katabasis*.

---

[71] This earlier variant also helps resolve the ambiguity of 'their' in 'all their eyes are ice'. This is often taken to refer to the eyes of the burial party. In the draft, however, the 'eyes' clearly belong to the frozen dead; Owen wrote 'We'll steal their boots; their feet are brick; their wide eyes, ice' (CPF 2.370).

'Apologia pro Poemate Meo' (1917)
(a) Text of poem [CPF 123, 1.124–5]

I, too, saw God through mud, —
  The mud that cracked on cheeks when wretches smiled.
  War brought more glory to their eyes than blood,
  And gave their laughs more glee than shakes a child.

Merry it was to laugh there —   5
  Where death becomes absurd and life absurder.
  For power was on us as we slashed bones bare
  Not to feel sickness or remorse of murder.

I, too, have dropped off Fear —
  Behind the barrage, dead as my platoon,   10
  And sailed my spirit surging light and clear
  Past the entanglement where hopes lay strewn;

And witnessed exultation —
  Faces that used to curse me, scowl for scowl,
  Shine and lift up with passion of oblation,   15
  Seraphic for an hour; though they were foul.

I have made fellowships —
  Untold of happy lovers in old song.
  For love is not the binding of fair lips
  With the soft silk of eyes that look and long,   20

By Joy, whose ribbon slips —
  But wound with war's hard wire whose stakes are strong;
  Bound with the bandage of the arm that drips;
  Knit in the webbing of the rifle-thong.

I have perceived much beauty   25
  In the hoarse oaths that kept our courage straight;
  Heard music in the silentness of duty;
  Found peace where shell-storms spouted reddest spate.

Nevertheless, except you share
  With them in hell the sorrowful dark of hell,   30
  Whose world is but the trembling of a flare
  And heaven but as the highway for a shell,

> You shall not hear their mirth:
> > You shall not come to think them well content
> > By any jest of mine. These men are worth   35
> > Your tears. You are not worth their merriment.

(b) Poem—date, form, and content

The poem was written in Scarborough in November–December 1917. It consists of nine quatrains, each with an ABAB rhyme scheme (with the rhymes changing in each stanza). Each first line consists six or seven syllables and the second, third, and fourth lines are iambic pentameter.

'Apologia' is often presumed to be a response to Robert Graves' 'Two Fusiliers' (Welland 1978: 67–8) and perhaps also to Graves' letter to Owen of 22 December 1917 in which he said that 'a poet should have a spirit above wars' (Owen and Bell 1967: 596). The poem was probably written before Graves' letter, but Stallworthy comments that 'Graves may have said much the same to WO earlier' (CPF 1.125). However, Norgate argues compellingly that Owen is responding to a series of articles by Horatio Bottomley, in which Bottomley claimed to have seen 'the hand of God' in the conditions at the trenches (2022).

(c) Reception commentary

This is one of two poems to which Owen gave Latin titles, the other being 'Dulce et Decorum Est'. Owen's motivation for choosing a Latin title (which references Cardinal Newman's defence of his religious opinions in *Apologia pro vita sua* [1864]) may have been to give his poem an air of authority or to underline the seriousness of the poetic credo he expressed in it, a seriousness further emphasized by the metalepsis that structures the poem. Whatever his reasons, the history of the poem's title encapsulates many of Owen's difficulties with Latin composition. A draft (CPF 2.278) shows the working title 'Apologia lectorem pro Poema Disconsolatia Mea', which cannot be construed grammatically. Clearly, Owen meant 'Apology/ Defence to the reader for my disconsolate poem' (or perhaps 'poetry'; Hibberd 2002: 293), but he uses the accusative *lectorem* instead of the dative *lectori* and the (unattested) noun *disconsolatia* instead of the adjective *disconsolata*. The fair copy in the British Library has the shorter title 'Apologia pro Poema Mea', which takes *poema* as a first-declension feminine noun, a reasonable assumption if Owen did not have a Latin dictionary at hand. In fact *poema* is a Greek loan-word, third declension, and neuter. Stallworthy notes that Sassoon 'corrected the faulty Latin grammar of WO's own title', presumably for the poem's publication in the 1920 edition (CPF 1.125).

The poem engages with classics in several ways beyond its Latin title. The second, third, and fourth stanzas recall a Homeric *aristeia*. Owen touches on the experience of the *aristeia* in an October 1918 letter to his mother, describing the action for which he won his Military Cross, where he says, 'I lost my earthly faculties and fought like an angel' (Potter 2023: 397), and he memorably represents an *aristeia* in the closing lines of 'Spring Offensive' (discussed above).

The sixth stanza's reference to 'the bandage of the arm that drips' (l. 23) suggests that Owen might have seen a reproduction of the famous Sosias cup of Achilles' bandaging Patroclus' arm (acquired by the Staatliches Museum, Berlin, in 1831). Given his interest in art, Owen could easily have come across this image. In any case, the strong homoerotic nature of several of his poems and the progression in this poem from the focus on 'happy lovers in old song' to the deeper bond of war comrades strongly evoke this image and its eroticized treatment of Patroclus in the mind of the reader.

The eighth stanza involves a glancing reference to the path of Helios' chariot across the sky: 'and heaven but as the highway for a shell' (32). With this evocation of the hanging motif of the sky as a pathway, Owen starkly underlines the way the war has emptied out the meaning of nature for the soldiers and has left them with only the mechanistic accoutrements of the war (flares, shells) as markers of their reality.

The last two stanzas form a kind of anti-*katabasis*. Rather than returning to tell what he knows of 'the sorrowful dark of hell', this narrator presents himself as still present in that hell, 'sharing' it with the soldiers, and he directly refuses to report to those outside what his companions in hell say or think.

Two working manuscripts for 'Apologia' have versions of the final stanza that include the lines 'Only to gods and men grown sick of earth / Hilarious sound the thunders of this storm' (available on FWWPDA).[72] Norgate argues that this draft represents Owen's latest work on the poem; if he is correct, then this version of the final stanza is important for our interpretation of the entire poem (2023). The 'gods' here recall the

---

[72] This manuscript is cited at CPF 2.278 but not reproduced there. CPF does reproduce a variant of this same stanza, 2.281.

fundamentally detached gods of the *Iliad*, who observe the battle but are only infrequently deeply moved by it. A letter from Owen to his younger brother Colin (23 August 1916) reflects a similar collocation of gods and men who are in some way detached from the battle. Owen writes, 'your tender age is a thing to be valued and gloried in.... [I]t puts you among the Elders and the gods, high witnesses of the general slaughter' (Potter 2023: 225). Owen's reference to 'the Elders' glances at the Trojan elders in *Iliad* 3, old men beyond the age of battle ('grown sick of earth'?) who look down from the walls of Troy to the battlefield. Owen apparently assumes the 16-year-old Colin will understand the reference.[73] In Homer, of course, the Trojan elders are themselves war veterans who understand the battle they are witnessing; Owen's refiguring of the scene seems to imply that both the old and the young are incapable of grasping the nature of this war. By classifying a boy too young to fight with elders too old to do so, and attributing a 'god'-like (that is, detached) attitude towards the general slaughter to both, Owen emphasizes the distance between the soldiers and all non-combatants. This version reorients the poem from a direct attack against one individual to a broader statement of the gap in understanding that divides soldiers and civilians.

(d) Associated works

The poem's intratextual connection with 'Dulce et Decorum Est' is under-scored by the shift from the first-person metalepsis to an accusatory 'you' in the final two stanzas of 'Apologia', paralleling the shift in 'Dulce'. The difference in purpose between the two second-person addresses is striking; the speaker in 'Dulce' tries to bring the soldiers' experiences vividly before the eyes of the civilian reader, but the speaker of 'Apologia' rejects the reader as unworthy of any such attempt. The speaker's refusal to describe what he and his companions undergo in the 'sorrowful dark of hell' connects 'Apologia' to 'Spring Offensive' as well, where this refusal to report is modified into the unanswered question of why 'the few who rushed in the body to enter hell ... speak not' about their dead comrades. The draft version of the final stanza, foregrounding a detachment that can find the 'thunders' of battle 'hilarious', recalls the detachment described in 'Insensibility', both of the unschooled boy and of soldiers who have grown numb to emotion.

---

[73] I owe this observation about Colin to Paul Norgate (personal communication, 24 August 2021).

'A New Heaven (To —— on Active Service)' (1916)
(a) **Text of poem** [CPF 72, 1.82]

> Seeing we never found gay fairyland
>> (Though still we crouched by bluebells moon by moon)
> And missed the tide of Lethe; yet are soon
>> For that new bridge that leaves old Styx half-spanned;
> Nor ever unto Mecca caravanned;   5
>> Nor bugled Asgard, skilled in magic rune;
> Nor yearned for far Nirvana, the sweet swoon,
>> And from high Paradise are cursed and banned;
>
> — Let's die home, ferry across the Channel! Thus
>> Shall we live gods there. Death shall be no sev'rance.   10
> Weary cathedrals light new shrines for us.
>> To us, rough knees of boys shall ache with rev'rence.
> Are not girls' breasts a clear, strong Acropole?
> — There our own mothers' tears shall heal us whole.

(b) Poem—date, form, and content

This is one of Owen's earliest war poems. One manuscript of the poem is dated September 1916, at which time Owen was in camp in England with the 5th Manchesters (CPF 1.82). The addressee of the sonnet remains unidentified. C. Day Lewis prints a different version, under the title 'To a Comrade in Flanders' (1963: 143); there are three fair copies with variant readings preserved.

This is a Shakespearean sonnet with the rhyme scheme ABBAABBA CDCDEE. Day Lewis says judiciously that this poem 'shows Owen at his most romantic in the octave, but moving towards his mature style in the sestet' (1963: 143).

(c) Reception commentary

One manuscript has the variant subtitle 'To a Comrade in ~~Athens~~ Flanders' (CPF 2.223), which implies that at one point Owen considered linking the poem more closely with the imagined classical world than with the current war. The title is a quotation from Revelation 21:1–4, marked as a quotation by the inverted commas. This sets the keynote of the sonnet, which ranges through a variety of beliefs about the afterlife.

The poem's connection to classics appears first in the references to two rivers of the Underworld, Lethe and Styx. Lethe is the river of forgetfulness;

according to Vergil, souls would drink from Lethe before being reincarnated and so would lose all memory of their former lives (*Aen.* 6.748–51). Styx forms the boundary of the Underworld, and to cross the Styx means to leave the land of the living entirely. Furthermore, the dead whose bodies are unburied cannot cross the Styx. This is exemplified by Elpenor in *Odyssey* 8 and Palinurus in *Aeneid* 6. In both instances, the soul of the unburied dead man implores his living companion to bury him so that he can make the transition to the Underworld.

In this sonnet's octave, Owen surveys a range of no-longer-credible legends about the afterlife, finding them all inadequate or at least inapplicable to his and his comrade's current circumstances. He moves from 'fairyland' through Greek and Norse mythology, interweaving references to Islam (Mecca), Buddhism (Nirvana), and Christianity (Paradise). In the case of the final example, he comments that he and his comrade are 'cursed and banned' from Paradise. This echo of Adam and Eve's expulsion from Eden perhaps gestures towards the status of Christianity as a faith he had held and abandoned rather than one amongst a list that was never truly an option for him or a matter of 'low intensity belief' (see Introduction pp. 19–20). The sonnet's title reframes Owen's lost Christian belief ironically; the New Heaven that Revelation says 'shall be' is transmuted, in Owen's sonnet, into purely human reactions to the soldiers' deaths.

In this list of unavailable beliefs about the afterlife, Lethe and Styx are notable for being listed first, and also perhaps for their underlying metaphorical significance in Owen's personal system of imagery. 'Missed the tide of Lethe' is an odd description of the psychological or spiritual state of two young men, but apparently implies that the speaker and the addressee were unable to forget something that they wanted to forget or ignore— their duty to enlist, perhaps, given Owen's hesitation to do so throughout the first year and a half of the war. The statement that they 'are soon / For that new bridge that leaves old Styx half-spanned' is one that Owen tried out in the MSS, rejected, and then resumed. The rough draft (CPF 2.224) shows the variant:

For ~~that new bridge that makes old Styx half spanned;~~

the

ships to Avilon ~~by which shall to grey spirits~~ manned;

the spirits

The variant 'For ships to Avalon the spirits manned' would introduce Arthurian legend into the poem. In the fair copy Stallworthy takes as the latest version, however, Owen has reinserted the image of Styx and the rather surprising idea of a 'new' bridge that 'half-spans' that river. The underlying idea seems to be of dead who cannot actually cross Styx, and so remain 'half' over that river and half not. This would correspond to the unburied dead who cannot enter the Underworld, and it seems likely that Owen here is gesturing at the horrifically high number of unburiable dead, both those whose deaths are known but whose bodies cannot be recovered and those who are 'missing—presumed dead'. In classical terms, those souls would not be able to cross the Styx, and Owen's vision of young (living) men who will 'soon' be on a bridge between life and death that leaves them halfway over the Styx is powerful, although not fully developed.

Reading 'old Styx half-spanned' as a reference to the unburied and unburiable dead clarifies the turn in the sestet to the idea of a ghostly, or spiritual, return to England. 'Ferry across the Channel' reiterates the connection with Styx, since the souls of the (buried) dead are ferried across that river by Charon. The progression of thought here is 'since the loss of our bodies will mean that we cannot be ferried across Styx, let's imagine our souls being ferried across the Channel instead.' The next statement 'Thus / Shall we live gods there' gestures to the role of the Styx as guarantor for an unbreakable oath for the Olympian gods, though (apart from the reference to the Acropolis in the penultimate line) Owen does not develop the idea of any connection with the Olympians.

(d) Associated works

Stallworthy calls lines 11–14 'an anticipation of…"Anthem for Doomed Youth"' (CPF 1.82). Day Lewis prints a different version, where the first line of the sestet begins 'Let's die back to the hearths we died for' (1963: 143), a reading that clearly anticipates the sixth stanza of 'Exposure' (discussed above). The mention of Styx also connects this poem with the final stanza of 'Insensibility', which alludes to Vergil's depiction of the dead on the banks of Styx (see above). The idea of ghosts or spirits returning home when the bodies of the dead are left elsewhere becomes a trope in First World War poetry.[74]

---

[74] See Introduction p. 15 on problematic *nostos* as part of the poetry of unease, and Vandiver 2010: 322–8.

'[An Imperial Elegy]' (1915 or 1916)
(a) **Text of poem** [CPF 69, 2.453]

And Not one corner of a foreign field

~~but a~~ But a span as wide as Europe

Deep as ~~the~~ grave

I looked and saw   titan's

~~dig delved~~

An appearance of a⟨ grave

And the length thereof a thousand miles

~~This is the path of glor~~

It crossed all Europe like a mystic road

Or as the Spirits Pathway lieth on the night

And I heard a voice crying

This is the Path of Glory

(b) Poem—date, form, and content

Stallworthy dates this fragment as 'sometime between September 1915 and the early summer of 1916' (CPF 2.454). The text reproduced here, which is preceded by several disjointed words and phrases, seems to represent a self-contained stanza, perhaps imagined as part of a longer poem that Owen never completed.

For so short a text, the lines contain a remarkable number of recognizable allusions and intertextual references. As so often in Owen's work, the biblical resonances are obvious in the archaic language and the direct echo of Isaiah 40:3 ('the voice of him that crieth in the wilderness') in 'I heard a voice crying'. There are also semi-quotations from Brooke's 'The Soldier' ('some corner of a foreign field', discussed above) and Gray's 'Elegy' ('the paths of glory lead but to the grave').

(c) Reception commentary

The poem's primary use of classics occurs in the striking image of 'a titan's grave', a thousand miles long, crossing Europe. As a nightmarish image of the Western Front, this is powerful. It also imparts a resonance and depth that lift the description out of the desolation of the immediate present. As Hibberd has said, Owen's 'allusions to the Titans, the very first war-makers, and to Isaiah illustrate the mythical, prophetic dimension he is reaching for'; Hibberd further comments that 'as in "Strange Meeting" later, he has in mind some titanic conflict that is and is not the Great War' (2002: 180; see also Vandiver 1999: 448–9).[75] Owen achieves a similar effect in the final line of 'The Old Man and the Young', a retelling of the biblical story of the binding of Isaac (the Akedah), when the Old Man rejects the 'ram of pride' and instead kills his son 'and half the seed of Europe, one by one'—a phrase that recalls the titan's grave that 'crossed all Europe'.

(d) Associated works

The reference to 'a titan's grave' links this poem to 'Strange Meeting' and 'The End', since these are the only instances of 'titan' or 'titanic' in Owen's work. Das calls the 'titan's grave' here 'an early attempt at the vision of the tunnel' in 'Strange Meeting' (1977: 49). The aerial view of the Western Front is reminiscent of the viewpoint in 'The Show'.

3.3 Myths retold

In two long poems, 'The Wrestlers' and 'Perseus', Owen set out to retell episodes of classical myth. 'The Wrestlers' survives in fairly complete form, while 'Perseus' exists only in fragments. The subject of 'The Wrestlers' (Heracles' battle with Antaeus) was chosen by Owen's therapist, Dr Brock. The 'Perseus' poem, in contrast, was a long-standing project which Owen planned for several years. Perseus is not the protagonist of any extant classical text, although his deeds are narrated in Ovid's *Metamorphoses* 4 and 5. It is perhaps telling that Owen chose not to put himself in direct competition with canonical epic by attempting to write a long narrative on Achilles, for instance, but chose Perseus instead. In this he was following his idol Keats, whose 'Endymion' and 'Hyperion' also drew upon Greek myth but featured characters who were not the protagonists of any extant classical poems.[76]

---

[75] These comments are a marked revision of Hibberd's earlier view of the reference to a 'titan's grave', which he had called 'absurd' and 'irrelevant' (1979: 33).

[76] I am grateful to the anonymous OUP reader for pointing out another likely influence on Owen's choice of hero here: Perseus' story was frequently featured in children's books, and was the first myth recounted in Kingsley's *The Heroes*, which Owen owned.

'The Wrestlers' (1917–18)
(a) **Text of poem** [CPF 138, 2.520–4; text given here as restored in Stallworthy 1986: 184–6]

So neck to neck and obstinate knee to knee
Wrestled those two; and peerless Heracles
Could not prevail nor catch at any vantage;
But those huge hands which small had strangled snakes
Let slip the writhing of Antaeas' wrists;   5
Those clubs of hands that wrenched the necks of bulls
Now fumbled round the slim Antaeas' limbs
Baffled. Then anger swelled in Heracles,
And terribly he grappled broader arms,
And yet more firmly fixed his grasping feet,   10
And up his back the muscles bulged and shone
Like climbing banks and domes of towering cloud.
Many who watched that wrestling say he laughed, —
But not so loud as on Eurystheus of old,
But that his pantings, seldom loosed, long pent,   15
Were like the sighs of lions at their meat.
Men say their fettered fury tightened hour by hour,
Until the veins rose tubrous in their brows
And froth flew thickly-shivered from both beards.
As pythons shudder, bridling-in their spite,   20
So trembled that Antaeas with held strength,
While Heracles, —the thews and cordage of his thighs
Straitened and strained beyond the utmost stretch
From quivering heel to haunch like sweating hawsers —
But only staggered backward. Then his throat   25
Growled, like a great beast when his meat is touched,
As if he smelt some guile behind Antaeas,
And knew the buttressed bulking of his shoulders
Bore not the mass to move it one thumb's length.
But what it was so helped the man none guessed,   30
Save Hylas, whom the fauns had once made wise
How earth herself empowered him by her touch,
Gave him the grip and stringency of winter,
And all the ardour of the invincible spring;
How all the blood of June glutted his heart;   35

And the wild glow of huge autumnal storms
Stirred on his face, and flickered from his eyes;
How, too, Poseidon blessed him fatherly
With wafts of vigour from the keen sea waves,
And with the subtle coil of currents —   40
Strange underflows, that maddened Heracles.
And towards the night they sundered, neither thrown.
Whereat came Hylas running to his friend
With fans, and sponges in a laving-bowl,
And brimmed his lord the beakerful he loved,   45
Which Heracles took roughly, even from him.
Then spake that other from the place he stood:
'O Heracles, I know thy fights and labours,
What man thou wert, and what thou art become,
The lord of strength, queller of perilous monsters,   50
Hero of heroes, worthy immortal worship,
But me thou canst not quell. For I, I come
Of Earth, and to my father Poseidon,
Whose strength ye know, and whose displeasure ye know.
Therefore be wise, and try me not again,   55
But say thou findst me peer, and more than peer.'
But Heracles, of utter weariness,
Was loath to answer, either yea or nay.
And a cruel murmur rankled through the crowd.
Now he whose knees propped up the head of him,   60
Over his lord's ear swiftly whispered thus:
'If thou could'st lift the man in air — enough.
His feet suck secret virtue of the earth.
Lift him, and buckle him to thy breast, and win.'
Up sprang the son of Perseus deeply laughing   65
And ere the crimson of his last long clutch
Had faded from that insolent's throat, again
They closed. Then he, the Argonaut,
Remembering how he tore the oaks in Argos,
Bound both his arms about the other's loins   70
And with a sudden tugging, easily
Rooted him up; and crushed his inmost bones.
Forth to the town he strode, and through the streets,
Bearing the body light as leopard-skins,

And glorious ran the shouting as he strode —   75
Some say his footfalls made an earthquake there
So that he dropped Antaeas: some say not:
But that he cast him down by Gea's altar
And Gea sent that earthquake for her son,
To rouse him out of death. And lo! he rose,   80
Alive, and came to Heracles
Who feasted with the people and their King.
And fain would all make place for him
But he would not consent. And Heracles,
Knowing the hate of Hylas for his deeds,   85
Feasted and slept; and so forgot the man,
And early on the morrow passed with Hylas
Down to the Argo, for the wind was fair.

(b) Poem—date, form, and content

Owen drafted this poem in July 1917, at the suggestion of his therapist Dr Brock, and revised it in early 1918, after he had left Craiglockhart. He wrote his mother in December 1917 that he had visited Edinburgh and seen Brock, 'whose first word was "Antaeas!" [*sic*] which they want immediately for the next Mag!' (Potter 2023: 344).[77] 'The Mag' refers to *The Hydra*. In the January 1918 issue Dr Brock, writing under the pseudonym Acturus, published an article about the Antaeus myth. In an endnote to this article, the current editor (George Henry Bonner) mentioned Owen's blank-verse treatment of the Antaeus myth and said he 'hope[d] to print' the poem in the next issue of *The Hydra*. No copy of the February 1918 issue was known until 2014; when a copy came to light, it showed that Owen's poem on Antaeus did not appear in that issue, nor in the March 1918 issue.[78] There is still no known extant copy of the April 1918 issue so it is possible that a version of 'The Wrestlers' was published there, but as Stallworthy

---

[77] Owen usually misspells Antaeus' name as 'Antaeas', but one draft manuscript (OEF 303–7) has the working title ANTAEVS (VERSUS HERACLES). This is crossed out and 'The Wrestlers' is substituted. Owen uses the correct spelling throughout this draft. The various manuscripts are available on FWWPDA.

[78] For an account of how John Garth came to find the February and March 1918 issues of *The Hydra*, see Garth 2014. These issues are now in the George Henry Bonner Papers, Magdalen College Archives, Oxford (https://archive-cat.magd.ox.ac.uk/records/P429). Garth has now revised his previous attribution of the January 1918 article 'Antaeus, or Back to the Earth' to Owen himself, rather than to Brock (personal communication, John Garth to Elizabeth Vandiver, 2 May 2021).

already noted, 'there is no evidence that the poem was ever finished and it seems unlikely to have been published in part during WO's lifetime' (CPF 2.524).

Brock's consulting room at Craiglockhart displayed an engraving of Heracles and Antaeus wrestling (Hibberd 2002: 254), and he saw the myth as a paradigm for shell-shocked soldiers. He summarized the myth in his *Hydra* article:

Antaeus was a young Libyan giant, whose parents were Gaia and Poseidon, Earth and Sea. In a wrestling combat he could not be over-thrown so long as his feet were on his Mother Earth. When he was raised off the earth his strength rapidly failed, only to be renewed again at the first contact with the soil. Finally Hercules, seeing this, lifted him bodily up in the air, and holding him there, crushed him to death in his arms. ([Brock] 1918: 3)[79]

Brock suggested that the soldiers he was treating would regain strength if, like Antaeus, they could renew their contact with the earth; in his interpretation, this meant finding useful and satisfying work:

Now surely every officer who comes to Craiglockhart recognises that, in a way, he is himself Antaeus who has been taken from his Mother Earth and well-nigh crushed to death by the war giant or military machine....

Antaeus typifies the occupation cure at Craiglockhart. His story is the justification of our activities....

We are all, to a large extent, creatures of our environment—that is, we are all offspring of earth.... And so our activities, in order to be healthy, must both bring us as far as possible back to natural conditions, and also have some relation to our surroundings ([Brock] 1918: 3).

Brock began treating Owen on 27 June 1917. As part of Owen's 'ergother-apy', Brock appointed him editor of *The Hydra* and also gave him the task of writing a poem on the Antaeus theme (Hibberd 2002: 253–7). Owen set to work on the poem quickly. In a letter of 17 July 1917 to his mother he says

[79] Somewhat surprisingly, the detail that Antaeus' strength depended on contact with the earth is not attested before Ovid, who alludes to it in *Met.* 9.183–4; it is fully recounted by Lucan 4.593–653 (Gantz 1993: 417). Brock quotes Lucan 4.593–5 as the epigraph to his article. His summary of Antaeus' story was probably taken from a reference book, perhaps one of the same 'dictionaries' that Owen refers to in a letter to his mother (see below).

that he has done 'about 50 lines' and quotes the first fourteen lines, and in an undated July letter to his cousin Leslie Gunston, he quoted six lines (32–7 in the text given above) with the comment 'Last week I wrote (to order) a strong bit of Blank: on <u>Antaeus v. Heracles</u>. These are the best lines, methinks' (Potter 2023: 299, 300; emphasis original). The versions in both these letters differ only in minor details from the text printed here. Apart from these two sources, there survive eleven manuscript pages that Stallworthy calls 'preliminary', four pages of a partially revised version, and two pages of an 'incomplete fair copy' (CPF 2.525). The text reproduced above is Stallworthy's reconstruction of the poem based on these sources. In fact, the poem's text is no more uncertain than that of many others that Stallworthy classifies as poems, not fragments.

The reconstructed version consists of eighty-eight lines of blank verse. The metre is fairly regular overall, preferring ten-syllable lines but including several eleven-syllable lines with feminine endings. Some lines have extra syllables (e.g. ll. 17 and 22, both twelve syllables) or are short (ll. 68 and 81, both eight syllables), and in some the rhythm is very awkward (e.g. l. 53). Presumably further revision would have modified these lines. There is frequent use of alliteration within single lines (e.g. l. 4, 'huge <u>h</u>ands which <u>s</u>mall had <u>s</u>trangled <u>s</u>nakes'; l. 10, 'firmly <u>f</u>ixed his grasping <u>f</u>eet') and several instances of internal pararhyme (e.g. 'pantings…pent', l. 15; 'thews…thighs', l. 22; 'suck secret', l. 63) and some sound effects that, while not actually pararhyme, are very close to it ('writhing…wrists', l. 5; 'straitened and strained…stretch', l. 23; 'strode'…'streets', l. 74).

The poem is Owen's only sustained retelling of an episode from classical myth, although it is possible that his planned long poem 'Perseus' (discussed below) would have contained similar narrative sections. 'The Wrestlers' describes the fight between Heracles and Antaeus, opening emphatically *in medias res* with the two already wrestling. Stallworthy comments that 'The violent verbs from which the poem derives much of its power are a clear legacy of the battlefield' (2013: 197). The poem details Heracles' fruitless efforts to subdue his opponent and his growing anger and weariness, and recounts that only Heracles' young companion Hylas knew the secret of Antaeus' strength and was able to tell Heracles that if he could lift Antaeus off the earth, he would be able to kill him. So far Owen follows the classical version, as recounted by Dr Brock, fairly closely. At the end of the poem, however, he adds the surprising detail that Antaeus was resurrected from the dead by Gea (Earth), his mother.

Owen may have invented this detail as an attempt to fit the myth more closely to the symbolic use Dr Brock wanted for it. An obvious objection to Brock's use of this myth as a paradigm for the treatment of shell shock is that Heracles kills Antaeus; the supposed resurrection of Antaeus would help alleviate this difficulty (Vandiver 2010: 127). But Owen says little about Antaeus after stating that he came back to life, and the poem, as it stands, is oddly anticlimactic. Clearly, Owen's focus throughout is on Heracles, not Antaeus, which makes the poem less than successful in illustrating Brock's idea that identifying with Antaeus could benefit shell-shocked patients.

(c) Reception commentary

The fact that his therapist chose the topic of 'The Wrestlers' for him meant that Owen had to familiarize himself with the details of the myth. The Heracles-Antaeus myth is not told at length by any extant classical poet, but is only referred to in passing (e.g. an allusion to Antaeus by Pindar *Isthm.* 4.52ff.).[80] In a letter of early July 1917, Owen wrote his mother 'On The Hercules-Antaeas Subject—there are only 3 or 4 lines in the Dictionaries. So I shall just do a Sonnet' (Potter 2023: 297). It is not clear which mythological dictionaries he had available to him at Craiglockhart, but the standard dictionaries of Lemprière and Smith include short entries on Antaeus, which give summaries very similar to Brock's for *The Hydra*. There was a library or reading room at Craiglockhart (Hibberd 2002: 252), which may have contained copies of these or other mythological dictionaries.[81]

Owen's decision to focus his poem more on Heracles than on Antaeus himself may have grown from his use of other sources beyond the dictionaries. Owen's portrayal of the wrestling draws on Vergil's description of Heracles and Cacus (*Aen.* 8.219ff.), and 'The Wrestlers' also includes several verbal echoes of Lang's translation of Theocritus' Idylls 24 and 25 (Vandiver 2010: 125–7). More tellingly still for Owen's debt to Theocritus, Hylas assumes a prominence that is not supported by most classical texts. Hylas is a very marginal figure in Heracles' overall myth and is usually associated

---

[80] In *Inferno* Canto 31, Antaeus is the giant who lifts Dante and Vergil in his arms and lowers them to the bottommost circle of Hell; his hands are described as those 'of which Hercules felt the great grasp' (l.132).

[81] It is possible that Owen's family sent him some of his own books, but his letters make no mention of this.

with Heracles only during the voyage of the Argo.[82] In Apollonius'
Argonautica he is mentioned briefly as one of the Argonauts, but the text
foregrounds him only in the story of his abduction by nymphs, which
motivates Heracles' absence for most of the Argo's voyage (since the Argo
sailed and left Heracles behind as Heracles searched for Hylas). He is
not normally associated with any of Heracles' canonical Labours or other
adventures, and has no connection at all to the Antaeus episode.[83] But
Theocritus' Idyll 13, while it describes Hylas' abduction by nymphs during
the voyage of the Argo, implies that Hylas was much more than merely
Heracles' squire for that voyage. The Idyll begins by presenting Hylas as
Heracles' beloved; it opens (in Lang's translation) 'Not for us only, Nicias,
as we were used to deem was Love begotten.... Nay, but the son of
Amphitryon, that heart of bronze, who abode the wild lion's onset, loved a
lad, beautiful Hylas—Hylas of the braided locks' (Lang 1889: 67). A few lines
later, the Idyll says that Heracles and Hylas were constant companions;
'never was he apart from Hylas' (67). A reader who was unfamiliar with
other ancient sources of Heracles' myth could easily presume that Hylas
(rather than Heracles' nephew Iolaus) accompanied Heracles through all his
Labours and adventures and that the homoerotic aspect of their relationship
was central to Heracles' myth, and this seems to be what Owen does in fact
assume. He preserves the connection with the voyage of the Argo at the end
of the poem, but he interpolates Hylas into the Antaeus myth and locates
Heracles' encounter with Antaeus immediately before the Argonauts' sailing
or perhaps even on shore during one of the Argo's stops, so that at the
poem's end Heracles and Hylas go 'Down to the Argo'.

The chronological relationship of 'The Wrestlers' manuscripts to Lang's
Theocritus translation is complicated.[84] Owen includes *Theocritus, Bion,
and Moschus* on a list of 'Books read at Scarborough Dec. 1917' and his
own copy of Lang's text is inscribed 'W. E. S. Owen / Scarborough / Dec:
1917'. But Hylas appears already in the earliest manuscripts of 'The
Wrestlers', which Stallworthy dates to July 1917, soon after Owen's arrival
at Craiglockhart. Furthermore, Hibberd 1986 and Reed 2006 both take
Bion's 'Lament for Adonis' as a source for 'Disabled', which was drafted in

---

[82] Owen's statement that 'the fauns' had made Hylas wise is curious. There seems to be no
classical source for a connection between Hylas and fauns. In fact, here as elsewhere Owen
actually wrote 'fawns', and Stallworthy assumes that he meant 'fauns'; but it seems just possible
that Owen was conflating Hylas with Heracles' son Telephus, who was suckled by a deer.

[83] For the variability in the 'canon' of Heracles' labours, see Stafford 2011: 24–30.

[84] Vandiver 2010 fails to take full account of the earlier manuscripts (125).

the summer of 1917 (see below). It seems clear, then, that Owen must have had access to a copy of Lang's text before he bought his own in Scarborough. Hibberd recognizes this point in his discussion of 'Disabled' and says that Owen 'might have glanced at [the Lang translation] before' buying his own copy (1986: 113). We can only speculate about where Owen might have seen a copy of Lang's translation; perhaps there was one in the Craiglockhart library, or perhaps Brock owned a copy and lent it to Owen.[85]

Stallworthy follows OEF 310V for the end of the poem (CPF 2.523). That manuscript has the words 'the hate of H for his deeds' for line 85. Stallworthy fills this 'H' out to 'Hylas', as he does the next one (in l. 87). But in another fragment, the phrase is clearly written as 'the hate of Hera for his deeds' (OEF 309; not reproduced in CPF, but available on FWWPDA), and Hylas is written out in full in line 87, where OEF 310V has only 'H'. There is no manuscript support for reading the 'H' of line 85 as Hylas rather than Hera. Najarian makes a great deal of 'the hate of Hylas for his deeds', reading it as evidence that 'for Owen, erotic bonds between men prevent recurring violence' (2002: 165; followed by Vandiver 2010: 128). But if we restore line 85 as 'knowing the hate of Hera for his deeds', then Heracles' motive for 'forgetting' Antaeus is one of self-preservation, to avoid Hera's wrath, rather than a demonstration of the soothing power of love. This reading is supported by a variant on the same manuscript OEF 309, where Heracles casts Antaeus down by Hera's altar, not Gea's, and a tentative reading seems to show that Owen considered attributing Antaeus' resurrection to Hera as well. Reading line 85 as 'knowing the hate of Hera for his deeds' also fits well with the canonical versions of Heracles' myth, in which most of his sufferings are caused by Hera's implacable hatred. There is no way to know how Owen might later have revised line 85, but given the manuscript evidence, it is wise to be cautious in giving too much weight to line 85 as an expression of Owen's beliefs about the calming power of same-sex love.

The Vergilian echoes of Heracles' wrestling match with Cacus appear in line 8, 'then anger swelled in Heracles', which recalls Vergil's 'then Heracles' resentment blazed up with rage and black bile' (*hic vero Alcidae furiis exarserat atro / felle dolor*, *Aen.* 8.219–20) and in line 64, where Hylas'

---

[85] Brock was a dedicated Hellenist and had published a translation of Galen, so the idea that he might have owned a copy of Lang's translation is plausible.

advice that Heracles 'lift him, and buckle him to thy breast' recalls Vergil's 'he grips him embraced in a knot' (*corripit in nodum complexus*, 8.260). The poem also shows clear debts to Homer. 'Neck to neck' and 'knee to knee' in the first line reproduce the Homeric figure called 'battle polyptoton', as seen for instance in *Iliad* 13.130–1: 'spear on spear, shield on close-pressed shield; buckler presses on buckler, helmet on helmet, man on man'. In the second line, the use of the epithet 'peerless' to describe Heracles recalls Homeric epithets such as *amumōn*. The overall tone of the opening two lines is thus deeply Homeric. The Homeric resonances are particularly marked in the poem's use of similes, and especially animal similes, to describe Heracles and Antaeus. The first twenty-five lines of the poem include four similes. Three concern Heracles: 'up his back the muscles bulged and shone / Like climbing banks and domes of towering cloud' (11–12); 'his pantings … / Were like the sighs of lions at their meat' (15–16); 'his throat / Growled, like a great beast when his meat is touched' (25–6). One refers to Antaeus: 'As pythons shudder, bridling-in their spite, / So trembled that Antaeas with held strength' (20–1). Later, a short simile describes Antaeus' body as 'light as leopard-skins' (74). This technique of comparing a hero to a wild animal, and especially to a lion, is one of the most characteristic aspects of Homeric epic (e.g. *Iliad* 3.23–8, 5.136–43, 10.485–8). One further Homeric touch is Owen's use of 'the son of Perseus' to refer to Heracles (l. 65); Heracles was, of course, the son of Zeus, but he was also Perseus' great-grandson, since Heracles' mother Alcmene was a granddaughter of Perseus. This use of a patronymic to refer to a male ancestor other than the father recalls Homer's use of Aeacides, 'son of Aeacus', to refer to Achilles (who was Aeacus' grandson).

(d) Associated works

Owen's description of Heracles' heavily muscled back may draw on the copy of the Farnese Heracles that stood in The Quarry, a park in Shrewsbury; the middle-aged Heracles' exaggerated musculature is especially noticeable on this statue's back. This statue features in 'Roundel' (discussed below).

Owen repeats the phrase 'the invincible spring' (34) in 'Exposure', l. 33: 'for God's invincible spring our love is made afraid'; see discussion above.

'[Perseus]'

(a) **Text of poem** [CPF 82, 2.464–71]

The inchoate long poem 'Perseus' occupies a unique position amongst Owen's writings; Hibberd calls it 'the most ambitious and irrecoverable of all Owen's poetic endeavours' (1986: 122).[86] Owen appears to have intended a major narrative poem on the Perseus myth and to have worked on it at various times from 1915 onward. Yet not even a skeleton of this crucial poem can be extracted in any coherent or accessible form from the manuscripts that remain, and it is not even entirely clear which of Owen's most fragmentary manuscripts are connected with 'Perseus'. Nevertheless, it is evident that in Owen's mind his 'Perseus' poem was of great importance for his poetic practice, so much so that Hibberd says 'through all this chaotic material Owen seems to be feeling his way towards a myth of his own life and identity, giving it shape in a pattern that is strangely close to that of his war poetry, so that the "Perseus" manuscripts . . . are a key to his eventual achievement' (1986: 43).

(b) Poem: date, form, and content

Stallworthy groups several fragments together under the heading 'Perseus', each of which contains the name 'Perseus' or 'Danae' in the text or has a marginal notation such as 'For Perseus' or 'Danae speaks'. Hibberd argues that two other fragments, CPF 59 ('About the winter forest loomed') and 60 ('The sun, far fallen') should also be considered as work for 'Perseus'; he bases this on the shared vocabulary and imagery of those fragments and the other 'Perseus' work. It is possible to trace several themes (Perseus' conception; his encounter with Medusa; his rescue of Andromeda) in the manuscripts, as well as, surprisingly, references to Persephone and an apparent descent to the Underworld. As Hibberd notes, in attributing a *katabasis* to Perseus Owen would be taking 'as many liberties with classical myth as Keats had done in writing about Endymion or Hyperion'—poems that were very likely models for Owen's work (1986: 46).

(c) Reception commentary

It is difficult to envisage what shape Owen would eventually have given this very fragmentary material. He does not seem to have intended merely a straightforward retelling of the myth, of the sort he did in 'The Wrestlers', although he may have planned some sort of introductory section summarizing Perseus' story; OEF 216 begins with several partial lines describing a man seizing a woman, identify this as 'Danae's . . . love', and say 'Of all this sprang the infant Perseus. / Fair from the moment of his birth' (CPF 2.464). A longer fragment, using imagery of fire and burning that might seem more appropriate to the myth of Semele than of Danae, is written in the first person and labelled 'Danae speaks' in the margin

---

[86] Hibberd's discussion of the Perseus fragments remains definitive (1986: 42–54).

(CPF 2.465–6). A third fragment (CPF 2.467–8) is also in the first person. It has the marginal annotation 'For Perseus' and begins:

> ~~What have I done, O God, what have I done?~~
>
> --
>   was
> One night I knew the thing ~~would~~ come at last
> I heard the heart of Eros[87] and his wings
>   ~~self-fanned with flames~~
> ~~Pant like a~~ furnaces ~~winnowed   by   great fans~~
>   Murmur

This too might seem to be in Danae's voice, but Owen complicates the reading by writing in the variants 'her' and 'him' for the speaker's 'love'. The lines seem to focus on a great sense of guilt:

>   ~~have~~ drop
> Let not the sun ~~be~~ sweetness on me more
> Nor let the moon be comforting by night
> Nor the clean sea have ~~washing~~ for my ~~woes.~~ scars

At this point, the words 'but cool Persephone' appear in the margin, and the speaker comments:

> To my great friends I said 'Unhand ~~me~~
> For I has [*sic*] touched the godess [*sic*], ~~and~~ touch me not.'

Persephone's name appears again in the margin several lines later. Interpretation is obviously very difficult here, but perhaps these words should be read as Danae's acceptance of her sexual relationship with Zeus. The clear echo of the resurrected Jesus' words to Mary Magdalen ('touch me not', John 20: 17) is striking, but puzzling in this context.

The overwhelming sense of sexual guilt and the ambiguity of gender represented by alternate pronouns continues in another first-person speech, where the speaker apparently rejects his/her lover, then finds him/herself in hell and confronted by both a 'haggled crone…Age herself' and Pluto,

---

[87] Owen wrote an upper-case 'E' just above the line and a lower case 'e' just under it, giving the dual reading 'Eros/eros'.

'reining [*sic*] in hell, being the most unhappy' (CPF 2.469–70). The final first-person fragment (CPF 2.470) is marked '<u>Speech for King</u>' and has the marginal note 'Perseus'. Who the 'King' is remains unclear, but it perhaps makes most sense to assume that he is Acrisius, Danae's father, who imprisoned her to try to prevent Perseus' conception.

Hibberd identifies 'The sun, far fallen' (CPF 60, 2.449–50) as a 'Perseus' fragment, based on its descriptions of the air as 'thick with gold' (1986: 49).[88] Crucially, this fragment, written in 1915, describes an arrogant emperor whose country is a 'Beast / Whose throat is iron & whose teeth are steel'. Hibberd connects this with Owen's description in a 1916 letter of his desire to join the RAF, in which he says:

> By Hermes, I will fly … and all you shall see me … and marvelling behold the pinion of Hermes, who is called Mercury, upon my cap.
>
> If I fall, I shall fall mightily. I shall be with Perseus and Icarus, whom I loved; and not with Fritz, whom I did not hate. To battle with the super-Zeppelin, when he comes, this would be chivalry more than Arthur dreamed of.
>
> Zeppelin, the giant dragon, the child-slayer, I would happily die in any adventure against him. (Potter 2023: 227)

Hibberd comments that 'The modern Perseus-pilot, born of Zeus (sunlight) and endowed with the power of Hermes, the winged messenger of the gods, would rescue Andromeda-France from the German dragon' (1986: 49). If Hibberd is right to take CPF 60 as a 'Perseus' fragment, then it appears that Owen did indeed, however briefly, envisage 'Perseus' as a war poem. But the relationship of the various fragments to one another remains very unclear, as does the final form that the poem would have taken had Owen continued to work on it; 'how he imagined he could include Danae, Perseus, Pluto, Persephone and Eros in a poem about the Great War, heaven knows' (Hibberd 1986: 50).[89] The main significance of the 'Perseus' fragments for our purposes here is that they indicate how deeply Owen had internalized the idea that a classical myth—perhaps especially one not associated with Homer, Vergil, or Greek tragedy, and therefore available to be treated in a

---

[88] In myth, Perseus was conceived when Zeus appeared to Danae in a shower of gold; see Gantz 1993: 300.

[89] The closest comparandum for such a wide-ranging and re-creative treatment of myth and legend in a long war poem is David Jones' *In Parenthesis* (1937).

free and unconstrained way—was the appropriate vehicle for a serious narrative poem.

(d) Associated works
Given the fragmentary nature of 'Perseus', it is difficult to identify clear intratextual associations. Most noticeable (and perplexing) are the references to Persephone, whose connection with the Perseus story is unclear.

4. Other classical interactions (in chronological order, following CFP)

This section briefly comments on a selection of poems that feature passing or incidental interactions with classical texts. The coverage here is not exhaustive; there are also classical interactions in 'The Fates', 'Happiness', 'Lines to a Beauty Seen in Limehouse', 'Has Your Soul Sipped', 'Cramped in That Funnelled Hole', 'Miners', 'Asleep', 'The Show', 'Training', 'The Next War', 'Elegy in April and September', and 'The Sentry'. For discussion of those poems, see Hardwick, Harrison, and Vandiver 2024 and its digital version.

'[Purgatorial Passions]' (1916)

[CPF 70, 2.455]
Hibberd identifies this fragment as possibly part of the draft work for 'Perseus' (Hibberd 1986: 67). 'Their necks were bowed like foxgloves all', line 2, glances at the Homeric image comparing a dying warrior's head to a drooping poppy (*Iliad* 8.306–8). The description of souls tormented in hell anticipates much of Owen's later work featuring shell-shocked and wounded soldiers, especially 'Mental Cases' and 'Strange Meeting'.

'[It was an evening]' (1916)

[CPF 71, 2.457]
This fragment consists of several heavily cancelled lines that are little more than jottings of phrases. Amongst the phrases are 'He found not Cybele' and 'He saw not Proserpine, for he was lost'. Those lines are both struck through,

but the page ends with the uncancelled lines 'I ~~said~~ thought my heart has failed, / As I desired, in sleep. And this is Hell'. The underlying idea seems to be the visit of a living man to Hell, in a dream or a vision, as in 'Strange Meeting'; the reference to Proserpine makes the hell a classical one. The mention of Cybele could perhaps be a reference to Catullus 63 and the self-castrated Attis.

'Roundel' (1917)

[CPF 78, 1.85]

This poem survives only in an undated letter, the first pages of which are missing, to Owen's cousin Leslie Gunston. Owen and Bell tentatively dated the poem to May 1914 (1967: 250), but Stallworthy and Hibberd both persuasively argue that it was probably written in May 1917 at the Casualty Clearing Station, where Owen had been sent with shell shock (CPF 1.85; Hibberd 1982: 281).

The poem discusses a statue, a reproduction of the Farnese Heracles that still stands in a park (called The Quarry) in central Shrewsbury.[90] The Farnese Heracles depicts a weary, heavily-muscled, middle-aged Heracles near the end of his Labours; his right hand, behind his back, holds the Apples of the Hesperides, which he gained as the result of his penultimate Labour. His left arm leans on his upright club, positioned as a crutch under his arm, and his overall stance is indicative of extreme weariness. He is nude, although in the Shrewsbury copy he has a loincloth; Owen says that he is 'attired' like a baby. In Owen's poem, Hercules is suffering from weariness and boredom due to his presence in Shrewsbury.

This poem is, thus, a reception of a reception; the Shrewsbury copy, labelled only 'Hercules' on its plinth, is itself a reception of a classical artefact. Owen clearly assumes that the hero's reputation for endurance throughout his Labours is common knowledge; the point is that Shrewsbury wearies *even* Hercules ('In Shrewsbury Town e'en Hercules wox tired', l. 1). The poem can be read as a comment on civilians' incomprehension of the suffering and labours of those who have been struggling on their behalf.

---

[90] An image of the Farnese Heracles is available at https://mannapoli.it/en/farnese-collection/#gallery-4.

'The Unreturning' (1912 or 1913; revised 1917 or early 1918)

[CPF 104, 1.107]

Owen revised this early sonnet while he was at Craiglockhart or shortly thereafter. The poem shares some features with 'Strange Meeting', in its presentation of a living man trying (here unsuccessfully) to contact the dead. One draft version has the variant line 'But not one sleeper out of Hades woke' (CPF 2.262), which increases the intratextual connection with 'Strange Meeting' (see Das 1977: 46; Hibberd 1986: 174). The presentation of the lightly personified 'indefinite unshapen dawn' as 'peer[ing] ... with vacant gloaming' evokes glancing associations with Homer's rosy-fingered Dawn.

The overall presentation of the dead as a thronging but inaccessible mass may owe something to Sorley's 'When you see millions of the mouthless dead' (discussed in this volume), since as noted above Owen probably knew Sorley's work.

'I saw his round mouth's crimson' (1917)

[CPF 122, 1.123]

Stallworthy dates this poem (or fragment) to November–December 1917, when Owen was in Scarborough. The poem consists of eight lines of varying lengths, arranged in couplets of a long line followed by a shorter one. The overall movement of the poem is predominantly iambic and spondaic, with frequent substitutions of anapaests or dactyls.

Reed has compellingly read this poem as 'a spectacular reworking' of the death of Camilla in the *Aeneid* (Reed 2006: 43). The poem also engages with two Vergilian descriptions of Pallas, like Camilla a young warrior cut down in his youth. The first of these is the description of Pallas' death where his bloody mouth strikes the earth (*Aen.* 10.499–8) and the second is Pallas' entry into battle, when he is compared to the morning star driving the shadows from the sky (*Aen.* 8.587–91). Owen's reworking of this second description so that it refers to 'cold stars ... old and bleak ... in different skies' stresses the distance of this nameless young soldier from Pallas, at whose death Jupiter reminds Hercules that *fama*, lasting reputation, is the recompense for the brevity of human life. Owen suggests that such a system of value belongs to an entirely different natural order ('different skies').[91]

---

[91] Mediating texts are also important for this poem; on Shelley's 'Adonais' and 'I saw his round mouth's crimson', see Kendall 2006: 63.

The imagery of a dying boy's bloodied mouth and of the 'draining away of vermilion and purple' (Hibberd 1986: 82) recurs in several of Owen's other poems, most notably in 'Has your soul sipped' and 'Disabled'. Hibberd convincingly links this intratextual imagery with Owen's private nightmares and comments 'the vision took an actual shape in 1917 when Owen saw a young man dying while bleeding at the mouth' (1986: 82).

'The Women and the Slain'/ 'The Ballad of Purchase Money'

[CPF 126, 2.500–9]

This fragmentary poem exists in many versions, with various titles: 'The Women and the Slain', 'The Ballad of Peace & War', 'The Ballad of Purchase-Money', and 'The Ballad of Kings and Christs'. Stallworthy's note on this poem reads 'Drafted in Bordeaux between June and August 1915, the latest revision of this poem (OEF 293–5) was made either at Craiglockhart in October–November 1917, or at Scarborough in November-December.... Between the first and last of those dates, it passed through several distinct phases' (CPF 2.502).

The relevant lines for our purposes appear in three of the drafts, and begin one of them, titled 'The Ballad of Purchase-Money' (OEF 289, CPF 2.507):

> O meet it is and passing sweet
>   To live in peace with others,
> But sweeter still and far more meet
>   To die in war for brothers.[92]

In two versions (OEF 287 and 288, CPF 2.504 and 505) these lines appear as Stanza III rather than Stanza I. In the second of those drafts, Owen has bracketed the lines and written 'Omit' in the margin. These versions are on paper stock that Stallworthy notes Owen was using in 1915. But OEF 289, where these lines form the first stanza, is on paper stock that Owen used for letters in November 1917 and January 1918 (CPF Appendix C, 2.541, 547). 'The Women and the Slain' also appears on two draft Tables of Contents that Owen drew up in 1918 (CPF Appendix C, 2.503), indicating that he intended to publish some form of this poem.

---

[92] Available on FWWPDA, under 'Archival Holdings/ English Faculty Library'. This manuscript is catalogued as 'June 1915–August 1915', but the source for that dating is unclear.

'O meet it is and passing sweet…To die in war' is very close to a direct translation of *dulce et decorum est pro patria mori*, which as we saw above Owen translated 'It is sweet and meet to die for one's country' when he sent a copy of his poem by that title to his mother in October 1917 (Potter 2023: 322). In his biography of Owen, Stallworthy assumed that the drafts containing these lines must be early versions, since the lines show 'as great an ignorance of the issues involved as anything from the pen of the maligned Rupert Brooke' (2013: 104). The original 1974 edition of the biography was written before he had done his crucial work of dating Owen's poems, but Stallworthy maintains this position in his edition of Owen's war poems (1994: xxxii) as well as in his 2013 revised edition of the biography. But in fact OEF 289 indicates that at some point in 1917 Owen was quoting an English version of *dulce et decorum est* unironically.

'Futility' (1918)

[CPF 153; 1.158]

One of only five poems printed during Owen's lifetime, 'Futility' was written at Ripon in 1918 and published in *The Nation* on 15 June 1918. The fourteen-line poem divides into two stanzas of seven lines, with lengths varying from six to nine syllables. It is in mixed pararhyme and rhyme, with the pattern ABABCCC DEDEFFF. The three closing lines of each stanza consist of a true rhyme flanking a pararhyme: snow/now/ know; tall/toil/at all. The metre is irregular but the main rhythm is largely iambic. The final line of each stanza is three iambs, consisting entirely of monosyllables.

The lightly personified sun is the key image of the poem (Das 2005: 159–62). The personification of the sun perhaps recalls stories in *The Greenwood Tree*, and the despairing question 'Was it for this the clay grew tall?' followed by the reference to 'fatuous sunbeams' waking living creatures glances at Ovid's account of creation in *Metamorphoses* 1.

The appearance of 'the kind old sun' as a vivifying and beneficent force invoked in the context of a young person's death triggers several glancing associations with classical texts. Euripides' Iphigenia and Sophocles' Antigone both bewail their own deaths specifically because they will be unable any longer to see the sun (Eur. *Iph. Aul.* 1218–19; Soph. *Ant.* 807–9). A related association is with Helios, the sun, seeing the abduction of Persephone and recounting what he saw to her mother Demeter; when Persephone returns each year, Demeter allows the sun to reawaken the seeds so that crops can grow. As Das notes, the idea of an elder male's touch warming a beautiful but inert and cold body into life also recalls Ovid's Pygmalion (2005: 162). All of these resonances, along with traces of Shakespeare, Donne, and Keats (Das 2005: 161) combine to focus the poem's attention on the word Owen uses for its title: the futility, in this instance, of thinking that anything could ever again raise this dead body into life.

'The End' also rejects the idea of any renewal for the dead, and 'A New Heaven' and 'Asleep' both question received ideas of the afterlife. The semi-personification of 'the kind old sun' recalls the sun as a 'friend' in 'Spring Offensive', where the hint at hope given by 'Futility' is directly repudiated.

'O true...' (1918)

[CPF 156; 2.528–30]

This fragment consists of many cancelled phrases and half-lines and lacks an overall narrative. It is clear, however, that it treats the theme of beauty (amongst other things) and draws on examples of ancient statues, buried bronzes, and ancient artefacts in general to connect beauty with antiquity. A reference to 'The breeze of pinioned-sandals' leads Hibberd to speculate that this, too, may be work connected with 'Perseus' (1986: 213n42).[93] The connection with the war appears in one section:

>   maybe
> As bronze ~~are~~ much beautified
>   es
>   ~~stale~~dark
> By lying in the ~~old~~ ⟋ damp soil,
>   fade   dust of
> So men who ~~rust~~ in ⟋ warfare, ~~but~~ fade
> Fairer, and sorrow ~~blooms~~ their soul.

---

[93] The attribution of winged sandals to Perseus goes back as far as the archaic 'Shield of Heracles' (*Aspis*), ll. 216–37; see Gantz 1993: 304.

'Mental Cases' (1918)

[CPF 163, 1.169]

Hibberd notes (1986: 169–70) that the setting is clearly in Hell or the Underworld. The primary influence is probably Dante, but the description of 'these hellish' as tortured souls whose identity must be described to a horrified, questioning visitor by a knowledgeable guide also recalls Aeneas' questions and the Sibyl's description of the souls tormented in Tartarus, *Aen.* 6.560–627. The line 'Dawn breaks open like a wound that bleeds afresh' (l. 22) is another glancing reference to the Homeric trope of the rosy-fingered Dawn. The Underworld setting ties 'Mental Cases' closely to 'Strange Meeting' and also to 'The Sentry', 'Exposure', and 'Spring Offensive'.

'The Send-Off' (1918)

[CPF 165; 1.172]

This twenty-line poem is divided into eight stanzas, alternating between three and two lines each. The lines are strongly iambic; the three-line stanzas have a long (nine to eleven syllables) first and third line and a short (four or five syllables) middle line, while the two-line stanzas have a long first and a short second line.[94] The poem describes a group of soldiers departing from an unnamed station 'secretly, like wrongs hushed-up' (l. 11). The final five lines describe their return:

> Shall they return to beating of great bells
> In wild train-loads?
> A few, a few, too few for drums and yells,
>
> May creep back, silent, to village wells,
> Up half-known roads.

---

[94] The long lines are more regular than this description might imply. The two eleven-syllable lines feature trisyllabic words that Owen may in fact have pronounced as disyllables: 'darkening' (l. 1) and 'casual' (l. 6). The only nine-syllable line is Stallworthy's version of l. 19, 'May creep back, silent, to village wells'. Earlier editors had read 'still village wells', which would make this line ten syllables. Given the overall regularity of the metre in the long lines, the reading 'still village wells' is probably preferable and seems to be supported by the manuscripts; see especially CPF 2.347, 350.

To a classicist, the final three lines strikingly recall Pindar's description in *Pythian* 8.85–7 of defeated contestants returning home:

> nor upon returning to their mothers did sweet laughter
> arouse joy all around; but staying clear of their enemies
> they shrink down alleyways, bitten by failure. (Race 1997: 347)

This may be another example of a reader-activated connection. But this ode is amongst Pindar's most famous and frequently anthologized poems; the lines quoted above occur slightly before the well-known section that begins 'Creatures of a day'. It is therefore quite possible that Owen had indeed come across this ode at some point in his reading. The connection of Owen's work with Pindar's appears also in 'Disabled', where Housman's 'To an Athlete Dying Young' provides a crucial mediating text between Pindar and Owen.

'Disabled' (1917–18)

[CPF 167; 1.175–6]
Owen drafted 'Disabled' in October 1917 and revised it in July 1918 (CPF 1.176). It is in regular iambic pentameter, with frequent examples of Owen's characteristic substitutions of choriambs for the first two feet and an occasional substitution of a dactyl or an anapaest, giving an eleven-syllable line (e.g. ll. 31, 'Aústria's', and 36, 'And sóon, he was dráfted'). Two lines (10 and 40) have an extra foot; this metrical fault was singled out as a blemish by Robert Graves, who saw a draft of the poem in October 1917 and wrote Owen about it (Owen and Bell 1967: 595).

The forty-six-line poem is divided by lines of asterisks into six stanzas of irregular length. The longest of these, the fourth stanza, is sixteen lines long, and the shortest, the fifth, is only three lines. The poem uses rhyme, in varying patterns that partially carry over from one stanza to the next. The poem describes a very young, grievously mutilated soldier, sitting in a wheelchair in a park at twilight. He has lost both legs and both arms. The poem is written as a third-person description of the soldier, but focuses on his own subjectivity and his memories of his life 'before he threw away his knees'.

The classical resonances in this poem have been thoroughly elucidated by Reed, whose sensitive reading of the underlying allusion to Adonis is exemplary. As Reed shows, lines 17–20 draw directly on Bion's 'Lament for Adonis', and specifically on Lang's translation of that poem (Reed 2006: 41). Reed draws out the similarities between Bion's dying Adonis and Owen's maimed youth: they are both very young; their wounding results in 'an irrevocable loss of youthful beauty and desirability'; and the soldier's twilight existence can be read as 'a development of Bion's persistent assimilation of immortal Aphrodite to dying Adonis'. Reed further identifies other common elements in Owen's poem and Bion's, such as the 'voices of boys...like a hymn' and the Erotes who are enjoined to sing the refrain of Bion's poem (Reed 2006: 42). Reed also explores Owen's use of 'certain themes in the Adoniac tradition', especially what he terms 'colorlessness' (43–4). The influence of Housman's 'To an Athlete Dying Young' is obvious and often noted; Housman himself was reworking the depictions of the homecoming of athletes in Pindar's epinicians.

'A Terre (being the philosophy of many soldiers)' (1917; revised 1918)

[CPF 168; 1.178–80]
This sixty-five-line poem is a monologue spoken by a blinded, mutilated, bed-ridden soldier to an unidentified visitor. It consists primarily of para-rhymed couplets in iambic pentameter, divided into eleven stanzas of uneven length, with occasional triplets instead of couplets and one ABBA quatrain. The fifth stanza (ll. 25–35) evokes associations with Achilles' words to Odysseus in *Odyssey* 11, where Achilles says that he would rather be the slave of a poor man than king over all the dead. Owen's disabled soldier thinks of his own servant, and comments that he now would welcome the chance to sweep floors or chimneys, or to take on any other form of manual labour: 'Who's prejudiced / Against a grimed hand when his own's quite dust [?]' (ll. 30–1). A further classical association appears in the penultimate stanza, lines 61–3:

> My soul's a little grief, grappling your chest,
> To climb your throat on sobs; easily chased
> On other sighs and wiped by fresher winds.

The description of the soul as a sob, a sigh, or a breath of wind glances at Homer's description of the *psychē* leaving the body at the moment of death (*Il.* 16.856–7 and 22.362–3) and Vergil's reworking of the same trope as the final lines of the *Aeneid*; cf. Rosenberg, 'Dead Man's Dump', lines 27–31 (discussed above).

'The Kind Ghosts' (1918)

[CPF 169, 1.181]

This highly Swinburnian poem of four three-line stanzas is dated 30 July 1918. It features an unidentified sleeping goddess who is unaware of or indifferent to her 'wall of boys on boys and dooms on dooms'. Stallworthy (1.181) and Hibberd (1986: 161) assume that the sleeping woman is Britannia and Das calls her 'England' (1977: 49), but Reed identifies her as 'Aphrodite as blithe destroyer…implicitly transposed to the Great War and its destruction of boys' (2006: 45). The penultimate line refers to 'her terraces, their hecatombs'. Stallworthy suggests that Owen may have thought 'hecatombs' meant 'places of sacrifice', or alternatively that he may have confused this word with 'catacombs' (1.181). Hibberd agrees that Owen likely thought 'hecatomb' referred to a place of sacrifice, and suggests that 'he probably had in mind pagan sacrifices such as those in *Salammbô*, where parents sacrifice their children to Moloch' (1986: 161). Owen had read *Salammbô* in France in the summer of 1915 (Potter 2023: 182).

Works Cited

Adams, M. [1910]. *Contes fabuleux de la Grèce antique*. Trans. Mlle Latappy (Paris: La Collection Stead).

Anon. 2014. *Art from the First World War* (London: Imperial War Museum).

Auden, W. H., 2009, *W.H. Auden, Selected Poems: Revised Edition*, ed. E. Mendelson (London: Faber).

Bäckman, S. 1979. *Tradition Transformed: Studies in the Poetry of Wilfred Owen*. Lund Studies in English 54 (Lund: C. W. K. Gleerup).

Balmer, J. 2009. *The Word for Sorrow* (Cambridge: Salt).

Beckett, L. C. 2015. *The Second I Saw You: The True Love Story of Rupert Brooke and Phyllis Gardner* (London: The British Library).

Beller, S. 2007. *Anti-Semitism: A Very Short Introduction* (Oxford: Oxford University Press).

Bird, G. 2018. 'Homer as Improviser?', in Macintosh, F., McConnell, J., Harrison, S., and Kenward, C. (eds) *Epic Performances from the Middle Ages into the Twenty-First Century* (Oxford: Oxford University Press), 228–49.

Bloom, H. 2003. *Poets of World War I: Rupert Brooke and Siegfried Sassoon* (Broomall, PA: Chelsea House).

Blunden, E. (ed.) 1931. *The Poems of Wilfred Owen* (London: Chatto and Windus).

Bottomley, G., and Harding, D. (eds) 1937. *The Collected Works of Isaac Rosenberg, with a Foreword by Siegfried Sassoon* (London: Chatto and Windus).

Brearton, F. 2013. '"But that is not new": Poetic Legacies of the First World War', in Das, S. (ed.) 2013, 229–41.

[Brock, A. J.] 1918. 'Antaeus, or Back to the Land', in *The Hydra: Journal of the Craiglockhart War Hospital* ns 3 (January 1918), 3–4 [to be found on FWWPDA].

Brooke, R. 1915. *1914 and other Poems* (London: Sidgwick and Jackson).

Brooke, R. 1918. *The Collected Poems of Rupert Brooke*. Ed. E. Marsh, with memoir (London: Sidgwick and Jackson).

Burrow, C., Harrison, S. J., McLaughlin, M., and Tarantino, E. (eds) 2020. *Imitative Series and Clusters from Classical to Early Modern Literature* (Berlin: De Gruyter).

Burt, R. A. 1986. *British Battleships of World War One* (Annapolis: US Naval Institute Press).

Butler, S. (ed.) 2016. *Deep Classics: Rethinking Classical Reception* (London: Bloomsbury Academic).

Campbell, G. 2010. *Bible: The Story of the King James Version 1611–2011* (Oxford: Oxford University Press).

Clarke, G. H. (ed.) 1919. *British and American Poems of the World War 1914–19* (London, New York, and Toronto: Hodder and Stoughton).

Corcoran, N. 2013. 'Isaac Rosenberg' in Das, S. (ed.) 2013, 105–16.

Currie, B. 2016. *Homer's Allusive Art* (Oxford: Oxford University Press).

Cuthbertson, G. 2014. *Wilfred Owen* (New Haven and London: Yale University Press).

Das, S. 2005. *Touch and Intimacy in First World War Literature* (Cambridge: Cambridge University Press).

Das, S. (ed.) 2013. *The Cambridge Companion to the Poetry of the First World War* (Cambridge: Cambridge University Press).

Das, S. B. 1977. *Wilfred Owen's Strange Meeting: A Critical Study* (Calcutta: Firma KLM Private Ltd.).

Dawe, G. (ed.) 2008. *Earth Voices Whispering: An Anthology of Irish War Poetry 1914–1945* (Belfast: Blackstaff Press).

Day Lewis, C. (ed.) 1963. *The Collected Poems of Wilfred Owen* (London: Chatto and Windus).

De Graef, O. 2017. 'Nudes Gibbering: Isaac Rosenberg Entrenched', *Image and Narrative* 18.1, 111–28.

Delany, P. 2015. *Fatal Glamour: The Life of Rupert Brooke* (Ottawa: McGill-Queen's University Press).

Dickson, R., Liddiard, J., McDougall, S., Moorcroft Wilson, J., and Williams, D. (eds) 2009. *Whitechapel at War: Isaac Rosenberg and his Circle* (London: Lund Humphries).

Douglas, K. 2011. *Complete Poems*. Ed. D. Graham with introduction by Ted Hughes (London: Faber).

Duffy, C.A. 2013. 'Last Post', in C.A. Duffy (ed.), *1914: Poetry Remembers* (London: Faber and Faber), 112–13.

Eidinow, E. 2019a. 'The (Ancient Greek) Subject Supposed to Believe', *Numen: International Review for the History of Religions* 66.1, 56–88.

Eidinow, E. 2019b. '"They Blow One Way, Now Another" (Hesiod *Theogony* 875): Winds in the Ancient Greek Imaginary', in Scheer, T. S. (ed.) *Natur—Mythos—Religion im antiken Griechenland* (Stuttgart: Franz Steiner Verlag), 113–33.

Eliot, T. S. 1920a. 'A Brief Treatise on the Criticism of Poetry', *The Chapbook: A Monthly Miscellany* 2 (March), 1–2.

Eliot, T. S. 1920b. *Poems* (New York: A. A. Knopf).

Farrell, J., and Putnam, C. J. (eds) 2010. *A Companion to Vergil's Aeneid and its Tradition* (Oxford and Malden: Wiley-Blackwell).

First World War Archive = The First World War Poetry Digital Archive, University of Oxford, www.oucs.ox.ac.uk/ww1lit. [to be found on FWWPDA].

Fishbane, M. 1985. *Biblical Interpretations in Ancient Israel* (Oxford: Oxford University Press).

Folsom, E., and Price, K. M. 2005. *Re-scripting Walt Whitman* (Malden and Oxford: Blackwell).

Foster, R. F. 2014. *Vivid Faces: The Revolutionary Generation in Ireland 1890–1923* (London: Penguin).

France, P. 2012. 'Scott Moncrieff's First Translation', *Translation and Literature* 21.3, 364–82.

Fussell, P. 1975. *The Great War and Modern Memory* (New York and Oxford: Oxford University Press).

Gantz, T. 1993. *Early Greek Myth: A Guide to Literary and Artistic Sources*. 2 vols (Baltimore and London: Johns Hopkins University Press).

Garth, J. 2014. 'Secrets of the Hydra: How Tolkien Research Uncovered Lost Wilfred Owen Magazines', https://johngarth.wordpress.com/2014/06/17/, accessed 30 April 2021.

Giddings, R. 1988. *The War Poets* (London: Bloomsbury).

Goldman, D. P. 2021. 'T. S. Eliot and the Jews', *First Things*, firstthings.com/articles/ 2021/03/t-s-eliot-and-the-jews, accessed 1 December 2022.

Graham, D. 1984. *The Truth of War: Owen, Blunden, Rosenberg* (Manchester: Carcanet Press).

Grant, J. 1967. *Harold Monro and the Poetry Bookshop* (Berkeley and Los Angeles: University of California Press).

Graves, R. 1960 [1929]. *Goodbye to All That* (Harmondsworth: Penguin).

Graziosi, B., and Greenwood, E. (eds) 2007. *Homer in the Twentieth Century: Between World Literature and the Western Canon* (Oxford: Oxford University Press).

The Greenwood Tree: A Book of Nature Myths and Verses [1903]. (London: Edward Arnold).

Grier, E. F. (ed.) 1984. *Walt Whitman: Notebooks and Unpublished Prose Manuscripts* (New York: New York University Press).

Griffin, J. 1980. *Homer on Life and Death* (Oxford: Oxford University Press).

Gurney = [Ivor] Gurney Archive, Gloucester Public Records Office.

Hale, K. 1998. *Friends and Apostles: The Correspondence of Rupert Brooke and James Strachey, 1905-1914* (New Haven and London: Yale University Press).

Hall, E. 2008. 'Navigating the Realms of Gold: Translation as Access Route to the Classics', in Lianeri, A., and Zajko, V. (eds) *Translation and the Classic: Identity as Change in the History of Culture* (Oxford: Oxford University Press), 315–40.

Hall, E., and Macintosh, F. 2005. *Greek Tragedy and the British Theatre, 1660–1914* (Oxford: Oxford University Press).

Hall, E., and Stead, H. 2020. *A People's History of Classics* (London: Routledge).

Hallett, C. E. 2021. 'The Heiress and the French Army', *Country Life: Gentleman's Life* (Autumn), 60–3.

Hardwick, L. 2015. 'Radicalism and Gradualism Enmeshed: Classics from the Grass Roots in the Cultural Politics of Nineteenth-century Britain', in Stead, H., and Hall, E. (eds) *Greek and Roman Classics in the British Struggle for Social Reform* (London: Bloomsbury), 20–36.

Hardwick, L. 2018. 'The Poetics of Cultural Memory: World War 1 Refractions of Ancient Peace' in Pender, E. (ed.) 2018, 393–414.

Hardwick, L. 2019. 'Epilogue: Seamus Heaney's Classical Ground' in Harrison, S., Macintosh, F., and Eastman, H. (eds) *Seamus Heaney and the Classics: Bann Valley Muses* (Oxford: Oxford University Press).

Hardwick, L., Harrison, S. and Vandiver, E. (2024), *Rupert Brooke, Charles Sorley, Isaac Rosenberg, Wilfred Owen: Classical Connections* (Oxford: Oxford University Press).

Harris, P. 1991. *Song of Love: The Letters of Rupert Brooke and Noel Olivier 1909–1915* (London: Bloomsbury).

Harrison, S. 2017. *Victorian Horace: Classics and Class* (London: Bloomsbury).

Harrison, T. 2007. *Collected Poems* (London: Viking).

Haubold, J. 2013. *Greece and Mesopotamia: Dialogues in Literature* (Cambridge: Cambridge University Press).

Heaney, S. 1966. *Death of a Naturalist* (London: Faber).

Heaney, S. 1972. 'Introduction' to *Soundings '72: An Annual Anthology of New Irish Poetry* (Belfast: Blackstaff Press).

Heaney, S. 2000. 'What Makes a Good Poet', *Portal* 2 (July), 5.

Heslin, P. (2016), 'The Dream of a Universal Variorum: Digitizing the Commentary Tradition', in Kraus and Stray, (eds.) 2016, 494–511.

Hibberd, D. (ed.) 1973. *Wilfred Owen: War Poems and Others* (London: Chatto and Windus).

Hibberd, D. 1976. 'The Date of Wilfred Owen's "Exposure"', *Notes and Queries* 23 (July), 305–8.

Hibberd, D. 1977. 'A Sociological Cure for Shellshock: Dr. Brock and Wilfred Owen', *Sociological Review* 25.2 (May), 377–86.

Hibberd, D. 1979. 'Wilfred Owen and the Georgians', *Review of English Studies* 30.117, 28–40.

Hibberd, D. 1982. 'Wilfred Owen's Letters: Some Additions, Amendments and Notes', *The Library* 4 (September), 273–87.

Hibberd, D. 1986. *Owen the Poet* (Houndmills and Basingstoke: Macmillan).

Hibberd, D. 1992. *Wilfred Owen: The Last Year 1917–1918* (London: Constable).

Hibberd, D. 2002. *Wilfred Owen: A New Biography* (London: Weidenfeld and Nicolson).

Hinds, S. 1998. *Allusion and Intertext: Dynamics of Appropriation in Roman Poetry* (Cambridge: Cambridge University Press).

Hipp, D. 2002. '"By Degrees Regain[ing] Cool Peaceful Air in Wonder": Wilfred Owen's War Poetry as Psychological Therapy', *Journal of the Midwest Modern Language Association* 35.1, 225–49.

Hobbs, A. (2018). 'Who Lied? Classical Heroism and World War I', in Pender, E. (ed.) 2018, 376–92.

Hornblower, S., and Spawforth, A. (eds) 2005. *The Oxford Classical Dictionary*. 3rd edn (Oxford: Oxford University Press).

Howarth, P. 2013. 'Poetic Form and the First World War', in Das, S. (ed.) 2013, 51–65.

Inge, W. R. 1900. 'The Permanent Influence of Neoplatonism upon Christianity', *American Journal of Theology* 4, 328–44.

Ingleheart, J. 2018. *Masculine Plural: Queer Classics, Sex, and Education* (Oxford: Oxford University Press).

Jones, N. H. 2014. *Rupert Brooke: Life, Death & Myth*. 2nd edn (London: Head of Zeus).

Julius, A. 2003 [2nd edn; 1st 1995]. *T. S. Eliot and the Jews: A Study in Antisemitism and Literary Form* (London: Thames and Hudson).

Kelly, F. S. 2004. *Race against Time: The Diaries of F.S. Kelly*. Ed. T. Radic (Canberra: National Library of Australia).

Kendall, T. 2006. *Modern English War Poetry* (Oxford: Oxford University Press).

Kendall, T. (ed.) 2013. *Poetry of the First World War: An Anthology* (Oxford: Oxford University Press).

Kennedy, K. 2021. *Dweller in the Shadows: A Life of Ivor Gurney* (Princeton and Oxford: Princeton University Press).

Kerr, D. 1993. *Wilfred Owen's Voices* (Oxford: Clarendon Press).

Keynes, G. (ed.) 1968. *The Letters of Rupert Brooke* (London: Faber and Faber).

Keynes, G. (ed.) 1970. *The Poetical Works of Rupert Brooke*. 2nd edn. (London: Faber and Faber).

Kraus, C. S., and Stray, C. (eds) 2016. *Classical Commentaries: Explorations in a Scholarly Genre* (Oxford: Oxford University Press).

Lang, A. (trans.) 1889. *Theocritus, Bion and Moschus Rendered into English Prose*. 2nd edn. Golden Treasury Series (London and New York: Macmillan).

Lanone, C. 2013. '(Dis)figuring Rebellion: Wilfred Owen and the Legacy of Outrage', *Études britanniques contemporaines: Revue de la Société d' Études Anglaises Contemporaines* 45, https://journals.openedition.org/ebc/583#bodyftn20, accessed 28 April 2021.

Leavis, F. R. 1932. *New Bearings in English Poetry* (London: Chatto and Windus).

Lewis-Stempel, J. 2016. *Where Poppies Blow: The British Soldier, Nature, The Great War* (London: Weidenfeld and Nicolson).

Liddiard, J. (ed.) 2003. *Isaac Rosenberg: Selected Poems and Letters* (London: Enitharmon Press).

Liebregts, P. 2019. *The Translations of Greek Tragedy in the Work of Ezra Pound* (London: Bloomsbury).

Logue, C. 2015. *War Music: An Account of Homer's Iliad* (London: Faber).

Longley, E. (ed.) 2008. *Edward Thomas: The Annotated Collected Poems* (Tarset: Bloodaxe Books).

Longley, M. 2006. *Collected Poems* (London: Cape Poetry).

Longley, M. 2014. *The Stairwell* (London: Cape Poetry).

Longley, M. 2020. *The Candlelight Master* (London: Cape Poetry).

MacCarthy, F. 2002. *Byron: Life and Legend* (London: Faber).

Mackay, J. A. (ed.) 1993. *The Complete Poems of Robert Burns, 1759–1796* (Darvel: Alloway Publishing).

Maggioni, E. 2016. '"Earth! Have they gone into you?": An Ecocritical Reading of the Relationship between Man, Nature and War in Isaac Rosenberg's Poems', *L'Analisi Linguisticae Litterarum*, Anno XXIV.2, 53–62, https://www.analisilinguisticaeletteraria. eu/index.php/ojs/issue/view/51.

Martin, M. 2012. *The Rise and Fall of Meter: Poetry and English National Culture, 1860–1930* (Princeton and Oxford: Princeton University Press).

Martindale, C. 1993. *Redeeming the Text* (Cambridge: Cambridge University Press).

Matzner, S., and Trimble, G. 2020. *Metalepsis: Ancient Texts, New Perspectives* (Oxford: Oxford University Press).

Michelakis, P. (ed.) 2020. *Classics and Media Theory* (Oxford: Oxford University Press).

Minogue, S., and Palmer, A. 2018. *The Remembered Dead: Poetry, Memory and the First World War* (Cambridge: Cambridge University Press).

Mythologie Gréco-Latine. n.d. 2 vols (Paris: Les Meilleurs Livres).

Najarian, J. 2002. *Victorian Keats: Manliness, Sexuality, and Desire* (Houndmills and Basingstoke: Palgrave Macmillan).

Nisbet, G. 2013. *Greek Epigram in Reception* (Oxford: Oxford University Press).

Noakes, V. (ed.) 2004. *The Poems and Plays of Isaac Rosenberg* (Oxford: Oxford University Press).

Noakes, V. (ed.) 2008. *Isaac Rosenberg.* 21st Century Oxford Authors Series (Oxford: Oxford University Press).

Norgate, P. 1989. 'Wilfred Owen and the Soldier Poets', *Review of English Studies* 40, 516–30.

Norgate, P. 2020. 'Five-Nines and Gas Shells: Working with Wilfred Owen's Manuscripts', *Wilfred Owen Association Journal* 2020 (2), 10–21.

Norgate, P. 2021. 'Wilfred Owen and the "Soldier's Friend" (1)', *Wilfred Owen Association Journal* 2021 (1), 5–15.

Norgate, P. 2022. '"Somewhere in Hell": Wilfred Owen and "The Soldier's Friend" (2)', *Wilfred Owen Association Journal* 2022, 35–47.

Norgate, P. 2023. 'Beyond Bottomley: A Revised Version of Wilfred Owen's "Apologia pro Poemate Meo"', *The Wilfred Owen Association Journal* 2023: 11–18.

O'Keefe, T. 1972. 'Ironic Allusion in the Poetry of Wilfred Owen', *ARIEL* 3, 72–81.

Orwell, G. 1940. *Inside the Whale and Other Essays* (London: Gollancz).

Oswald, A. 2021. 'Sidelong Glances', Oxford Professor of Poetry Lecture (27 May).

Owen Archive = Archive of Wilfred Owen and Family Members. c.1820–2003. Oxford, Bodleian Libraries. MSS. 12282/1–59; MSS. 12282 photogr. 1–10; JL 977–84.

Owen, H. 1963–5. *Journey from Obscurity: Wilfred Owen 1893–1918.* 3 vols (Oxford: Oxford University Press).

Owen, H., and Bell, J. (eds) 1967. *Wilfred Owen: Collected Letters* (Oxford: Oxford University Press).

[Owen, W.] 1917. 'Editorial', in *The Hydra: Journal of the Craiglockhart War Hospital* 10 (1 September 1917), [7], http://ww1lit.nsms.ox.ac.uk/ww1lit/collec tions/document/3132, accessed 19 December 2021.

Palaima, T. 2021. 'Pound and Owen: A Correction', *Paideuma* 45, 243–8.

Parker, L. 1999. *The Georgian Poets: Abercrombie, Brooke, Drinkwater, Gibson and Thomas* (Plymouth: Northcote House).

Parsons, I. (ed.) 1979. *The Collected Works of Isaac Rosenberg: Poetry, Prose, Letters, Paintings, and Drawings, with a Foreword by Siegfried Sassoon* (New York: Oxford University Press).

Pender, E. (ed.) 2018. 'Classics and Classicists in World War 1', *Classical Receptions Journal Special Issue* 10.4, 393–414.

Poole, A. 2013. 'David Jones', in Das, S. (ed.) 2013, 144–55.

Potter, J. 2014. *Wilfred Owen: An Illustrated Life* (Oxford: Bodleian Library).

Potter, J. (ed.) 2023. *Selected Letters of Wilfred Owen* (Oxford: Oxford University Press).

Race, W. H. (ed. and trans.) 1997. *Pindar, Olympian Odes. Pythian Odes.* Loeb Classical Library 56 (Cambridge, MA: Harvard University Press).

Ramsey, J. T. (ed.) 2013. *Sallust. The War with Catiline. The War with Jugurtha.* Trans. J. C. Rolfe. Loeb Classical Library (Cambridge, MA: Harvard University Press).

Reed, J. D. 2006. 'Wilfred Owen's Adonis', in Dufallo, B., and McCracken, P. (eds) *Dead Lovers: Erotic Bonds and the Study of Premodern Europe* (Ann Arbor: University of Michigan Press), 39–56.

Reilly, C. (ed.) 1997. *Women's War Poetry and Verse* (London: Virago Press).

Riley, K. 2021. *Imagining Ithaca: Nostos and Nostalgia since the Great War* (Oxford: Oxford University Press).

Rudd, N. (ed. and trans.) 2004. *Horace. Odes and Epodes.* Loeb Classical Library (Cambridge, MA: Harvard University Press).

Samet, N. 2012. 'On Agricultural Imagery in Biblical Descriptions of Catastrophe', *Journal of Ancient Judaism* 3, 2–14.

Sassoon, S. 1975 [1929]. *Memoirs of a Fox-Hunting Man* (London: Faber).

Sassoon, S. 1997 [1930]. *Memoirs of an Infantry Officer* (London: Faber).

Saunders, T. 2000. *Bucolic Ecology: Virgil's Eclogues and the Environmental Literary Tradition* (London: Duckworth).

Schroder, J. 1970. *Catalogue of Books and Manuscripts by Rupert Brooke, Edward Marsh & Christopher Hassall* (Cambridge: Rampant Lion Press).

Schuchard, R. 2003. 'Burbank with a Baedeker, Eliot with a Cigar', *Modernism/Modernity*, vol. 10, January, special section 'Eliot and Antisemitism: The Ongoing Debate'.

Sedley, D. 2016. 'An Introduction to Plato's Theory of Forms', *Royal Institute of Philosophy Supplements* 78, 3–22.

Seldon, A. 2022. *The Path of Peace: Walking the Western Front Way* (London: Atlantic Books).

Silkin, J. 1972. *Out of Battle: The Poetry of the Great War* (Oxford: Oxford University Press).

Silkin, J., ed. 1981 [1979]. *The Penguin Book of First World War Poetry* (London: Allen Lane).

Sitwell, E. (ed.) 1919. *Wheels 1919: Fourth Cycle* (Oxford: B. H. Blackwell).

Sitwell, E. (ed.) 1920. *Poems by Wilfred Owen* (London: Chatto and Windus).

Sitwell, E. 1922. 'Review of *Poems by Isaac Rosenberg*, ed. G. Bottomley', *The New Age: A Weekly Review of Politics, Literature and Art* 31.13, 161.

Slavitt, D. (trans.) 2014. *Horace. Odes* (Madison: University of Wisconsin Press).

Sorley, C. H. 1916a. *Marlborough and Other Poems* (Cambridge: Cambridge University Press).

Sorley, C. H. 1916b. *Letters from Germany and from the Army* (Cambridge: privately printed).

Sorley, W. R., and Sorley, J. S. (eds) 1919. *The Letters of Charles Sorley* (Cambridge: Cambridge University Press).

Stafford, E. 2011. *Heracles* (London: Routledge).

Stallworthy, J. (ed.) 1983 [rev. edn 2013]. *Wilfred Owen: The Complete Poems and Fragments*. 2 vols (London: Chatto and Windus).

Stallworthy, J. (ed.) 1986. *The Poems of Wilfred Owen* (New York and London: Norton).

Stallworthy, J. (ed.) 1994. *The War Poems of Wilfred Owen* (London: Chatto and Windus).

Stallworthy, J. 2008. *Survivors' Songs from Maldon to the Somme* (Cambridge: Cambridge University Press).

Stallworthy, J. 2013. *Wilfred Owen* (rev. edn., London: Pimlico).

Stallworthy, J., and Potter, J. (eds.) 2011. *Three Poets of the First World War: Ivor Gurney, Isaac Rosenberg, Wilfred Owen* (London: Penguin).

Stevenson, D. 2014. 'Supply and Logistics', www.bl.uk/world-war-one/articles/supply-and-logistics.

Stewart, R. 2016. *The Marches*, London: Random House.

Stobart, J. C. 1911. *The Glory That Was Greece: A Survey of the Hellenic Culture and Civilisation* (London: Sidgwick and Jackson).

Stobart, J. C. 1912. *The Grandeur That Was Rome: A Survey of Roman Culture and Civilisation* (London: Sidgwick and Jackson).

Stovall, F. (ed.) 1963–4. *Walt Whitman's Prose Works 1892* (New York: New York University Press).

Stray, C. A. 1998. *Classics Transformed: Schools, Universities and Society in England, 1830–1960* (Oxford: Clarendon).

Taylor, P., and Cupper, P. 2000. *Gallipoli: A Battlefield Guide* (Kenthurst, NSW: Kangaroo Press).

Thomson, J. A. K. 1915. *The Greek Tradition: Essays in the Reconstruction of Ancient Thought* (London: Allen and Unwin).

Vandiver, E. 1999. ' "Millions of the Mouthless Dead": Charles Hamilton Sorley and Wilfred Owen in Homer's Hades', *International Journal of the Classical Tradition* 5, 432–55.

Vandiver, E. 2010. *Stand in the Trench, Achilles: Classical Receptions in British Poetry of the Great War* (Oxford: Oxford University Press).

Vandiver, E. 2018. 'Dulce et Decorum Est: Wilfred Owen's Latin', http://ww1centenary.oucs.ox.ac.uk/?p=4261.

Vandiver, E. 2019. 'Classics, Empire, and War', in Haynes, K. (ed.) *The Oxford History of Classical Reception in English Literature*, Vol. 5: *After 1880* (Oxford: Oxford University Press), 170–99.

Welland, D. 1978. *Wilfred Owen: A Critical Study*. Rev. edn (London: Chatto and Windus).

West, M. L. 1966. *Hesiod: Theogony* (Oxford: Clarendon).

West, M. L. (ed. and trans.) 2003. *Greek Epic Fragments: From the Seventh to the Fifth Centuries BC*. Loeb Classical Library (Cambridge, MA: Harvard University Press).

White, R. H. 2022. *Wroxeter: Ashes under Uricon: A Cultural and Social History of the Roman City* (Oxford: Archaeopress).

Williams, R. D. (ed.) 1972. *The Aeneid of Virgil. Books 1–6.* (Basingstoke and London: Macmillan, St. Martin's Press).

Wilson, J. M. (ed.) 1985a. *The Collected Poems of Charles Hamilton Sorley* (London: Cecil Woolf).

Wilson, J. M. 1985b. *Charles Hamilton Sorley: A Biography* (London: Cecil Woolf).

Wilson, J. M. (ed.) 1990. *The Collected Letters of Charles Hamilton Sorley* (London: Cecil Woolf).

Winkler, M. M. 2000. '*Dulce et decorum est pro patria mori?* Classical Literature in the War Film', *International Journal of the Classical Tradition* 7.2, 177–214.

Winter, J. 2013. 'Beyond Glory: First World War Poetry and Cultural Memory', in Das, S. (ed.) 2013, 242–55.

Yeats, W. B. 1921. *Michael Robartes and the Dancer* (Dublin: Cuala Press).

Yeats, W. B. 1940. *Letters on Poetry from W. B. Yeats to Dorothy Wellesley* (London: Oxford University Press).

Index of Classical Writers

For the benefit of digital users, indexed terms that span two pages (e.g., 52–53) may, on occasion, appear on only one of those pages.

Aeschylus
  Agamemnon 435–6, 452–5 35–6
Apollonius
  Argonautica 195–6

Bion
  Lament for Adonis 120–1, 196–7, 209–10

Caesar
  De bello Gallico 116
Catullus
  11.22–4 84
  63 202–3 [on p.203]
Cicero
  Pro Archia 24 39

Euripides
  Bacchae 72 152
  Hippolytus 228–231 31
  Iphigenia in Aulis 1218–19, 1509 168,
    206–7

Herodotus
  History 1.31 39
Hesiod
  Theogony 148
  Works and Days 106–201 75
Homer
  Iliad 3 184
  Iliad 3.23–28 197–8
  Iliad 3.443 50
  Iliad 5.136–43 197–8
  Iliad 5.340 97
  Iliad 5.541–53 35
  Iliad 6 160–1
  Iliad 6.27–8 87–8
  Iliad 6.146–50 152–3
  Iliad 8.306–8 83–4, 87–8, 152–3, 202
  Iliad 8.337 87–8
  Iliad 10.485–8 197–8

  Iliad 11.67–71 76, 145
  Iliad 13.130–1 197–8
  Iliad 13.553 ff. 108
  Iliad 16.665–85 39, 170–1
  Iliad 16.856–7 96–7, 210–11
  Iliad 18.174 49–50
  Iliad 20.75 and 168 136
  Iliad 20.106–7 53–4
  Iliad 20.390–1 35
  Iliad 20.499–502 160
  Iliad 20.588ff 76
  Iliad 21 160–1
  Iliad 21.214–21 35
  Iliad 22.147–56 160
  Iliad 22.159–61 54–5
  Iliad 22.362–3 96–7, 210–11
  Iliad 22.395–440 97–8
  Iliad 23.69 157–8
  Iliad 24.18–23 97–8
  Iliad 24.495 39
  Iliad 24.629–32 54
  Odyssey 1.58–9 50
  Odyssey 1.93 50
  Odyssey 3.481–97 49
  Odyssey 4.47–58 49
  Odyssey 4.220–28 50
  Odyssey 4.240–58 49
  Odyssey 6.154 152
  Odyssey 8 185–6
  Odyssey 8.62–82 49–50
  Odyssey 10 103
  Odyssey 11 53, 157–9, 171–2, 210
  Odyssey 11.42 53
  Odyssey 11.48–50 159
  Odyssey 11.467–540 159–60
  Homeric Hymn to Aphrodite
    218–38 148
  Homeric Hymn to Demeter
    32–3 178
    480 152

Homeric Hymn to Pan
2, 37 32
Horace
Epistles 1.2 47–8 [p.48]
Epistles 1.10.49 50–1
Epistles 1.20.23–8 50–1
Epodes 2.1 152
Odes 1.9 147–8
Odes 1.14.1–2, 9 145
Odes 1.24 51
Odes 1.34.5–8 147–8
Odes 2.1.29–31 36
Odes 2.3.1–2 125–6
Odes 3.2.1–4 136
Odes 3.2.13 126, 206
Odes 3.2.13–16 130–2
Odes 3.30 141

Livy
Ab urbe condita 2.10 139
Lucan
De bello civili 4.593–653 193

Ovid
Metamorphoses 1 32, 206
Metamorphoses 2.272–300 148
Metamorphoses 3. 342ff 101–2
Metamorphoses 4 189
Metamorphoses 5 189
Metamorphoses 9.183–4 193
Metamorphoses 9.331–93 167–8
Metamorphoses 15.876–9 141, 143

Pindar
Isthmians 4.52–4 195
Pythians 8.85–7 209
Plato
Phaedo 117a-e 55
Republic 10.614b-621b 157–8
Propertius
2.13.35–8 34

Sallust
Bellum Catilinae 61.7–9 179
Simonides
AP 7.249 34
Sophocles
Antigone 338–9 55
Antigone 807–9, 879–80 168,
206–7
Statius
Achilleid 1.133–34 148

Theocritus
Idyll 13 195–6
Idylls 24, 25 195–6
Tibullus
1.3.55–6 34

Vergil
Aeneid 1.1 135
Aeneid 1.462 153–4
Aeneid 2.270 157–8
Aeneid 2.271, 773 158
Aeneid 2. 304–5 76
Aeneid 6 25, 159, 161–2, 185–6
Aeneid 6.126–9 171
Aeneid 6.237, 262 158–9
Aeneid 6.314 153
Aeneid 6.371 161–2
Aeneid 6.390 158–9
Aeneid 6.560ff 208
Aeneid 6.580–4 158–9
Aeneid 6.748–51 185–6
Aeneid 8.219–267 195–6 [= pp. 196, 197],
197–8
Aeneid 8.260 198–9
Aeneid 8.587–91 204
Aeneid 10.488–9 204
Aeneid 12.951–2 210–11
Eclogues 4.6–7 39
Georgics 1.491–2 36, 145–6
Georgics 2.490–2 152

Index of Biblical Passages

For the benefit of digital users, indexed terms that span two pages (e.g., 52–53) may, on occasion, appear on only one of those pages.

Hebrew Bible (Old Testament)
  Exodus 3:8 75–6
  Ezekiel 1 147–8
  Genesis 22: 1–19 18–19
  Hosea 6:11 76–7
  Isaiah 16.9 76–7
  Isaiah 17:11 76–7
  Isaiah 18:4–6 76–7
  Isaiah 35:1 55, 76–7
  Isaiah 40: 3 188
  Isaiah 40: 6–7 152–3
  Jeremiah 5:17 76–7
  Jeremiah 9:21 66–7
  Jeremiah 12:13 76–7
  Jeremiah 19:5 170
  Jeremiah 50:16 76–7
  Jeremiah 51:33 76–7
  Job 1. 15–19 157–8
  Job 5:5 76–7

Joel 3: 13 76–7
1 Kings 10–12 78–9
1 Kings 10:23 78–9
1 Kings 11:3 78–9
1 Kings 11:7 170
Psalms 37:1–2 88–9
Psalms 103 97–8
Psalms 103:14–16 88–9, 96–7
Song of Songs 78–9

New Testament
  Apocalypse 147–8
  John 13:1–7 17–18
  Luke 6:20–2 152
  Matthew 5:3–12 152
  Matthew 26: 14–39 17–18
  Matthew 27:29 96–7
  1 Peter 24 152–3
  Revelation (*see* Apocalypse)

Index of Poems

For the benefit of digital users, indexed terms that span two pages (e.g., 52–53) may, on occasion, appear on only one of those pages.

Brooke, Rupert
  'Clouds' 101
  'Dust' 25–6
  'Fragments written on the voyage to
      Gallipoli' 25, 36, 38–9
  'Goddess in the Wood, The' 25, 33
  'Hauntings' 25
  'It's Not Going to Happen Again' 25, 32
  'Jealousy' 25
  'Menelaus and Helen' 25
  'Mutability' 25, 32
  '1914' (sonnets) 33–4
    I. 'Peace' 33 n.5, 170
    II. 'Safety' 33 n.5
    III. 'The Dead' 33 n.5, 39, 144–5
    IV. 'The Dead' 33–4
    V. 'The Soldier' 15, 25–6, 33–8, 140,
      144 n.38, 145–6, 188
  'Old Vicarage, Grantchester, The' 1–2,
      24–33, 42–3, 47–8, 128 n.25
  'One Day' 25
  'Sonnet' (1909) 25
  'Sonnet' (1913) 25
  'Tiare Tahiti' 25–6

Owen, Wilfred
  'A Terre (being the philosophy of many
      soldiers)' 121, 210–11
  'Anthem for Doomed Youth' 17 n.25, 121,
      143–4, 144 n.39, 187
  'Apologia pro Poemate Meo' 20, 125,
      132–3, 170, 172–3, 181–4
  'Arms and the Boy' 125–6, 130, 133–7
  'Asleep' 149, 202, 207
  'Chances, The' 121
  'Cramped in that funnelled hole' 202
  'Dead-Beat, The' 121
  'Disabled' 121, 196–7, 205, 209–10
  'Dulce et Decorum Est' 9–10, 12, 109–10,
      121–2, 125–34, 137–9, 169, 182–4, 206

'Earth's wheels' 162–3
'Elegy in April and September' 202
'End, The' 19–20, 103, 125–6, 146–9,
      163, 189, 207
'Exposure' 89–90, 117–18, 125, 132–3,
      146, 172–80, 187, 198, 208
'Fates, The' 202
'From My Diary, July 1914' 174–5
'Futility' 117–18, 121, 149, 168, 172–3,
      180, 206–7
'Happiness' 202
'Has your soul sipped' 161 n.53, 202, 205
'Hospital Barge' 121
'I saw his round mouth's crimson' 81 n.27,
      204–5
'[Imperial Elegy, An]' 103, 125, 149, 163,
      188–9
'Insensibility' 125–6, 149–54, 165, 184, 187
'[It was an evening]' 163, 202–3
'Kind Ghosts, The' 211
'[Lines to a Beauty Seen in
      Limehouse]' 202
'Mental Cases' 157–8, 162–3, 202, 208
'Miners' 121, 143–4, 202
'New Heaven, A' 125, 154, 162, 180,
      185–7, 207
'Next War, The' 118, 121, 202
'1914' 125–6, 144–6
'O true…' 207
'Parable of the Old Man and the Young,
      The' 18 n.32, 188–9
'[Perseus]' 89–90, 125, 139–40, 180, 189,
      194, 198–202, 207
'[Purgatorial Passions]' 162–3, 202
'Roundel' 203
'Schoolmistress' 125–6, 133, 137–40
'Send-Off, The' 208–9
'Sentry, The' 117–18, 121, 162–3, 172–3,
      202, 208
'Show, The' 121, 189, 202

'Smile, Smile, Smile' 164 n.54
'Song of Songs' 118, 121
'Spring not, spring not in my wild eyes' 154
'Spring Offensive' 6–7, 125, 132–3,
    163–73, 183–4, 207–8
'Strange Meeting' 9, 11, 25 n.2, 52, 98, 103,
    121, 125, 135, 143–4, 149, 154–63,
    171–3, 189, 202–4, 208
'To Poesy' 113
'Training' 54–5, 202
'Unreturning, The' 162–3, 204
'Uriconium: An Ode' 115–16, 154–5
'With an Identity Disc' 125–6, 140–4
'Women and the Slain, The'/'The Ballad of
    Purchase Money' 132–3, 146, 162,
    180, 205–6
'Wrestlers, The' 118, 125, 139–40, 177,
    189–200

Rosenberg, Isaac
    The Amulet (verse play) 77–8, 97, 99
    'August 1914' 73–7, 78 n.24, 97, 108–10, 145
    'Break of Day in the Trenches' 12, 16,
        64–5, 69–70, 72–3, 80–90, 104–5, 110,
        152–3, 178–9
    'Daughters of War' 103, 105–6
    'Dead Man's Dump' 7 n.14, 11, 64, 72, 76–7,
        81, 90–9, 105, 111, 160 n.52, 210–11
    'Destruction of Jerusalem by the
        Babylonian Hordes' 77–8
    'Dusk and the Mirror' 101–2

'Girl to Soldier on Leave' 103, 163
'Girl's Thoughts, A' 69
'Heart's First Word' 69
'Immortals, The' 102, 104
'In the Trenches' 80–5, 87–8, 90, 96–7, 102
'Jew, The' 70, 72, 86 n.32
'Louse Hunting' 59, 102, 104
'Marching—as seen from the left file'
    69–70, 102
Moses (verse play) 69–70
'On Receiving News of the War: Cape
    Town' 15, 99–101, 144–5
'Returning, we hear the larks' 7 n.14,
    16 n.24, 64–5, 81, 100, 103, 108
'Soldier Twentieth Century' 103
'[Worm fed on the heart of Corinth, A]'
    77–80, 100–1, 105
'Wedded' 69
Sorley, Charles Hamilton
    'All the hills and vales along' 42, 55
    'I have not brought my Odyssey' 9,
        41–51, 54
    'In Memoriam S.C.W., V.C.' 54
    'J. B.' 51
    'Marlborough' 51
    'Quis desiderio' 42, 51
    'Song of the Ungirt Runners, The' 42,
        51, 54–5
    'To Germany' 42, 51, 54
    'When you see millions of the mouthless
        dead' 42–3, 51–4, 161 n.53, 204

General Index

For the benefit of digital users, indexed terms that span two pages (e.g., 52–53) may, on occasion, appear on only one of those pages.

Abbreviations:
  CS = Charles Sorley
  IR = Isaac Rosenberg
  RB = Rupert Brooke
  WO = Wilfred Owen
For individual poems by CS, IR, RB, and WO,
  see the 'Index of Poems'

Abercrombie, Lascelles 23–4, 69
Achilles 4–5, 9, 15, 35, 49, 53–4, 76, 98,
        103, 148, 160, 169–70, 176, 183,
        189, 197–8
  Hector, pursuit of 54–5, 160
  Hector's body, defiles 97–8
  Lycaon, slays 52–4, 160–1
  Odysseus in Underworld, speaks to
        159–60, 171–2, 210
  Patroclus appears to in dream 157–8
  Priam, meeting with 54, 153–4
  tomb of 34, 39
Acrisius 200–1
Acropolis (Athens) 187
Actaeon 136–7
Adam and Eve, fall of 136 n.32, 186
Adonis 120–1, 167–8, 196–7, 209–10
Aeacus 197–8
Aeneas 9, 35, 153–4
  conversations in Underworld 25, 160–2
  dream appearances to 157–8
  katabasis of 153–5, 157–9, 161–2,
        171, 208
Aeschylus 10, 16 n.24, 59, 62–3, 102
  Agamemnon 35–6, 59 n.6, 109–10
  Eumenides 35 n.6
affinities 6–7, 10–11, 20, 47–8, 64, 66–7,
        74–5, 98–9, 111
  see also *Oxford Classical Reception
        Commentaries*, taxonomy
afterlife 36, 52–3, 105–6, 148–9, 154, 159–60,
        185–7, 207
  Christian 19–20, 52–3, 148, 186
  see also heaven; hell; Paradise; Underworld

Agamemnon 12–13, 18, 49, 66–7, 171–2
Age (personified) 19–20, 148, 200–1
Ajax 171–2
Akkadian literature 66–7
Alcinous 49
Alcmene 197–8
Aldington, Richard 2–3
  and Imagism 74–5
Alexander the Great 39
alliteration 75, 78–9, 81–2, 94–5, 151–2, 194
allusion 4–10, 14–15, 17–18, 19, 24, 78 n.23,
        79 n.26, 109–10, 195
  in CS 42, 50, 54–5
  indirect 9, 12–13, 87–8
  in IR 58–63, 67, 74–7, 80, 87–8, 95,
        97–103, 105
  in RB 25, 34
  submerged 8–9, 148
  triangulation of 98, 109–10
  types of 9
  in WO 119–21, 126, 148, 157–8, 160–2,
        167–8, 178–9, 188–9, 209–10
  see also *Oxford Classical Reception
        Commentaries*, taxonomy
Amazons 103
ambrosia 75–6, 90, 96
America 23, 105–6, 122
Amphitryon 195–6
Andromeda 199, 201–2
Antaeus 118, 139–40, 177, 189, 192–8
anti-Semitism 86–7
  and T. S. Eliot 70 n.20, 86 n.31
  toward IR 2 n.4, 62, 69–71, 86 n.32, 87–8
  and Ezra Pound 70, 109–10
Antwerp 24
Apelles 32
Aphrodite 31, 209–11
  see also Venus
Apollo 23–4, 39, 97–8
Apollonius
  Argonautica 195–6
Apulia 142

Arcas 136–7
Argo 195–6
Argonauts 24, 195–6
aristeia 169–70, 173, 183
Armistice, the 21, 89 n.36, 119
Artemis 31
    see also Diana
Arthur (King) 187, 201
Arts and Crafts School, Stepney Green
        (London) 57–8
Artists' Rifles 117, 131
Asia Minor 39, 77–8
Asquith, Violet 34–5
associations 4, 6–13, 16–19, 20 n.36, 21, 99,
        108, 110–11
    IR and 58–63, 75 n.22, 76–83, 81 n.27,
        86–90, 94–101, 108, 110–11
    reader-activated 10–11, 58–9, 109–10,
        180, 209
    religious 17–19, 100–1, 147–8
    WO and 120–1, 145, 147–8, 202, 204,
        206–7, 209–10
    see also *Oxford Classical Reception
        Commentaries*, taxonomy
Assyrian literature 66–7
Athens 31, 185
Attis 202–3
Auden, W. H. 111, 122–3
Aurora 176
    see also Dawn; Eos
author, role of 7–8, 12

Baal 170
Babylon 77–80
Bain, John 41–3, 48–51
Bainbrigge, Philip 24 n.1, 36–7, 118–19
    'If I should die' 36–7
Balmer, Josephine 3–4, 7–8
Bantam Battalions 67, 86 n.32
Berg, Alban 122–3
Berg Collection, New York Public Library 73
Bible 114 n.1, 120–1
    agricultural imagery in 66–7
    allusions, associations, and connections to
        and CS 55
        and IR 10, 57–9, 62–3, 66–7, 71–2,
            76–9, 87–9, 96–7, 99
        and WO 114 n.1, 120–1, 136 n.32,
            147–8, 152–3, 157–8, 170, 188
    and ancient Near Eastern literature 66–7
    flowers, as motif in 88–9, 96–7, 152–3
    grass, as motif in 88–9, 96–7, 152–3

harvest and reaping, as motif in 66–7,
        76–7, 152–3
    editions, versions, and translations:
        Authorized version (King James
            Bible) 8–9, 57, 88–9
        Hebrew (Tanakh) 18, 57, 62–3, 66–7,
            76–9, 87–8, 96–7, 170
        New Testament 62–3
        Septuagint 57
        Vulgate 57
Binyon, Laurence 58, 68–9, 104–5
birds 72–3, 136–7
    as motif 9, 64
    see also larks
Birkbeck College (London) 57–8, 68–9, 105
Birkenhead Institute 113–14
Blake, William 9, 57–8, 62–3, 69, 72, 80, 105
    as artist 105
    IR's evaluation of 105
    'Echoing Green, The' 88–9
    'Jerusalem' 101
    'London' 78–9
    'Marriage of Heaven and Hell, The' 98
    'Milton' 101
    'Sick Rose, The' 78–80, 100–1
    'Tyger, The' 87–8
Bloomsbury 58, 68
Bloomsbury Group 23–4
Blunden, Edmund 110–11, 121, 124, 128–9,
        142, 144 n.39, 174–5
    'Vlamertinghe: Passing the Chateau,
        July 1917' 20 n.36
Board School, Baker Street (London) 57–8
Bodleian Library (Oxford) 115–16, 123
    English Faculty Library 124, 124 n.18
    Weston Special Collections
        Library 115 n.4, 124, 124 n.18
Boer War 35, 131
Boland, Eavan 3–4
Bomberg, David 69
    *Sappers at Work: Canadian Tunnelling
        Company, R 14, St Eloi* 94
Bonaparte, Napoleon 103
Borden, Mary 3, 20
    Forbidden Zone, The 3 n.5
    'Hill, The' 108
    'Song of the Mud, The' 20, 107–8
    'Where Is Jehovah?' 18 n.32, 107 n.52
Botticelli, Sandro 102
Bottomley, Gordon 58–9, 69, 80–1, 85–7,
        86 n.32, 102, 105–6
Bottomley, Horatio 127 n.24, 182

Britain 3, 24, 74, 78–9, 85 n.30
    Roman occupation of 115–16
    see also England
Britannia (personified) 211
British Library 26, 86–7, 123, 182–3
British Museum 72
    Prints and Drawings Department 69, 73
Brittain, Vera 3
    'Perhaps—(*To R.A.L. Died of Wounds in
        France, December 23rd
        1915*)' 106–7
    Testament of Youth 107 n.50
Britten, Benjamin
    War Requiem 121
Brock, A. E. (WO's therapist) 118, 193–4,
        196–7
    Antaeus
        article on 192–5
        assigns to WO as topic for poem
            ('The Wrestlers') 118, 189, 192–4
        interpretation of myth of 193, 195
    classical knowledge 193 n.79, 197 n.85
    and 'ergotherapy' 118
Brooke, Rupert Chawner 1–3, 11–13, 15,
        61–2, 72, 75–6, 132, 144–5, 206
    and Aeschylus' *Agamemnon* 35–6
    appearance of 23–4, 37–8
    and Catullus 25
    class, social 2
    and classical associations of Gallipoli 18,
        24, 36, 38
    CS on 42–3
    and the dead 34–6, 38–9
    death of 2, 24, 33–4
    education of 2, 7–8, 23, 25, 132
    and English landscape 30–2
    emotional and sexual life 23–6
    enlistment 24
    and Euripides 25, 31–3
    family
        daughter in Tahiti, possible 23
        parents 23
    funeral of 18
    grave of 18, 24, 144–5
    and Greek epigram 25, 33–4, 36
    and Herodotus 39
    and Homer 18, 23–5, 34–5
    and *Homeric Hymn to Pan* 32
    intratextuality in 32–3, 36
    IR on 75–6, 101
    and love elegy, Latin 34

    and Lucretius 23, 25
    metres
        iambic pentameter 33–4
        iambic tetrameter 30–1, 47–8
    military service 24
    and Neoplatonism 36
    1914 sonnets 33–4, 39, 44, 75–6, 101
    and Ovid 23, 32
    paramaterial 26
    posthumous reputation 24–6, 122 n.15, 206
    publication history 24, 26, 33–4
    receptions, later 24–6, 101
        P. Bainbrigge 36–7
        musical settings of poems 25–6
        W. B. Yeats 23–4, 36–8
    rhyme, feminine 30–1
    and Sappho 18, 23–4
    sonnet form, use of 25, 33–4, 39, 169
    and Sophocles 23
    travel
        in Germany 30–1
        in North America, the Pacific, and
            Tahiti 23
    Trojan war, in poems of 25, 34–6, 38–9
    and Vergil 25, 36, 39
    WO's opinion of 144–5
Browne, Sir Thomas
    Religio Medici 104–5
Browning, Robert
    'Home Thoughts, from Abroad' 30–1
Buddhism 186
burial 39, 153, 177–8, 180
    in foreign territory 35–6
    see also dead, the; death; funeral rites;
        mourning and commemoration
Burns, Robert
    'Jolly Beggars' 102
    'To a Louse' 102
Butler, Samuel
    Hudibras 30–1, 47–8
Byron, George Gordon, Lord 32

Cacus 195–8
Caesar, Julius 103, 116, 119–20
Cain 79 n.26
Calleva Atrebatum. *See* Silchester
Callisto 136–7
Calypso 50
Camilla 204
Cannan, May Wedderburn 3
    'August 1914' 106–7

Cape Town, South Africa 59–60, 67
Carlisle Art Gallery 59–60, 73
Carthage 153–4, 170, 211
catastrophe 16 n.24, 64–5, 76–7
catastrophe literature 65–7
Catullus 25, 84 n.29, 152–3, 202–3
censorship of soldiers' letters, military 24, 68, 72
chance 16–17, 19 n.33, 64–5
Chapman, George
    translation of Homer 119–20, 160–1
Charon 153, 158–9, 187
chivalry 4, 101, 201
Christianity 18–20, 36, 52–3, 62–3, 136–7,
        147–8, 169–71, 178–9, 186
    in First World War poetry 16–18
    Hell 158–9, 171–2
    Paradise 186
    Providence 16–17
    see also afterlife; Bible; religion
Churchill, Winston 24, 34–5, 69
Cicero 39, 48 n.19
Circe 103
civilians and non-combatants 178–9
    attitude toward First World War 3, 6, 16,
        183–4, 203
    veterans among 183–4
    WO's view of 132–3, 138–9, 183–4, 203
class, social 4–5, 58–61, 64–5, 67, 69–70,
        138–9
    and culture 4–5
    and education 7–8, 60–1, 64–5, 113
    and war poets 2, 5, 60–1, 64–5
classics as 'cultural capital' 132
Clytie 167–8
code-switching 58 9, 63, 129–30
Cohen, Mrs. Herbert 74–6, 105–6
Columbia University (New York City) 123
comparative analysis 7–9, 13, 21, 57, 65, 104–11
consolation 35–6, 53–4
    Christian 52–3, 170–1
    futility of 53, 152–3, 170–1, 173
Corinth 77–80
Cornford, Frances 23–4
cowardice 3, 130–1
Cowley, Abraham 154
    'Happy the Man...' 152
Craiglockhart War Hospital 22, 118–20, 132,
        135 n.31, 192–3
    WO's poems written at 127, 137, 140, 147,
        151, 177, 193–4, 196–7, 204–5, 209
    reading room/library 195–7

Crethon 35
Creusa 158
culture, popular 4–5
Currie, Bruno 67 n.19
Cybele 202–3
Cyparissus 167–8

Danae 199–202
Dante 171, 208
    The Divine Comedy 157–9, 195 n.80
        H. F. Cary's translation 119–20, 157–8
    katabasis of 157–8, 171
Daphne 167–8
Dardanelles campaign 4–5, 34–5, 38
    see also Gallipoli
Das, Santanu 169–70, 171 n.63, 206–7
Dawn (goddess) 32, 176, 204, 208
    see also Aurora; Eos
Day Lewis, C. 121, 128–9, 142, 180, 185, 187
dead, the 11, 33–4, 38–9, 52–3, 89–90, 95–8,
        105, 140, 143–4, 152–3, 162, 168,
        171–2, 175–6, 179–80, 184, 204, 207
    attempts by living to contact 52–3, 204
    conversations with 25, 53, 159–62, 171,
        185–6, 210
    despoiling of 107, 179–80
    and fertility of land 36, 145–6, 180
    in Greek epigram 34
    as happy 39
    in Homer 159–60, 171, 210
    and Lethe 185–6
    and Styx 153–4, 185–7
    unburied 93, 97–8, 106–7, 153–4, 161–2,
        180, 185–7
    in Vergil 153, 161–2, 185–7
    see also dreams and visions; dying, the;
        ghosts
death 34, 64–5, 96–7, 175–6
    in battle 34–6, 52, 132–4, 152–3, 169–71
    far from home 15, 34–5, 175–6
    finality of 206–7
    glorification of 52, 54, 101, 132, 170–1
    own, poet imagines or foresees 15, 34–8,
        110, 175–7
    personified 170–1
    and preservation of future 145–6, 177–80
    see also burial; consolation; mourning and
        commemoration; sacrifice
Debussy, Claude 32
Demeter 89–90, 206–7
Demodocus 49–50

Diaghilev, Sergei 32
Diana 136–7
    see also Artemis
Dido 9, 25
Diomedes 160–1
Donne, John 62–3, 85–8, 102, 104–5, 206–7
    IR's opinion of 85, 104–5
    'Break of Day' 85
    'The Flea' 87–8, 104
Doolittle, Hilda (H.D.) 3–4, 74–5
    'Hermes of the Ways' 74–5
Douglas, Keith 3–4, 71, 110
    'Desert Flowers' 71, 110
dreams and visions 52–3, 175–7, 202–3
    appearances of ghosts in 157–8
    WO's 'Strange Meeting' as 157–9,
        161–2
Dryden, John
    translation of Horace's *Odes* 3.29 154
    translation of Vergil's *Georgics* 36
Dryope 167–8
Duffy, Carol Ann
    'Last Post' 133–4
dulce et decorum est pro patria mori 109–10,
        129–30, 133, 136
    in 19th and early 20th-century British
        culture 130–2, 206
    on gravestones and monuments 131
    interpretation of, WO's influence on 9–10,
        122, 133–4
    meaning in Horace 9–10, 122, 130–1
    and Ezra Pound 109, 133
    WO and 129–34, 206
Dunsden (Oxfordshire) 114–16, 125–6
dying, the 5, 93, 152–3, 175–9, 202, 204–5,
        209–10
    see also dead, the; death

Earth (personified) 6–7, 19–20, 55, 91, 94–5,
        148, 163, 165–6, 173, 177, 193
    see also Gea; Gaia
East End (London) 57–8, 68–70
ecocritical poetics 13, 21, 61–2, 65–6
Eden 136 n.32, 186
Edinburgh 118, 123–4, 192–3
education, classical, *see* public schools,
        English
Eidinow, Esther 18–19
elders
    Greek 35–6
    Trojan 183–4

Eliot, T. S. 3–4, 76
    anti-Semitism of 70 n.20, 86 n.31
    on IR 71
    'Burbank with a Boedeker: Bleistein with
        a Cigar' 86 n.31
    'Gerontion' 86 n.31
    'Sweeney among the Nightingales' 86 n.31
    Waste Land, The 109–10
Elpenor 171, 185–6
empire 4
    British 5 n.12, 78–9, 78 n.23
England 3, 41, 50, 54–5, 67, 72
    'betrothal' of 78–9
    CS and 47–50, 54–5
    and Georgian poetry 1–2, 24–5
    IR and 75–80, 101
    landscape of 1–2, 15, 20, 24–5, 30–1,
        48–50, 65, 75–6, 108–9
    nostalgia for 30–1, 47–8
    and pastoral 65, 75–6
    personified 211
    RB and 30–2, 34–5, 37–8, 47–8
    and Troy 4–5
    WO and 117–19, 185, 187
Enna 178
environment 6–7, 13, 32, 72–3, 193
    First World War poetry and 13, 18–21,
        61–2, 65–6, 106–8
    as motif 14–15
    war's impact on 4, 20–1
    see also ecocritical poetics; England,
        landscape of; natural world
Eos 148, 176
    see also Aurora; Dawn
Epic Cycle, the 77–8, 103, 176
epigram, Greek 25, 31 n.3, 32 n.4, 34
    and sonnets 33–4, 36, 140
epistles, poetic 30–1, 47–8, 50–1
Er, myth of 157–8
erasure 58–9
Eros 200–2, 209–10
Euripides
    Bacchae, The 152
    Hippolytus 31–3
    Iphigenia in Aulis 168, 206–7

fame 140, 171, 204
    personified 142–3
    poet's desire for 142–3
fate 16, 152
Fauns 32, 196 n.82

First World War
    in art 64, 76–7, 89–90
    contemporary attitudes to 6
    poetry as source for study of 1–6, 72
    and Trojan War 4–5, 11, 38, 79–80, 100–1,
        110–11
    see also civilians and non-combatants,
        attitude to First World War;
        Western Front
First World War Poetry Digital Archive
        (FWWPDA) 13 n.21
    IR's materials in 68, 70 n.21, 73
    WO's materials in 123–4, 127, 142, 156,
        166, 174 n.65, 183–4, 192 n.77,
        197, 205 n.92
Fitzgerald, F. Scott
    This Side of Paradise 25–6
Flanders 18 n.32, 20, 34–5, 83, 89–90,
        94 n.41, 185
Flaubert, Gustave
    Salammbô 170, 211
flowers, as motif 71, 81–2, 87–9, 96–7,
        108–11, 152–3, 166, 169
Fox, George
    *Guide to the Roman City of
        Uriconium* 115–16
Frazer, J. G.
    The Golden Bough 145–6
free verse 93, 96, 105–6, 151
Freston, Rex 133–4
funeral rites 34, 95–8
    Christian 18
    in *Iliad* 34–5, 97–8
    see also burial; consolation; mourning and
        commemoration
Fuscus 50–1

Gaia 193
    see also Earth (personified); Gea
Gallipoli 4–5, 7, 24–5, 34–6, 38, 131
    and Trojan War 4–5, 11, 35, 38
    Turkish casualties at 39
    see also Dardanelles campaign
Gea 194, 197
    see also Earth (personified); Gaia
Georgian Poetry 69, 103
Georgian poets 1–2, 23–5, 61–2, 65, 75–6, 108
    and English landscape 1–2
ghosting 11, 21, 63, 83–4, 153
    see also *Oxford Classical Reception
        Commentaries*, taxonomy

ghosts 159, 211
    appearances to living 157–8
    nostos of, imagined 175–7, 180, 187
    speechless 53, 159
    unhappy 153
    see also dead, the; dreams and visions
Gibson, Wilfred 144 n.39
    'Wheels' 98
glancing 11, 25, 63, 83–4, 100, 125, 144–5,
        147–8, 154–5, 157–8, 161–2,
        167–70, 177–8, 183–4, 202, 204,
        206–8, 210–11
    see also *Oxford Classical Reception
        Commentaries*, taxonomy
Glaucus 160–1
glory 4 n.9, 54, 75–6, 101, 132, 136, 138–9,
        142, 145, 160, 169–73, 188
    see also *kleos*
Glory of the Kings, The (*Kebra Nugast*;
        Ethiopian epic) 78–9
God
    Christian 136–7, 140, 148, 169–71, 177–9,
        181–2, 198
    Hebraic 76–7, 100–1
gods
    classical 16–18, 32, 75–6, 97, 102–3,
        114–15, 136–7, 145–6, 152, 176,
        183–4, 187, 200–2
    Near Eastern 66–7
Gorgythion 83–4, 87–8, 90 n.39
Grantchester (Cambridgeshire) 30–2
Grantully Castle, the (ship) 18, 24
Graves, Robert 2–3, 24–5
    on CS 43, 161 n.53
    and WO 2, 118–19, 161 n.53,
        182, 209
    Goodbye to All That 43
    'Sorley's Weather' 43
    'Two Fusiliers' 182
Gray, Thomas
    'Elegy Written in a Country
        Churchyard' 188
Greek (language)
    in public-school curriculum 4–5
    WO's desire to learn 113–15
Gregory, Robert (Major) 37–8
Grenfell, Julian 2–3, 133–4
    'Into Battle' 169 n.61, 173
Gunston, Leslie (WO's cousin) 115–16, 147
    WO's letters to 122–3, 153, 173 n.64,
        193–4, 203

Gurney, Ivor 2–3, 5, 14–16, 64 n.13, 88 n.35,
    144 n.39
  social class and education 60–1
  '*Iliad* and Badminton, The' 61 n.7
  'Silent One, The' 16–18, 90 n.37
  'To His Love' 90 n.38, 106–7
  'To the Poet before Battle' 14–15

Hades (god) 177–8
  see also Pluto
Hades (Underworld) 89–90, 115–16, 153–5, 204
  see also hell, *katabasis*, Tartarus
Hardy, Thomas 2–3, 108–9
  'Drummer Hodge' 35
Harrison, Tony 3–4
  'Cold Coming, A' 95 n.43
Harry Ransom Center, University of Texas at
    Austin 124
harvest and reaping, as motif 9, 66–7, 75–7,
    145, 152–3, 180
  in Hebrew Bible 66–7, 76–7, 152–3
  in *Iliad*, simile for death in battle 76
  in Sumerian literature, simile for death in
    battle 66–7
  see also motifs, 'hanging'
Headlam, Walter 23
Heaney, Seamus 111, 122–3
  'Personal Helicon' 101–2
  'Requiem for the Croppies' 89–90
heaven 36, 52, 104–5, 173, 186
  as sky 20, 33, 183
  see also afterlife; hell; Paradise
Hebrew literature 17 n.26, 57–9, 61–2, 70–1,
    74–5, 75 n.22, 97–8
  and ancient Near Eastern literature 61–2,
    74–5
  see also Bible; Near Eastern literature, ancient
Hector 95 n.43, 96–7
  Achilles' pursuit of 54–5, 160
  body dragged behind Achilles' chariot 97–8
  burial and tomb of 39
  dream appearance to Aeneas 157–8
Helen 25, 78–80
  abduction by Paris 77–80
  and Menelaus 48–50
Helenus 39
Helios 183, 206–7
hell 109–10, 157–9, 170–2, 178, 183–4,
    195 n.80, 200–3, 208
  see also Hades (Underworld); *katabasis*;
    Underworld

Hellespont 32
Hera 197
Heracles 53–4, 118, 139–40, 154–5, 189, 193–8
  Farnese statue of 198, 203
  and homoeroticism 197
  and Hylas 194–7
  Labours of 195–6, 203
  see also Hercules
Herbert, George
  'Virtue' 87–8
Hercules 193, 195, 203–4
  see also Heracles
Hermes 74–5, 201–2
  WO's statue of 115–16
  see also Mercury
Herodotus 39
heroes, mythical 17–18, 24, 97–8
heroism 100–1
  ancient 4, 15, 24, 49–50, 64–5, 169–70
  glorification of 15, 61–2, 101
  medieval 101
  modern 15, 24, 101, 164–5
  and First World War 61–2, 100–1,
    164–5
Hesiod 75, 119–20, 148
  Five Ages in 75
Hibberd, Dominic 114–15, 119, 119 n.13,
    121, 124, 135, 142, 145–7, 151 n.45,
    158 n.49, 161 n.53, 166 n.56,
    182–3, 188–9, 196–7, 203, 211
  on WO's draft 'Preface' 164–5
  on WO's 'Dulce et Decorum Est' 128–9
  on WO's experiences on Western
    Front 117–18
  on WO's 'Exposure' 176–8
  on WO's imagery 205
  on WO's manuscripts 156, 166, 178,
    199, 201
  on WO's 'Perseus' fragments 198–9,
    201–2, 207
  on WO's 'Spring Offensive' 164–6, 170–2
'high intensity' cultural awareness 10 n.19,
    19–20
  of classics 19–20
'high intensity' religious belief 19–20, 148,
    178–9
  see also religion
Hinds, Stephen 8–9
Hippolytus 31, 33
Hodgson, Noel 133–4
homecoming, see *nostos*.

Homer 4, 9–12, 18, 21, 23–5, 32, 38–9, 41–2,
        51, 54, 58–9, 62–3, 77–8, 87–8,
        96–7, 105–6, 108, 119–20, 154–5,
        169–70, 173, 176, 183, 201–2, 204,
        208, 210–11
    battle polyptoton 197–8
    epithets 32 n.4, 49–50, 66–7, 83–4, 197–8
    and Near Eastern literature 58–9, 66–7
    and *nostos* 15, 176–7
    patronymics 197–8
    poetics of 21, 66–7, 74–5, 108
    and poppy 83–4, 87–8, 90, 110–11, 152–3, 202
    Iliad 4–5, 9, 12, 34–5, 52–4, 61 n.7, 97–8,
        136, 152–4, 160–1, 183–4
    Odyssey 9, 15, 42, 47–50, 52–3, 103, 171–2,
        176–7
    see also similes; specific entries in 'Index of
        Classical Writers'
Homeric Hymns 32, 148, 152, 178
Hopkins, Gerard Manley 95
    'God's Grandeur' 95 n.42
Horace 8–10, 109–10, 132–3, 135, 139, 154
    and CS 42, 47–8, 50–1
    as 'cultural capital' 132
    meaning of *dulce et decorum est pro patria
        mori* in 130–1, 133–4
    military service of 130–2
    in public-school curriculum 25
    RB's allusions to 25, 36
    'Ship of State' in 145
    WO's allusions to 122, 125–6, 129–31,
        133, 135–7, 141–5, 147–9,
        152, 154
    WO's knowledge of 119–20, 125–6, 130,
        136–7, 141–3, 154
Horatius Cocles 133, 138–9
    companions of 139
Housman, A.E. 2–3
    A Shropshire Lad 117
    'To an Athlete Dying Young' 209–10
Hughes, Ted 3–4
Hulme, T. E. 69, 71
Hyacinthus 167–8
Hydra, The 119–20, 192–3, 195
    extant issues of 123–4, 192–3
    WO as editor 118–20, 123–4, 193–4
Hylas 194–7
    abduction by nymphs 195–6

Icarus 201
ichor 90, 97–8

idealization
    of Graeco-Roman past 145
    of natural world 6–7, 20, 94–5
    of pastoral 61–2
Imagism 74–5, 109–10
Imperial War Graves Commission 68
Imperial War Museum (IWM) 59–60, 72–3,
        81, 89 n.36
imperialism, *see* empire
improvising 12, 62–3, 74–5, 83, 97–8
    see also *Oxford Classical Reception
        Commentaries*, taxonomy
Inge, W. R. (Dean) 33–4, 36
Ingleheart, Jennifer 118–19
intertexts, biblical
    and CS 55
    and IR 16 n.24, 18, 58–9, 62–3, 74–9,
        87–9, 96–8
    and WO 120–1, 147–8, 152–3, 157–8,
        170, 188
intertexts, classical
    and CS 9, 42, 47–55, 154–5
    and IR 10, 16 n.24, 58–9, 62–3, 74–8,
        83–4, 87–90, 96–8, 101–2
    and RB 31–6
    and WO 9, 119–20, 122, 125–6, 129–31,
        133, 135–7, 141–9, 152–4, 157–62,
        167–72, 176–80, 183–7, 195–8,
        202, 204, 206, 208–11
intertexts, post-classical
    in IR 85, 87–8, 98, 100–1, 103–6
    in RB 30–2, 35–6
    in WO 120–1, 127, 140 n.37, 145–6,
        152–4, 157–8, 160–1, 169, 173,
        176–7, 178 n.70, 182–3, 188,
        206–10
intertextuality 3, 9–10, 14, 59–60, 62–3, 66–7,
        75–7, 83–4, 96, 103–6, 109–10,
        125–6, 136, 143, 176–7, 188
    see also *Oxford Classical Reception
        Commentaries*, taxonomy
intratextuality 10, 14, 96
    in CS 51, 54
    in IR 10, 63, 77, 83–4, 96–7, 99
    in RB 33, 36
    in WO 139, 154–5, 168, 172–3, 177, 180,
        184, 187–9, 198, 202, 204–9
    see also *Oxford Classical Reception
        Commentaries*, taxonomy
Iphigenia 12–13, 18, 168, 206–7
Iphition 35

iron, as motif
    IR's use of 75–7
    in Near Eastern literature 67
    in myth of sequence of 'ages' 75
Isaac, binding of (Akedah) 188–9
Islam 186
Ithaca 15, 48–50

Jerusalem, destruction of 78 n.24
Jesus Christ 17–18, 96–7, 200
    crown of thorns 96–7
    as trope for soldiers' suffering 16–18, 68,
        96–7, 105–6
    see also Christianity
Jewish East End Celebration Society 68
Jewish Educational Aid Society 58
Joergens, Olwen 147
Johannesburg, South Africa 67
Jones, David 2–3, 4 n.9, 5, 61 n.8
    as artist 11
    In Parenthesis 87 n.33, 201 n.89
Jupiter 147–8, 158–9, 204
    see also Zeus
Jupiter Capitolinus, Temple of (Rome) 142

katabasis 11, 125, 154–5, 157–8,
        161–2, 171
    in Aeneid 159–62, 171–2
    in CS's poems 52–3, 154–5
    in Dante's Divine Comedy 157–8, 171
    in Odyssey 159–60, 171–2
    in WO's poems 125, 154–5, 157–63,
        167–8, 171–3, 177–8, 180, 183, 199
    in Plato's Republic 157–8
    see also Hades (Underworld); hell;
        Tartarus; Underworld
Keats, John 105, 120–1, 157–8, 167 n.58,
        206–7
    grave of in Rome 142–3
    WO's admiration for 119–20, 142, 176, 189
    'Endymion' 189, 199
    'Hyperion' 189, 199
    'Ode to a Nightingale' 176
Kelly, Frederick 18
Kendall, Tim 85
Keynes, Geoffrey 24
King's College, Cambridge 23, 26, 30–1
King's School (Gloucester) 60–1
Kingsley, Charles
    Heroes, The 120–1, 189 n.76

Kipling, Rudyard 2–3, 16
    'Common Form' 16 n.23
    'Recessional' 78 n.23
kleos 54, 171–2
    see also fame; glory

Lang, Andrew
    translation, Theocritus, Bion and
        Moschus 119–21, 195–7,
        209–10
larks, as motif 7 n.14, 16 n.24
    in IR 7 n.14, 16 n.24, 20, 64–5
    see also birds
Latin
    in public-school curriculum 4–5, 132
    WO's knowledge of 113–16, 182–3
Leander 32
Ledwidge, Francis 21
Leftwich, Joseph 69
Lethe 185–6
Letts, Winnifred M. 3
Lewis, Wyndham
    Battery Shelled, A 94
lice 10, 59, 102, 104
Life (personified) 19–20, 148
Liddiard, Jean 70–1
Livy 133, 138–9
Logue, Christopher
    War Music: An Account of Homer's
        Iliad 12
Lollius 47–8, 50–1
Longley, Edna 106–9
Longley, Michael 3–4, 10, 21–2, 101–2, 110–11
    and Homer 10, 110–11
    and IR 110–11
    poppy as motif, use of 10, 110–11
    metalepsis in 21, 110–11
    temporalities in 110–11
    and Vergil 10, 110–11
    'Ballyboley' 99, 111
    'Campfires' 108 n.54
    Candlelight Master, The 21
    'Orpen' 21
    'Ors' 21–2
    'Pebble, A' 111
    'Poetry' 110–11
    'Poppy, A' 10, 90 n.39, 110–11
    Stairwell, The 111
    'War Graves' 110–11
Lotis 167–8

love elegy, Latin
  in public-school curriculum 34
'low intensity' cultural awareness
  of classics 10 n.19, 19–20, 58–9, 148, 178–9
'low intensity' religious belief 19–20,
      178–9, 186
  see also religion
luck 16–17, 64–5
Lucretius 23, 25, 59
Lycaon 52–4, 160–1

Macaulay, Thomas 138
  'Horatius at the Bridge' 138–9
  Essays and Lays 113–14, 138–9
  Lays of Ancient Rome 138–9
McCrae, John
  'In Flanders Fields' 34–5, 83
MacNeice, Louis 3–4
makarismos 152
Mallarmé, Stephane
  'L'Après-Midi d'un faune' 32
Marlborough (Wiltshire) 48–51
Marlborough College 41, 43, 48, 51, 54
Mars 75–6, 102, 102 n.48
Marsh, Edward 34–5, 58–9, 67, 73, 85–6, 93,
      101, 104–6, 118–19
  patron of IR 67–9, 103
  patron of RB 24, 34–5
  Georgian Poetry 1916–1917, edits 103
Marvell, Andrew 93
masculinity 4, 160–1
Masefield, John 43
Mecca 186
Medusa 199
  see also Gorgon
Memnon 176
memorialization, *see* mourning and
      commemoration
Menelaus 49, 77–8
  and Helen 25, 48–50
Mercury 201
  see also Hermes
metalepsis 12, 21, 63–5, 81–4, 96, 110–11,
      128, 164–5, 182–4
metre
  blank verse 192–4
    feminine endings in 194
  iambic 114–15, 151, 175, 204, 206, 208
    pentameter 33–4, 128–9, 135, 138, 147,
      157, 165, 175, 182, 209–10

tetrameter 30–1, 47–8
    trimeter 147
Meynell, Alice
  'Summer in England 1914' 106–7
Milton, John 62–3, 101, 172
misogyny 138
Modernism 2, 74–5, 121, 151 n.45
Moloch 170, 211
Monro, Harold 117, 157–8
  Children of Love 117
Monroe, Harriet 69–70
Morley, Edith 116
motifs 61–3, 120–1
  hanging 9, 58–9, 63–4, 98 n.45, 106–7,
      110–11, 136 n.32, 183
  transferred 63, 79–80
  see also birds; eagles; grass; harvest and
      reaping; iron; larks; mud; *Oxford
      Classical Reception Commentaries*,
      taxonomy; poppy
mourning and commemoration 34–6,
      52–4, 131
  in Aeschylus 35–6
  CS and 52–4
  Iliad, in 34–5
  RB and 34–6
  WO and 142–3, 148–9, 152–4, 171–2, 206–7
  see also burial; consolation; death; funeral
      rites
mud, as motif 20, 68, 72, 89–90, 99, 107–8,
      174, 181
Muses 49, 143
  Melpomene 142–3
myth
  classical 18, 58–60, 65, 77–8, 89–90, 97,
      101–2, 178–9, 187, 189
  in First World War Poetry 18
  Norse 186

Naiads 32
Najarian, James 197
Narcissus 101–2, 167–8
narratology 12
Nash, Paul
  Menin Road, The 94 n.41
  Wire 94
  Ypres Salient at Night, The 94
Nation, The 206
National Portrait Gallery (London) 73
nationalism 87–8

natural world 6–7, 9, 15, 18–20, 61–2, 65–6,
        76, 80, 89–90, 100–1, 114–15,
        136–7, 166–9, 173, 177, 183, 193
    see also environment; England, landscape of
Nature (personified) 165–7, 169, 172–3
Nausicaa 152
Near Eastern literature, ancient 58–9, 61–2,
        66–7, 105
    and Greek literature 66–7
    and Hebrew Bible 66–7
    and Homeric epic 66–7
    and IR 58–9, 61–2, 66–7, 74–5
nectar 75–6
Neoplatonism 36
Nestor 49
New Numbers 33–4, 98
Newman, J. H. (Cardinal)
    Apologia pro vita sua 182–3
    'Lead, kindly light' 52–3
Nirvana 186
Nisus 136–7
no man's land 86–9, 108 n.54, 117–18
Norgate, Paul 126 n.23, 127 n.24, 129, 182–4
nostalgia 2 n.3, 15, 30–1, 47–8, 74–6,
        85–6, 108
nostos 15, 35, 48, 50, 175–7, 187, 187 n.74, 208
Novello, Ivor
    'Keep the Home Fires Burning' 176–7
nymphs 32, 167–8, 195–6

Odysseus 15, 48–50, 103, 152, 176–7
    conversations in Underworld 53, 159–60
        with Achilles 159–60, 171–2, 210
        with Agamemnon 171–2
        with Ajax 171–2
        with Anticlea 53
        with Elpenor 171
    katabasis of 53, 154–5, 157–60, 171
        describes to Phaeacians 157–8, 171
    and *nostos* 15, 48, 50, 176–7
    Penelope, reunion with 176–7
Olympians, *see* gods, classical
onomatopoeia 94–5
oral literature 58–9
Orpen, William 21, 64, 108 n.53
    Harvest 1918 77
    *To the Unknown British Soldier in
        France* 89 n.36
    *View from the old British Trenches at La
        Boisette* 89–90

Orsilochus 35
Oswald, Alice 3–4, 11, 83–4
    Sidelong Glances 11
Ovid 7–8, 23, 32–3, 101–2, 119–21, 136–7,
        141, 143–4, 148, 189, 193 n.79,
        206–7
    human-to-animal metamorphoses
        in 136–7
    human-to-plant metamorphoses in 167–8
Owen, Colin (WO's brother) 183–4
    WO's letters to 140, 170, 183–4
Owen, Harold (WO's brother) 116 n.9,
        124, 130
    WO's letters censored by 116 nn.7,8, 124
Owen, Mary (WO's sister) 116
    WO's letters to 116, 116 n.7, 125–6
Owen, Phyllis (Harold Owen's widow) 124
Owen, Susan (WO's mother) 19–20, 113–14,
        119, 124
    religious beliefs of 19–20, 114 n.1, 147–8
    WO's letters to 78 n.23, 114–18, 116 n.7,
        123, 127, 130, 132, 144, 158 n.50,
        170–2, 174–5, 180, 183, 192–5, 206
Owen, Tom (WO's father) 60–1, 113–14,
        119 n.13
Owen, Wilfred Edward Salter 6–7, 9–11,
        21–2, 24–5, 64–5, 78 n.23, 98,
        109–10
    alliteration, use of 151–2, 194
    as autodidact 113, 159, 195
        anxiety about classical learning 113
        classical texts, reading of 119–21,
            195–7, 209–10
        mediating texts, reading of 120–1
    and Bible
        allusions, associations, and
            connections 120–1, 136 n.32,
            147–8, 152–3, 157–8, 170, 188–9
        study of 114 n.1, 120–1
    and Bion 120–1, 196–7, 209–10
    and H. Bottomley 127 n.24, 182
    Brock, A. E. (therapist) 118, 189, 192–7
        chooses topic for WO's poem 'The
            Wrestlers' 118, 192–4
    and Catullus 202–3
    and children, educational indoctrination
        of 132, 138
    civilians and non-combatants, attitude
        towards 132–3, 138–9, 183–4, 203
    class, social 2, 60–1, 113–14

classical literature and culture
  belief in importance of 113
  knowledge of 119–21, 153, 195–6
  retellings of myths 189, 194, 198–9,
    201–2
and A. Cowley 152
at Craiglockhart War Hospital 22, 118–20,
    127, 132, 135 n.31, 137, 140, 147,
    151, 177, 192–7, 204–5, 209
and CS 161 n.53, 204
and Dante 157–9, 171, 195 n.80, 208
  H. F. Cary's translation 119–20, 157–8
death of 2, 21, 119, 172
and C. Dickens 177 n.69
and J. Donne 206–7
and J. Dryden 154
dulce et decorum est pro patria mori
  comments on 130
  familiarity with, sources of 130–1
  interpretation of 132–3, 206
Dunsden, lay assistant in 114–16, 125–6
education 2, 60–1, 113–14, 116
in France as teacher and tutor 116, 144, 205
and J. G. Frazer 145–6
Germans, attitude toward 201
and R. Graves 43, 118–19, 182, 209
and T. Gray 188
Greek (language)
  desire to learn 113–15
  terminology, use of 114–15, 160–1
and J. Grenfell 169 n.61, 173
and Hesiod
  allusions to 119–20, 148
  knowledge of 119–20
and Homer
  allusions and references to 9, 98,
    119–20, 136, 152–4, 157–61,
    167–70, 176–7, 183–4, 197–8,
    202, 208, 210–11
  G. Chapman's translation 119–20,
    161–2
  knowledge of 119–20, 161–2
  poetic engagement with 171–2, 183
  rejection of concept of glory 171–2
and *Homeric Hymns*
  mediated reception of 148, 152, 178
homoeroticism in poems 183, 197
and Horace
  allusions to 122, 125–6, 129–31, 133,
    135–7, 141–5, 147–9, 152, 154

  influence on modern readings of 9–10,
    130–4
  knowledge of 119–20, 125–6, 130,
    136–7, 141–3, 154
  poetic engagement with 126, 129–31,
    136, 141–3, 145
  quotations from 122, 125–6, 130–1
  rejection of view of war 129–32
and A. E. Housman 209–10
Hydra, The, edits 118–20, 123–4, 193–4
intratextuality in 139, 154–5, 168, 172–3,
    177, 180, 184, 187–9, 198, 202, 204–9
and *katabasis* 125, 154–5, 157–63, 167–8,
    171–3, 177–8, 180, 183, 199
and J. Keats
  admiration for 119–20, 142–3, 176, 189
  allusions and references to 157–8, 176,
    189, 206–7
and C. Kingsley 120–1, 189 n.76
Latin
  efforts to learn and knowledge of 113–16
  mistakes in 182–3
library, personal 119–20, 124–6, 144–6,
    189 n.76
manuscripts 123–4, 127–9, 140 n.37,
    142, 147 n.41, 148, 153, 156,
    158–9, 166, 174–5, 177–80,
    182–7, 193–4, 196–202, 205–6,
    208 n.94, 209
and material culture, ancient 115–16
mediating texts 120–1, 136–9, 153, 160–1,
    176, 178 n.70, 189 n.76, 195,
    204 n.91, 209
  dictionaries, classical 193 n.79, 195
  handbooks, mythological
    Contes fabuleux 120–1, 136–7
    Greenwood Tree, The 120–1, 136–7,
     167–8, 176, 178, 206
    Mythologie Gréco-Latine 158 n.51
metalepsis, use of 12, 128, 132, 164–5, 168,
    183–4
metre
  blank verse 192–4
  choriambs, frequent use of 128–9, 138,
    151, 157, 165, 175, 209
  iambic 151, 175, 204, 206, 208
  iambic pentameter, use of 128–9,
    135, 138, 157, 165, 175, 182,
    209–10
  iambic trimeter, use of 147

Owen, Wilfred Edward Salter (*cont.*)
  military service 117–18, 140, 164–6
    in camp in England 185
    commissioned in Manchester Regiment,
      5th Battalion 117–18
    considers applying for home service 163
    enlistment 117
    RAF, wishes to join 201
    stationed at Ripon 119, 135, 151, 206
    stationed at Scarborough 119, 147, 151,
      174–5, 182, 196–7, 204–5
  Military Cross, wins 119, 132, 172, 183
  and J. Milton 172
  and H. Monro 117, 157–8
  nature imagery, use of 6–7, 20, 114–15,
    135–7, 152–3, 166–9, 173, 183, 204
    seasons 144–6
  odes 115–16, 151
  and Ovid
    allusions and references to 120–1,
      136–7, 141, 143, 148, 167–8, 206–7
    knowledge of 120–1, 143
    and mediating texts 167–8, 189
  paramaterial 123–4
  pararhyme, use of 122–3, 135, 151, 157,
    166, 175, 206, 210
  'Perseus' project, importance of 198–9
  poetic aspirations 113–15, 117–21
    classical knowledge essential to 119–21
    self-training for 113, 117, 119–21
  and A. Pope 154
  Preface, draft 122, 129–30, 135, 152–3
  publication history 121, 206
  as pupil-teacher 113–14
  and RB 144–5, 169, 188
  receptions, later 121–3, 133–4
    B. Britten, *War Requiem* 121
    C. A. Duffy, 'Last Post' 133–4
    M. Longley, 'Ors' 21–2
    of pararhyme 122–3
  religious beliefs 114 n.1, 148, 169–71,
    178–9, 186
    and crisis of faith 116
  rhyme, use of 128–9, 138, 140, 144, 147,
    165–6, 175, 182, 185, 206, 209
    feminine 128, 135, 157, 165
  Roman Britain, interest in 115–16
  and Romantic poetry 167, 185
  and S. Sassoon 118–19, 124, 135, 144, 163
    allusions to 138–9, 157–8

    corrects Owen's Latin 182–3
    letters to 122, 124, 164–5
  and W. Shakespeare 140 n.37, 146 n.40,
    206–7
  and P. Shelley 121, 157–8, 167 n.58,
    204 n.91
  soldiers, descriptions of 128, 164–5, 183–4,
    dead 153, 180, 206–7
    dying 128, 132–3, 152–3, 169–71,
      175–9, 204–5
    wounded, disabled, shell-shocked 122,
      202, 209–10
  sonnet form, use of 140, 144, 147,
    185–6, 195, 204
    on set subjects (with L. Gunston and
      O. Joergens) 147
  Table of Contents, drafts 135, 205
  and A. Tennyson 120–1, 176–7
  'thick' reception in 147–8
  and J. A. K. Thomson 153, 160–1, 178 n.70
  Underworld, depiction of 125, 154–5,
    157–62, 208
  university, efforts to attend 60–1, 113–16
  University College (Reading)
    fails scholarship examination 116
  University of Oxford, desire to
    attend 113–14
  and Vergil
    allusions to 135, 145–6, 152–4, 157–62,
      171, 185–7, 195–8, 204, 208, 210–11
    knowledge of 119–20, 135
  war, attitude towards 3, 24–5, 122, 132–5
  and C. Wesley 154
  Western Front, experiences on 117–19,
    140, 172
    shell shock, develops 118, 203
    shelters in shell-hole (1917) 117–18
    suffers concussion (1917) 117–18, 140
  wheels as motif, use of 98, 160, 162
  and W. Wordsworth 151
Owen Archive (Bodleian Library,
    Oxford) 115–16, 124, 124 n.18
Oxford Classical Reception Commentaries
    (*OCRC*)
  aims of 4–6
  format of 13–14
  *Rupert Brooke, Charles Sorley, Isaac
    Rosenberg, Wilfred Owen: Classical
    Connections* (Hardwick, Harrison,
    and Vandiver 2024) 1–2, 7–8, 125

taxonomy used in 2–3, 7–13, 58–9, 62–5
    'stretched' 58–9
    see also affinities, allusion, associations,
        intertextuality, intratextuality,
        ghosting, glancing, improvising,
        metalepsis, riffing, trace

Palinurus 161–2, 185–6
Pallas 204
Pan 32
Paradise 87 n.33, 186
paramaterial 13, 26, 43, 59–60, 72–3, 123–4
Paris (Trojan prince) 49
    abduction of Helen 77–80
Passmore Edwards Library (London) 57–8
pastoral 61–2, 65, 76, 108, 165–6
patriotism 37–8, 101
Patroclus 5, 15, 39, 53–4, 96–7, 157–8, 183
Peisistratus 49
Penelope 176–7
Penthesilea 103
Perdix 136–7
Persephone 89–90, 153, 177–80, 199–202,
        206–7
    see also Proserpine
Perseus 189, 198–201
personification 19–20, 50–1, 136, 143, 173,
        193, 201–2
    of age 19–20, 147–8, 200–1
    of dawn 32, 176, 204, 208
    of death 170–1
    of life 19–20, 148
    of earth 19–20, 55, 91, 94–5, 148, 163,
        165–6, 177, 193–4
    of nature 165–6, 172–3
    of sleep 170–1
    of sun 168, 172–3, 178, 180, 206–7
    of time 143
Phaeacia 49, 157–8
Phaedra 31–2
Phaethon 148, 167, 176
Philomela 136–7
Pindar 195, 209–10
place, sense of 6–7, 18, 21, 65
    see also environment
Plato 25, 55, 157–8
    and Forms 32
Plutarch 119–20
Pluto 178, 200–2
    see also Hades (god)

Poe, Edgar Allen
    'To Helen' 145
Poetry Bookshop, The 117–18
Poetry: A Magazine of Verse 69–70,
        84–5, 102
Pope, Alexander
    'Ode on Solitude' 154
Pope, Jessie 127, 139
poppies 7 n.14, 20
    as motif
        in Catullus 84 n.29, 152–3
        in First World War poetry 9, 83,
            88 n.35, 90, 108 n.53
        in Homer 83–4, 87–8, 90, 202
        in IR 12, 64, 81–4, 87–8, 90, 96–7,
            152–3
        in M. Longley 10, 90 n.39, 110–11
        in Sappho 152–3
        in Vergil 152–3
        in WO 152–3, 202
    as symbol of remembrance 83, 87–8,
        110–11
    see also motifs, hanging
Poseidon 193
Potter, Jane 60–1
Pound, Ezra 3–4, 65 n.15, 69, 76,
        109–10
    anti-Semitism of 70, 109–10
    and *dulce et decorum est pro patria
        mori* 109–10, 133
    foreign correspondent for *Poetry: A
        Magazine of Verse* 70, 85
    and Imagism 74–5, 109–10
    and IR 70, 109–10
    'Hugh Selwyn Mauberly' 109–10, 133
Priam 39, 78–9, 83–4
    meeting with Achilles 54, 153–4
priamel 151
Procne 136–7
Prometheus 103
Proserpine 178, 202–3
    see also Persephone
protest, poetry of 3, 6 n.13, 16–17, 24–5,
        132–4, 152–3
    anger in 64–5, 130, 184
    see also War poetry (First World War)
Protestant Cemetery (Rome) 142
psychē (soul) 210–11
public schools, English 2, 24–5, 113
    curriculum, classics in 4–5, 34, 36, 42, 132

Pygmalion 206–7
Pylos 48–50

Queen Elizabeth (ship) 38

rat, as motif 64, 70 n.20, 85–9, 104
reader, agency of 6–13, 67
    see also associations, reader-activated;
        reception studies; triangulation
reader-response theory 9–10
Reading (Berkshire) 115–16
reaping, as motif. *See* harvest and reaping,
        as motif
reception studies 1–2, 7–8, 58–9
    biblical 66–7
    classical 10 n.18, 58–9, 99
    heightened receptivity 10 n.19, 19–20
    'intermediate' reception 59–60
    mediated reception 9, 58–60, 96, 120–1,
        136–8, 154, 158 n.51, 160–1,
        167–8, 176, 178, 189, 195, 206,
        209–10
    'thick' reception 10, 21 n.38, 59, 61–2,
        66–7, 87–8, 96, 106, 147–8
    see also associations; comparative
        analysis; 'high intensity' cultural
        awareness; 'low intensity' cultural
        awareness;
Reed, J. D. 204, 209–11
Reilly, Catherine 3
religion
    ancient Roman 142–3
    as cultural framework 16–19
    and ritual 16–18
    and theology 16–18
    in First World War poetry 16–19
    see also Christianity; gods, pagan; 'high
        intensity' religious belief; 'low
        intensity' religious belief;
        Olympians; sacrifice
return, see *nostos*
rhyme, feminine 30–1, 128, 135, 157,
        165, 194
riffing 12, 63, 75–6
    see also *Oxford Classical Reception
        Commentaries*, taxonomy
Riley, Kathleen 15
Ripon (North Yorkshire)
    WO stationed at 119
    poems written at 135, 151, 206

Roberts, William RA
    Burying the Dead after a Battle 64
    Study for 'Crucifixion' 64
Rodker, John 69, 103
Romantic poetry 62, 65, 69–70, 158 n.49,
        167, 185
Rome 47–8, 77–80, 142, 145
    Capitoline Hill 142–3
Rosenberg, Annie (later Wynick; sister
        of IR) 72, 85–6
Rosenberg, Isaac 2, 6–7, 10, 15, 24–5, 144–5
    and Aeschylus 10, 16 n.24, 59, 62–3
    agricultural imagery in 65–6, 75–6, 89–90
    alliteration, use of 75, 78, 81–2, 94–5
    anti-Semitism and 2 n.4, 61–2, 69–71,
        87–8
    as artist 2, 11, 57–60, 64, 70, 94
        landscapes 64, 72–3
        portraits 64, 67, 72–3
        self-portraits 64, 72–3, 111
    as autodidact 59–60, 64–5
    and Bible
        allusions, associations, and
            connections 10, 57–9, 63, 67,
            71–2, 76–9, 87–9, 96–8
    and W. Blake 9, 57–8, 62–3, 69, 72, 78–80,
            87–9, 98, 100–1, 105
        allusions to 79–80, 98, 100–1, 105
    and R. Burns 102
    Christ, references to 68, 81, 96–7
    class, social 2, 5, 57–61, 68
        and poverty 57–8, 61, 67–8
        prejudice towards based on 70
    and classical literature and culture
        allusions, associations, and
            connections 58–60, 62–3, 70–1,
            75, 79–81, 95–6, 99–101
        classical and biblical references,
            interactions of 61–2, 70–2, 75, 99
    comparative analysis
        with M. Borden 107–8
        with W. Gibson 98
        with E. Thomas 107–9
    cultural range of 69–70
    death and burial of 2, 68
    'deep classics' in poetry of 96
    and J. Donne 62–3, 85, 87–8, 104–5
    and ecocritical poetics 61–2, 65–6
    education 2, 57–61, 64–5
    family of 57

Greek tragedy, knowledge of 59
harvest as motif, use of 75–6
health and physique 67–8
and Hesiod 75
and Homer 59, 66–7, 74–5, 83–4, 87–8, 90,
    96–9, 102, 105–6
intratextuality in 10, 63, 77, 83–4, 96–7, 99
iron as motif, use of 75–7
Judaism and 2, 18, 57–9, 61
lark, as motif 7 n.14, 16 n.24, 20, 64–5
letters:
    anti-Semitism, discussion of 70, 86 n.32
    censorship of, military 68, 72
    description of military experience 10, 72
    and poems 72
and lice 10, 59, 102, 104
Lucretius, knowledge of 59
mediating texts, importance of 9,
    58–60, 96
metalepsis 63–5, 81–4, 96, 110–11
military service of 64
    enlistment in Suffolk Bantams 67, 86 n.32
    motives for enlisting 67
    physical suffering during 68
    in Royal Engineers 93
and Milton 62–3
mud as motif, use of 68, 72, 89–90, 99,
    107, 174
nature imagery, use of 15, 20, 61–2, 65,
    72–3, 80, 89–90, 100–1
    and landscape paintings 72–3
and Near Eastern literature 58–9, 66–7,
    74–5
neglect of, by critics 71
and Ovid 101–2
paramaterial 72–3
patrons 58–60, 67–9, 74
persona, poetic, of 61–2, 64–5, 72, 90
phases in poetry of 62, 79–81
plays by 69, 77–8, 99
poetics
    enjambement 74, 86–7
    and 'perversity' of poet 60–3, 65, 90,
        97–8
    rhyme, use of 77–8, 94–6
    'thickness' in 61–2, 87–8, 96, 106
    and war service 68
poppy as motif, use of 20, 64, 81–4, 87, 90,
    96–7, 152–3
prose writings of 58, 60–2, 72, 105

publication history 67, 69, 84, 102
Rabbinic background of family 57
rat as motif, use of 70 n.20, 85–9, 104
RB, opinion of 75–6, 101
receptions, later
    K. Douglas 71–2, 110
    M. Longley 99, 110–11
sexualized imagery in poetry
    of 77–8, 105
in South Africa 67, 100–1
Trench poems 58–9, 61–3, 66–7, 70–3, 93,
    96, 111
and Vergil 102
wheels as motif, use of 96–8, 160 n.52
and Whitechapel Boys 57–8
and W. Whitman 105–6
Yiddish as first language 57
Rosenberg, Peretz (uncle of IR) 67
Ross, Robert 118–19
Royal Air Force (RAF) 201
Royal Military Academy Sandhurst 131
Rugby School 23

sacrifice 15
    in ancient religion 16–17, 159,
        170, 211
    animal 53–5, 159, 211
    human 16–18, 145, 170, 211
    redemptive (Christian) 18, 178–9
    voluntary, by soldiers 16 n.23, 18, 42–3,
        100–1, 168–70, 177–9
    of war dead, celebrated 87–8, 100–1
St Pancras New Church (London) 131
St Paul's Cathedral (London) 33–4, 36
Sallust 179–80
Sappho 18, 23–4, 152–3
Sarpedon 39, 170–1
Sassoon, Siegfried 2–3, 5 n.12, 6–7, 20, 24–5,
    41–2, 64–5, 135
    anger at conduct of war, expression of 16,
        17 n.25, 64–5
    and IR 70–1, 85–6
        writes foreword for 1937 edn of IR's
            poems 70–1
    and WO 2, 118–19, 122, 124, 138–9, 144,
        157–8, 161 n.53, 163–5
        corrects WO's Latin 182–3
        and 1920 edn of WO's poems 121,
            182–3
    'Christ and the Soldier' 17 n.25

Sassoon, Siegfried (*cont.*)
  'How to Die' 17 n.25
  *Memoirs of a Fox-Hunting
    Man* 5 n.12, 20
  Memoirs of an Infantry Officer 7 n.14
  Old Huntsman, The 118–19, 135 n.31
  'Redeemer, The' 17 n.25
  'They' 17 n.25
Scamander (river) 35, 169–70
Scarborough (North Yorkshire)
  German shelling of 117
  WO stationed at 119–21, 196–7
  WO's poems written or revised at 119,
    147, 151, 174–5, 182, 204–5
Schiff, Sydney 69, 86 n.32, 104–5
Schoenberg, Arnold 122–3
Scott, Marion 16, 88 n.35
Scott Moncrieff, C. K. 118–19
  dedicates *Song of Roland* translation to
    WO 118 n.12
Seaton, Winifreda 69, 104–5
Second World War 3 n.6, 4 n.7, 71, 76,
    79 n.26, 107
Semele 199–200
Shakespeare, William 8–9, 206–7
  Sonnet 97 146 n.40
  Sonnet 104 140 n.37
Shaw, George Bernard 135
Shaw-Stewart, Patrick 3, 15, 24
Sheba, Queen of 78–9
shell shock 118, 193, 195, 202–3
Shelley, Percy Bysshe 57–8, 120–1, 157–8,
    167 n.58
  'Adonais' 204 n.91
Shrewsbury 113–16
  Hercules, statue of (copy of Farnese
    Heracles) 198, 203
  Museum 115–16
  Quarry, The (park) 198, 203
Shrewsbury School (public school) 118–19
Shrewsbury Technical School 113–14
  Pupil-Teacher Centre 113–14
Sibyl, Cumaean 153, 158–9, 171, 208
  cavern of 158–9
Silchester (Roman Calleva Atrebatum) 115–16
similes 6–7, 10–11, 168
  Biblical 96–7, 152–3
  Homeric 74–6, 90, 110–11, 145, 152–3,
    167–8, 197–8
Simonides
  Thermopylae epitaph 34

Sinclair, May 3
  'Dedication' 58 n.3
Sitwell, Edith 121, 151 n.45
  dedicates *Wheels* (1919) to WO 121
  edition of WO's poems 121, 128–9, 133
  on IR 71
  'Still Falls the Rain' 79 n.26
Sitwell, Osbert 17 n.27, 121
Skyros 18, 24, 144–5
Slade School of Fine Art (London) 58, 64,
    68–70, 73
Slavitt, David 134
sleep, personified 38, 170–1
Socrates 55
Solomon 78–9
Solon 39
Somme, Battle of the 5 n.12
sonnets 14–15, 36–7, 118 n.12
  CS's use of 42–3, 51–2, 54
  epigram and 33–4, 36, 140
  Petrarchan 33–4, 52, 144
  RB's use of 25, 33–4, 36–9, 42–3, 52, 75–6,
    101, 144–5, 169–70
  Shakespearean 128, 140, 185
  war poets' use of 144 n.39
  WO's use of 128–9, 140–2, 144–5, 147,
    170 n.62, 185–6, 195, 204
Sophocles 23, 168, 206–7
Sorley, Charles Hamilton 2, 9
  attitude to war 42–3
  biblical allusions (KJV) 55
  class, social 2, 41–2
  death of 2, 41–2, 52
  education 2, 41–2, 132
  family 41–2
  and Homer 9, 42–3, 47–50, 52–4, 154–5
  and Horace 42, 47–8, 50–1
  iambic tetrameter, use of 47–8
  internment at Trier at outbreak of
    war 41–2
  intratextuality 51, 54
  memorial at Loos, Dud Corner
    Cemetery 41–2
  military service 41–2, 48–52, 54–5
  musical settings of poems 43
  and Plato 55
  publication history 42–3
  RB, opinion of 42–3, 47–8, 52
  receptions, later
    R. Graves 43
    N. McPherson 43

sonnet form, use of 42–3, 51–2, 54
  and Sophocles 55
  travel in Germany 41–2, 54
  Underworld, depiction of 52–3, 154–5
  Western Front, experiences on 52–3
  WO's knowledge of 161 n.53, 204
Sosias cup 183
Sparta 34, 48–50, 77–8
Spencer, Stanley 104–5
Spitalfields (London) 57
Stallworthy, Jon 60–1, 121, 124, 144–5,
    174–5, 182, 187, 192–3, 204, 211
  and WO's manuscripts 121, 174–5, 193–4,
    197, 199, 205–6
  WO's poems, dating of 121, 147, 156,
    174–5, 204
Stewart, A. T. Q. 99
Strachey, Lytton 23–4
Streets, Will 133–4
Styx 32, 148, 153–4, 185–7
Sumerian literature 66–7
'summer of 1914' trope 74, 106–7
survival, poetry of 14, 16, 20, 62, 64–5, 72, 90,
    97, 147, 164–5
  and poetics of chance and fate 16
Sutherland, Millicent 3
Swift, Jonathan 30–1, 47–8
Swinburne, Algernon Charles 211
Syrinx 32

Tartarus 158–9, 208
  see also Hades (Underworld); hell;
    katabasis, Underworld
Tate Britain (London) 73
Teiresias 171
Telemachus 49
  visits Menelaus and Helen 48–9
temporalities 6–7, 21, 110–11
  in IR 65–6, 106–7
  in WO 134
Tennyson, Alfred (Lord) 120–1
  'Lotos-Eaters, The' 176–7
Tereus 136–7
Theocritus 119–20, 195–7
Theseus 31
Thetis 148
Thomas, Edward 2–3, 6–7, 23–4, 108,
    110–11
  and English landscape 15, 65, 65 n.16,
    106–7
  place, sense of 65

'As the Team's Head Brass' 6–7, 108–9
'In Memoriam, Easter, 1915' 108–9
'Sun used to Shine, The' 106–7
Thomson, J. A. K.
  The Greek Tradition 153, 160–1, 178 n.70
Time (personified) 143
Times Literary Supplement 33–4
Titanomachy 103, 158–9, 163
Titans 103, 148, 163, 188–9
  in Underworld 158–9
Tithonus 148
trace/tracing 12–13, 63, 148, 153, 169, 178–9,
    206–7
  see also *Oxford Classical Reception
    Commentaries*, taxonomy
tradition, classical 4, 15, 64–5
tragedy, Greek 25, 31, 35–6, 41, 59, 201–2
Treacher, Llewellyn 115–16
Trench poems 58–9, 61–3, 64 n.13, 66–7,
    70–3, 93, 96, 111
trenches 3–4, 21, 48–51, 54–5, 59, 81–2,
    85–6, 89–90, 129–30, 174–5, 182
  see also Western Front
Trevelyan, R. C. 59, 70, 85–6
  translation of Lucretius by 59
triangulation 72–3, 98, 109–10
  see also reader, agency of
Trojan Cycle, the, *see* Epic Cycle, the
Trojan War 4–5, 9, 12–13, 25, 42,
    49–50, 76–80, 97–8, 153–4, 160,
    176, 183–4
  and Gallipoli 4–5, 11, 34–6, 38
  and war poetry 4–5, 11, 38, 79–80, 100–1,
    110–11
Troy 4–5, 11, 18–19, 34–5, 38–9, 49–50, 80,
    97–8, 103, 153–4, 160, 183–4
  rivers of 35, 169–70
  sack of 39, 76–8, 153–4, 158, 160
Tyche, *see* chance
Tynan, Katherine 3

Underworld 52–3, 125, 154–5, 157–9, 163,
    171, 185–7, 208
  in *Aeneid* 25, 153, 157–62, 171, 185–6, 208
  in *Odyssey* 52–3, 157–60, 171
  see also Hades (Underworld); hell;
    katabasis; Tartarus
unease, poetry of 4–5, 14–16, 20, 62, 64–5,
    100–1, 106–7, 136–7, 144–5,
    164–5, 176 n.68, 187 n.74
United Kingdom, *see* Britain; England

United States, *see* America
University College, Oxford 41–2
University of London 113–14, 116
Uriconium (modern Wroxeter) 115–16
    Underworld, and 154–5
    WO's visits to 115–16

Vandiver, Elizabeth 34, 53, 59–60
Venus
    Anadyomene 32
    see also Aphrodite
Vergil 10, 25, 119–20, 135–6, 153, 186
    in public-school curriculum 36
    civil war battlefields, description of 36
    relationship to Homer 10, 110–11, 153–4
Vestal virgins 142
Viriconium, *see* Uriconium
Voluntary Aid Detachments (VADs) 3,
        107 n.50
Vorticism 64 n.14, 94
Vulcan 75

Walcott, Derek 3–4, 122–3
War Office 67, 119 n.13
war poetry (First World War) 1–3,
        105–6, 156
    anthologies of 1–2, 5 n.10, 43, 121, 131
    and anti-war assumptions of modern
            readers 122, 132
    canon of 6 n.13
    Christ as trope for soldiers 16–18, 96–7,
            105–6
    and classical traditions 4–5, 129–30
    definition of (in WO's work) 125, 147
    as genre 1–2
    hanging motifs in 64
    and Greek epigram 25
    and Greek tragedy 25
    and Homer 25, 108
    modern intertexts with 3–4, 21, 76,
            109–11, 133–4
    nostos in 15
    and religious associations 16–20
    in school curricula (British) 1–2
    as source for study of First World
            War 6, 72
    and Trojan War 4–5, 11, 79–80, 100–1,
            110–11
    tropes in 106, 187
    and Vergil 25

by women 3, 106–8
    see also protest, poetry of; survival,
            poetry of; Trench poems;
            unease, poetry of
war poetry (Second World War) 4 n.7, 71,
        79 n.26, 110
warfare, ancient 130–2
    athletics and, in Homer 54–5
    idealization of 61–2, 138, 171–2
warfare, modern 53, 61–2, 129–30, 132, 139,
        155, 169, 171–2
Warner, Sylvia Townsend 3
Webster, John 23
Wesley, Charles 154
West, M. L. 66–7
Western Front 34–5, 41–2, 52–3, 117–18,
        149, 163, 169, 188–9
    and lice 10, 59, 102
    and mud 20, 68, 72, 78 n.25, 89–90, 99,
            107–8
    and poppies 7 n.14, 20, 83–4, 88 n.35
    as 'titan's grave' 149, 163, 188–9
Westminster Abbey 142
    tablet commemorating war poets 41–2,
            68, 142
wheels, as motif in First World War
            poetry 64, 97–8, 160 n.52
Wheels 121, 151
Whitechapel Boys 57–8, 69
Whitman, Walt
    IR and 59, 105–6
    'By the Bivouac's Fitful Flame' 105–6
    'Drum Taps' 59, 105–6
Wilson, Margaret Adelaide
    'Gervais (*Killed at the Dardanelles*)' 5
women
    in combat zones 3
    as nurses 3
    as war poets 3–5, 20, 106–8
Woolf, Virginia 23–4
Wordsworth, William
    'Ode on Intimations of Immortality'
            36, 151
Wright, Alice 57–8, 69, 104–5
Wroxeter, *see* Uriconium

xeinia 160–1

Yeats, W. B. 2–3
    and IR 69–70

RB, opinion of 23–4, 37–8
WO, opinion of 158–9
'Easter 1916' 5 n.12, 88 n.34
'Irish Airman foresees his Death,
    An' 36–8
'Leaders of the Crowd, The' 88 n.34
'Meditation in the Time of
    War, A' 88 n.34
*Michael Robartes and the
    Dancer* 88 n.34
'Rose Tree, The' 87–8
'Second Coming, The' 88 n.34

'Sixteen Dead Men' 88 n.34
'Towards Break of Day' 88 n.34
Yiddish 57
youth (stage of life) 5, 17 n.25, 75–7, 83–4,
    87–9, 97, 144–6, 170, 183–4, 204
youth (young man) 4–5, 130–1, 145–6, 168,
    176, 186–7, 204–5, 209–10

Zeppelin (personified as monster) 201
Zeus 39, 103, 158–9, 170–1, 197–8, 200–2,
    201 n.88
    see also Jupiter

The manufacturer's authorised representative in the EU for product safety is Oxford University Press España S.A. of El Parque Empresarial San Fernando de Henares, Avenida de Castilla, 2 – 28830 Madrid (www.oup.es/en or product.safety@oup.com). OUP España S.A. also acts as importer into Spain of products made by the manufacturer.

Printed in the USA/Agawam, MA
January 8, 2026

899493.098